Out of History:
Essays on the Writings of Sebastian Barry

Out of History:
Essays on the Writings of Sebastian Barry

Edited by
Christina Hunt Mahony

Carysfort Press, Dublin

The Catholic University of America Press
Washington, D.C.

A Carysfort Press Book in association with Peter Lang
Out of History: Essays on the Writings of Sebastian Barry
Edited by Christina Hunt Mahony
First published in Ireland in 2006 as a paperback original by
Carysfort Press, 58 Woodfield, Scholarstown Road,
Dublin 16, Ireland
ISBN to 978-1-78874-950-3

Typeset by Carysfort Press

This book is published with the financial assistance of The Arts Council (An Chomhairle Ealaíon), Dublin, Ireland

Published in North America by
The Catholic University of America Press
620 Michigan Ave., N. E. / 240 Leahy Hall
Washington, DC 20064

Library of Congress Cataloging-in-Publication Data
Out of history : critical essays on the writings of Sebastian Barry
edited by Christina Hunt Mahony.
p. cm.
Includes bibliographical references (p.) and index.
ISBN-13: 978-0-8132-1459-7 (pbk. : alk. paper)
ISBN-10: 0-8132-1459-9 (pbk. : alk. paper) 1. Barry, Sebastian, 1955---
Criticism and interpretation. I. Mahony, Christina Hunt, 1949- II. Title.
PR6052.A729Z84 2006
828'.91409--dc22
2005033357

Contents

Acknowledgements

As the editor of *Out of History: Essays on the Writings of Sebastian Barry* I would like to thank the publishers, Carysfort Press, in the persons of Dan Farrelly and Lilian Chambers, for fostering a thoroughly pleasant and productive working environment. Similar thanks, also, to Alan Bennis of Bennis Design, whose highly creative talent resulted in such an excellent cover design. Thanks to David McGonagle and Beth Benevides at The Catholic University of America Press, colleagues of many years with whom I forged a new professional relationship upon the co-publication of this volume.

Acknowledgement and thanks for permission to reprint photographs to - Amelia Stein, John Haynes, Lebrecht Music and Arts Photo Library, and to the Abbey Theatre, Out of Joint Theatre Company, The National Theatre, London and the Royal Court Theatre; and to *Eire-Ireland* for permission to reprint the essay by Elizabeth Butler Cullingford. My personal thanks to Graham Cowley, John Fairleigh and Max Stafford-Clarke of Out of Joint Theatre Company for helpful information on several occasions.

To Nora Mahony for help with indexing the volume and for tolerating a Dublin roommate for a term; to Robert Mahony for good-naturedly taking over the reins in Washington; to Lucinda Bray for supplying transportation and lodging; to Nicholas Grene and Bruce Stewart for practical help and inspiration; to Roy, Aisling and Nora Foster for London lodgings, and to all my excellent contributors. Most of all, my thanks to Sebastian Barry for his patience and good will, and, most importantly, for his artistry.

Christina Hunt Mahony
Washington and Dublin 2006

Illustrations

Cover: Courtesy of Out of Joint Theatre Co./Royal National Theatre
Photograph: John Haynes

1 | Introduction

Christina Hunt Mahony

Sebastian Barry was born in 1955 and therefore celebrated his fiftieth birthday shortly before this volume went to press. It is the first volume of essays on his work to be published, and seems a belated offering as such. The contributions reflect Barry's achievement in various genres and highlight his unquestioned success as a contemporary Irish dramatist.

Barry began as a poet, and remains a poet. His earliest work, and that for which he is credited in *The Field Day Anthology of Irish Writing*, published only a decade ago, is as a lyric poet. In *The Water-Colourist* (1983), *The Rhetorical Town* (1985), and *Fanny Hawke Goes to the Mainland Forever* (1989) the reader finds the seeds of his continuing life's subject – an investigation of his family in its complex relationship to Ireland as an emerging and evolving nation. Peter Denman's analysis of the poems provides the first comprehensive view of this work in its relation to the drama and the narrative prose which followed. Denman assesses the journeyman writer and noteworthy poet who began to be published at a very early age. The task of finding a voice is a prerequisite for a writer, and Barry found his early, making the decision to expand his work beyond the lyric parameters.

But Barry's first book, and a continuing interest while he was beginning to publish as a poet, took the form of fiction for young readers. As Éilís Ní Dhuibhne remarks in her valuable contribution to our understanding of Barry's development as a writer, Barry's early juvenile fiction also yields thematic and linguistic threads which he will weave throughout his mature work. *Macker's Garden* and *Elsewhere: The Adventures of Belemus* are the work of an author in his early twenties, close enough to the childhood adventures of the boys' world he captures to write with a seeming ease, while appealing equally for an authenticity in the difficult task of writing books for the young which the adult reader can find equally rewarding. *Macker's Garden* is an identifiably autobiographical work in its milieu and period, and shares with the much more fantastical *Belemus* a lovingly portrayed Dublin where adventures of a plausible or more highly imaginative sort are played against a real landscape of Dublin's inner city and suburbs.

Bruce Stewart approaches Barry's early move to narrative fiction for adults. His study of *The Engine of Owl-Light* benefits from their shared student experience and places this early prose work into the context of the maturing writer and his experimentation with multiple narratives and linguistic dialects both old and new. The ambition and scope of this early work proves a daunting read, and while the book is not entirely successful in its aims, it is more than sufficient evidence of a major writer in the making. Based in part on the same autobiographical setting as Barry's children's fiction, *The Engine of Owl-Light* journeys far into the colonial landscape and the underside of New World adventures undertaken by young male protagonists which reappear, transformed, in Barry's prose and drama in more recent years.

David Cregan explores Barry's maintenance of hope in his work for the stage, viewing it from a spiritual perspective removed from the confines of institutional religion in an Irish context. His choice to look first, and crucially, at the specifics of Barry's stage directions for his plays, finds poeticism where we least expect to encounter it in a playwright. In *Prayers of Sherkin* and *Fred and Jane*, two early plays, the life in community is sensitively portrayed, and the heightened spirituality that is the aim of that life is signaled in the playwright's specific directions for actors, directors and readers. From this starting point Cregan places Barry's initial dramatic urge into a context that writes the past into a contemporary future. The latter play is unusual in Barry's dramatic corpus in that it remains completely outside his familial project, relying solely on the community experience of religious orders, a context which is combined in the former.

Barry's gentle character portrayals are unique in the harder-edged reality with which contemporary Irish writing must contend. It is a given that Irish society is riven with rapid changes, and is still reeling from the shock of these. It is the task of contemporary writers to record these seismic indications of cultural upheaval and to record that loss which is an integral part of change. Although Barry writes many characters who are Victorian in upbringing and whose world changed violently in the early decades of the twentieth century, he also creates others who dwell in an Ireland that is more recent, but still irrevocably gone. Barry infuses these with an innocence that can seem at first at odds even with the earlier reality of their lives. He makes his innocents credible by coupling their unshakeable belief in the goodness of others with their adherence to their own belief systems. Barry's people don't simply carry on and bear their burdens (which are at times insupportable) they can rise to moments of illumination and clarity which the more fortunate among us can envy. In my own essay, 'Children of the Light amid the Risky Dancers', I have argued that these are not exercises in fantasy nor escapism from existentialist awareness, but fleeting moments of vision which place human aspiration and endeavour in a broad, nearly cosmic, humanist perspective which is both historical and postmodern. Barry's humanist naïf is best exemplified by the eponymous hero of *The Whereabouts of Eneas McNulty* (1998), a homeless and condemned wanderer who journeys through the morass of much of the twentieth century peculiarly unarmed for the fray.

Sebastian Barry has been writing for the theatre long enough now that the need for the revival of some of his work for the stage becomes an issue. Anthony Roche makes an eloquent case for *The Only True History of Lizzie Finn*, a play which contains its own revivalist project by incorporating lost traditions of the Irish theatre within its structure. It is a play keenly aware of the theatricality of its subject. *Lizzie Finn* has a unique dual perspective – the rare contemporary Irish play which actually has characters on stage in both Ireland and in England. Although the Irish/English experience is the stuff of much modern Irish writing this dual perspective rarely gets an outing on the physical stage; and *Lizzie Finn*, with its contrasting elements of class, gender and political viewpoint, is a rich tapestry which incorporates elements of the theatre of an earlier era with those of today's dramatic concerns and techniques. *Lizzie Finn* was produced for the stage in the same year as *The Steward of Christendom,* and the latter play's runaway success overshadowed the particular contribution of Barry's 'theatrical' play with its self-awareness and its active engagement in Irish theatrical history. The inclusion of its character Birdy Doyle, a tribute to veteran music-hall performer Birdy Sweeney, inscribes that tradition into the 'legitimate' theatre. Patrick Mason's production of the play a decade ago also relied on dual perspective, as classes perceive each other across social and gender gaps.

The Steward of Christendom became canonical with its first performances on the stage. It is Barry's most acclaimed achievement to date. John Wilson Foster takes the play beyond its Irish parameters by placing it side by side with the master work of Japanese writer Kazuo Isihguro, *The Remains of the Day*, and reconfiguring the reading of *The Steward of Christendom* outside the limits of a specifically postcolonial interpretation to allow for a historical approach which includes that perspective, but broadens it to the wider discussion of the now discountenanced ideas of service and loyalty. The mindsets of Barry's and Ishiguro's protagonists are difficult for contemporary readers and audiences to grasp in all their complexity and seeming contradictions. Dunne and Stevens are conflicted figures, each living in a world which no longer values the codes of conduct in which they have been trained to believe. Each finds himself stranded in a newer polity, and although their situations are not identical, each is forced to confront ideas of nationalism, and its obverse, treason.

The Steward of Christendom is a work which provokes a multiple response, and Elizabeth Butler Cullingford, benefiting from being the first scholar to make effective use of the cache of valuable Barry papers now in the Harry Ransom Humanities Research Center at the University of Texas at Austin, traces the genesis and ideological transformation of the play from its family origins to its apologia for the lost narratives of the formative years of the Irish state. As this is the site of the most contested area of Irish historical studies Barry's gradual movement toward a position at variance with the main nationalist narrative places him in a position which will remain contentious. Michael Collins is a figure who haunts contemporary Irish writing, and none more so than Sebastian Barry's, and Cullingford peels back Barry's ideological overlay in his representation of family history in the play to an authorial decision to focus in part on Collins' taking over of Dublin Castle – an historic moment in the shift of power from British control to Irish self-governance – and to keep offstage a less glorious moment in Irish history – the Dublin Lockout of 1913. Thus Barry reorders audience reaction to historical events of lingering emotional impact in Ireland today.

The figure of Thomas Dunne and his nuclear family, although only a part of Barry's family story, is the most prominent. Two of his children have now become protagonists in their own novels, the first of these his daughter, who lends her name to the title of his novel *Annie Dunne*. Nicholas Grene's essay pertinently argues that the character of Annie, as established in *The Steward of Christendom*, would have been unequal to the task of reciting her story on stage for an audience, and required the intimacy and exposition of the novel to articulate her progress through life. Within this genre the reader follows Annie into a perilous old age and finds her in the stewardship of a great nephew and niece, surrogates for the children she would never have. The change in venue from Dublin to rural Wicklow gives Annie, Dublin-reared, a valuable connection with her past and with nature, and with a sense of imperilled continuity which she attempts to pass on to the future generations within the limited sphere of her influence and waning powers.

Roy Foster brings the literate historian's perspective to bear on Barry's corpus, returning to Barry's cornerstone work, *The Steward of Christendom,* and following Barry's updated narrative of family in *Our Lady of Sligo,* which sees the descendants of Thomas Dunne through marriage, the would-be inheritors of the promise of the new Irish state, yet again disappointed and disenfranchized through choice and circumstance. The latter play brings the story up to the generation of his grandparents and his mother and is set in 1950s Ireland, a bleak period from any perspective. Foster has written in his introduction to that play that here 'As in so much of Barry's work, acceptance and redemption comes through the transfiguring power of memory, pouring in with the waves of language, unlocking the calcification of time … '

When Barry moves to present day Ireland history becomes news and *Hinterland* posed a new set of problems for Irish theatre-goers. It is one thing to 'revise' history, it is something else to set about presenting ongoing political factionalism in the national theatre in the guise of the age-old saga of fathers and sons. Colm Tóibín examines *Hinterland* in the fraught context of its immediate reception, drawing insight from the Abbey's literary manager, Jocelyn Clarke's, valuable record of inhouse discussions of the play with audiences irate at the representation of his protagonist, Johnny Silver, with his obvious parallels to former Taoiseach Charles Haughey. Tóibín also places Barry's play, insightfully, in the wider, and often overlooked, context of the first years of this century which saw the appearance of several new plays and playwrights who also took as their focus the portrayal of failed fathers.

Like *Fred and Jane,* Barry's most recent play, *Whistling Psyche*, veers from the family history undertaking which has long been the subject of his work in various genres, to take up two historical figures linked by profession, gender and overlapping historical periods. Claire Gleitman addresses Barry's dual character study for the stage – the strange case of James

Miranda Barry, a doctor and an Irish woman, trapped in the guise of a man, as 'he' argues the gains and losses of his unique dilemma in a dual monologue with the formidable Florence Nightingale, a generation younger, avowedly female, English and successful in causes to which they both devoted their lives. What could have become a study of the poison of resentment, missed chances and defeat, becomes instead, in Barry's hands, a transformative experience of redemption and forgiveness.

Out of History: Essays on the Writings of Sebastian Barry provides readers with a record of Sebastian Barry's achievement by supplying a full bibliography of his works and a representative selection of works written about him. Fintan Walsh provides, in addition, an invaluable list of first stagings of Barry's plays with their production details.

Sebastian Barry's corpus of thirty years shows a range of talent that boasts a continuous thread which lends it a coherence unusual in contemporary Irish writing. A poet first, he found a distinctive voice thereafter in both prose fiction and for the stage. His poeticism reigns supreme and his signature language has found its place in the history of literature in Ireland. There are many references in this volume to John Millington Synge, whose language has become a referral point in the discourse on Irish writing, defining poetic writing for nearly a century. Sebastian Barry's writing takes on that mantel for the years to come.

2 | From Rhetoric to Narrative: The Poems of Sebastian Barry

Peter Denman

Sebastian Barry published three volumes of poems during the 1980s: *The Water-Colourist* (1983), *The Rhetorical Town* (1985), and *Fanny Hawke Goes to the Mainland for Ever* (1989).[1] The third collection was to have been one entitled *The Grammatical History of Everiu*; a book with that title was signalled as 'forthcoming' in *The Inherited Boundaries*, the 1986 anthology edited by Barry.[2] The non-appearance may have been associated with the closure of the Dolmen Press, publisher of Barry's first two volumes and of *The Inherited Boundaries*. After an interval of fifteen years, during which Barry established himself as a playwright and the author of two successful novels, he published *The Pinkening Boy* (2004).[3] This was a pamphlet of two dozen short poems dominated by themes of birth and death, especially the birth of a child, Tobias, and the death of a friend, the actor Donal McCann. The poems in *The Pinkening Boy* are little more than occasional pieces confirming that Barry's poetry up to and including *Fanny Hawke Goes to the Mainland for Ever* represents the full range of development in his use of the genre. In that earlier poetry, the change of plan in which the intended *Grammatical History* was replaced by *Fanny Hawke Goes to the Mainland for Ever* marked a significant shift in Barry's poetry. As the titles indicate, there was a move away from overt foregrounding of modes of artistic and verbal expression and towards a concentration on character and experience. His first two collections display an increasingly elaborate organization of themes and language, in which a mannered self-consciousness is not always held in balance with the seriousness of the intent. The title of *The Grammatical History of Everiu* and the two short uncollected poems in *The Inherited Boundaries*, suggest an intention to continue in this style. But the actual third collection, *Fanny Hawke Goes to the Mainland for Ever* represents a radical departure in style and organization of the poetic work, a departure which opens the way for the flowering of Barry's career as playwright and novelist but also establishes an individual and effective mode of poetic expression.

The three poetry collections in the 1980s represent Barry's earliest published work for adults, apart from the novel *The Engine of Owl-Light.* It is customary to regard the poetry as a sort of literary proving ground, in which he can be seen testing and stretching his range before moving on to the more achieved drama and fiction. The poetry collections stand in close relation to his subsequent work in other genres, given the recursive mining of the past that constitutes Barry's themes, and are a sort of prolegomenon to the main writing career. Even as a poetic writer, he is considered to have found fuller expression in his writing for the stage, as indicated by articles on his work such as '"Such a Sense of Home": The Poetic Drama of Sebastian Barry' and 'The Poetic Theatre of Sebastian Barry'.[4]

Barry's mining of family history emerges as a concern of his first collection, *The Water-Colourist.* The painter in water-colours, who gives the book its title and is the subject of the poems at its centre, is his grandfather. The poems about him, 'Call', 'Sketch from the Great Bull Wall' and 'The Water-Colourist', are investigations of the reach of memory. In taking the figure of the painter as central, Barry deliberately transmutes the activities of his family forebears, and the associations of memory, into art. The phrase 'he paints', highlighting an artistic process, is repeated insistently through 'Sketch from the Great Bull Wall'. From the outset Barry is defining or discovering a voice by means of his familial predecessors. Two priorities are immediately apparent as they animate these early poems, and will characterize much of Barry's later writing in fiction and drama. Firstly there is the reference to a genealogical framework, in which characters, events and accomplishments that have come down from the immediately preceding generations are used to support the burden of the poem's experience. This genealogical framework is not a reverent homage to the past simply because it has produced the writer and his present. The knowledge and sense of the present are delineated by establishing it with reference to the past as it is exposed. Secondly there is the use of memory as a vehicle of sense experience. Memory in Barry's poems does not act as a nostalgic filter, but is used to assemble the material; this is to be seen at its most developed in 'Self', the final poem of the book. Although the poems in *The Water-Colourist* are motivated by recollections of the past, most of them are in the present tense. This anticipates the present tense narrative used for the autobiographical recall of *Annie Dunne*, and the lengthy passages describing the past given to characters present on the stage in *The Steward of Christendom.*

There is a hesitant, almost deferential quality in Barry's approach to poetry in this volume, displaying a clear sense of a poet trying out various possibilities of form and language. At one point the looming presence of T.S. Eliot becomes overwhelming, and 'Songs Against Winter' reads almost as a pastiche combining elements of 'Preludes', 'The Love Song of J. Alfred Prufrock' and 'The Waste Land':

> Do you listen for the key's turn?
> The recent action, in tossed hair,
> plays about your head (*TWC*, p.39).

and

> The wind blows. The leaves move a little.
> I saw my father by the Grand Canal (*TWC*, p.40).

The appeal to the sister art of painting contributes to the search for a poetic method. Similarly, the insistent use of landscape as a background on which to set out emotions and ideas achieves a mannerist persistence. 'Rocks', 'trees', 'forest', 'valley', and like words are used repeatedly to map the contours of the early poems, with titles such as 'The Quarry' and 'A Device of Hills' indicative of the material. The opening poem, 'Introduction to Rhetoric', begins:

> All my woods have been domestic.
> It was chance mostly that brought me
> down the tracks to the farmed woods,
> and it ends –
> And so my poems have been small (*TWC*, p.11).

The title of the poem emphasizes both its initiatory quality and a consciousness of the materiality of language as a medium. Rhetorically, it employs the orator's opening device of modesty, a sort of 'unaccustomed as I am ... ' Grammatically, the poem is cast in the present perfect tense – an unusual choice, although it is employed again elsewhere in the volume for the translated passage from Propertius, 'Cassibus Impositis Venor'. The present perfect sets up a link between the past and the present. As a tense it is thus consonant with Barry's later concerns with memory. At this early juncture in his career there is an awareness of the sensibility still in a formative stage: 'chance mostly that brought me/down the tracks', he says here, and in the next poem, 'The Quarry', he starts: 'Once you see it you look for sense'. 'Introduction to Rhetoric' is an introductory poem, and yet it refers to activity in the past, and ends by describing poems that have already been written. They are described deferentially as 'small' and, it is suggested, they are excursions into rhetoric. This is an idea not fully pursued in *The Water-Colourist*, other than perhaps being obliquely apparent in the references to and translations from classical poets. The idea of rhetoric becomes more significant in the next volume, *The Rhetorical Town*, as indicated by the title of the collection and other references in it, although the rhetorical emphasis in the poems is more notional than actual, and does not go beyond a meta-linguistic awareness of the constituents of language. The suggested equivalence between language and trees that is proffered in 'Introduction to Rhetoric' is repeated in a more developed treatment in the opening poem of *The Rhetorical Town*, in a poem called 'The Tree Alphabet':

> Each tree in this autumn script
> Shadows the white drawing of a letter (*TRT*, p.49).

Later, the final poem in *Fanny Hawke Goes to the Mainland Forever* is called 'First Letter', and also uses the image of a tree alphabet. This conjunction of trees and alphabets is not based on the elaborate Celtic system of correspondences as traced by Robert Graves in *The White Goddess*, but on a more general idea of language and the working of it as a sort of forest through which the poet tracks his way and gets delightfully lost. This equivalence between language and woodland is developed in the poems 'Two Brothers Up' and 'The Burden' (*TWC*, p.46, p.50). Real woods, such as those of Coollattin in Wicklow, figure in both the first collection and as 'the lost pillars of Coollattin' in the opening poem of *The Pinkening Boy* – and indeed elsewhere, as at the end of *The Steward of Christendom.*

A rhetorical figure occasionally employed by Barry is that of repetition of a phrase or line. Although it does contribute effectively to the overall stylistic impact of the poem, the technique in Barry's hands is more properly described as rhetorical rather than poetic. His use of repetition does not act as a refrain, but as a nodal or summary statement around which the poem clusters. The device is evident in the early poems 'Sunday Down the Town', 'The Piece of Bog Oak' and 'The End of the Year' (all *TWC*), and 'The Park' (*TRT*), but emerges with full power in 'Little Ithaca', the opening poem of *Fanny Hawke Goes to the Mainland Forever* . 'Little Ithaca' announces a move away from travelling the great cultured cities of the world and from the 'melancholy of the wanderer', opting instead for a return to the home and the known. Ithaca, as home land, is presumably Dublin.

> ... I come like a poor respectful friend
> of gentling Catullus to the pretty pass
> of praising your local colour in my own city
> that I abandoned as ordinary, ordinary.

> But you have made by grace of extended welcome
> my home extraordinary, extraordinary, truly (*FH*, p.13).

The falling rhythm of the closing lines is sustained and strengthened by the grace of the repeated words. Although rhyme is not a feature that Barry normally uses with any great sophistication, here there is a buried rhyming effect that operates powerfully not just between the proximate repeated words themselves but across the lines in the revision and expansion of 'ordinary' into 'extraordinary'.

A further feature of the final stanza of 'Little Ithaca', distinguishing it from the two preceding stanzas, is the switch to the second person, implicating and acknowledging a companion. 'New Song' (*TWC*) and 'Christ-in-the Woods' (*TRT*) are examples of extended pieces in this grammatical form. The presence of an implied addressee is frequent in Barry's poems. In part this conjuring of an audience goes hand in hand with the rhetorical strategy; it can also be seen as prefiguring the writing for the stage, where the audience is integral to the genre.

The poems in *Fanny Hawke Goes to the Mainland Forever* are mostly poems in a new manner, marking a significant advance on the poems in the two earlier collections. 'Little Ithaca', is a transitional piece, announcing a new start in turning back to the substance of local and personal material, but also a final exercise in the manner of the earlier pieces. As did the first poem in *The Water-Colourist*, it strikes a deferential or deprecating note with which to begin the collection. The adjective 'little' in the title sets the tone, and as well as announcing a fresh start there is an implied admission that the focus of the previous poems has been over-reaching and digressive.

The classical Mediterranean reference of 'Ithaca' is a continuation of labyrinthine allusions to classical myth in *The Rhetorical Town*, and its Daedalus connection also reminds us of Joyce's superscription of the Homeric myth on Dublin. The classical strain started early with the versions of Propertius and Juvenal in *The Water-Colourist*, and continued with the elaborate organization of *The Rhetorical Town* in which reference to the Bull no longer refers to the Bull Wall but to the Minotaur and the Cretan labyrinth. The two translations in the first collection are extracted from much longer poems. The lines from Propertius read as follows:

> cassibus impositis uenor: sed harundine sumpta
> autor plumoso sum deus aucupio.
> est etiam aurigae species Vertumnus et eius
> raicit alterno qui leue pondus equo.
> suppetat hic, piscis calamo praedabor, et ibo
> undus demissis institor in tunicis.
> pastorem ad baculum possum curuare uel idem
> irpiculis medio puluere ferre rosam.

These eight lines of Latin yield twenty in English, as Barry improvises around the base text. The extract is placed after the more intimate poem, 'Two Brothers Up', which also evokes Propertius. The poet depicts himself reading while his young brother is setting off to fish:

> Again, little brother, you appear below,
> a fishing-rod flicks above your shoulder (*TWC*, p.46).

This scene foreshadows aspects of the translation that follows it, and is exemplary of the way in which many of Barry's poems have a reach that extends beyond the self-containment of the form, touching on other works by him.

The poem at the end of *The Water-Colourist*, 'Self', is composed of an assembly of unpunctuated short notes and images. Internal organization is apparent in the way some of the sections correspond to each other through recurring motifs. A number of the details mentioned correspond to elements of Barry's biography: Longford Terrace in Dun Laoghaire is mentioned, and 'Papa Barry', and Aunt Annie who also figures, for instance, in *Fanny Hawke Goes to the Mainland Forever* and *Annie Dunne*. 'Self' demonstrates the construction of a character – the poet's own – understood through a gathering of contingencies: 'my books fall and a cat slips from the wall/a ginger cat'; 'a room of mirrors a room of wood statues on/the water I leant over with a small camera'; 'I went as far as the white quarry its shadow/in the air'. This self is linked to specific named places: Maynooth, Longford Terrace, the Rue de la Montagne Ste-Genevieve, Slane Castle, Hampshire. The combination of the range of geographical references with the disjointed form of the poem ensures that there is a scope in which the individual extends beyond the immediate self. The poem traces the emergence of a concern with the creation of an individual who is evoked by psychological fragments and glimpses of memory, as yet left inchoate. The apparent randomness of the associations runs counter to the rhetorical intent and painterly composition implied in the remainder of the book.

The Rhetorical Town is the most elaborately organized of Barry's books of poems. The three self-consciously titled sections, 'The Geometry of the Bull', 'The Diagram of Knossos' and 'The Room of Rhetoric' allude to Mycenaean culture and the myth of the minotaur. The organization in the poems themselves is far from clear, however, and the language can overreach itself. 'Christ-in-the Woods' begins:

> You never bearded more than syllables
> on the gray terrace of the cleric valley
> imagining perhaps I was not impressed
> by you being the thinned in your estate (*TRT*, p.27).

This is resistant to meaning. Poets such as John Ashbery have shown us that poems can be made operative in ways that are aside from the normal exigencies of language, and Barry attempts in *The Rhetorical Town* to free metaphors and images into a quasi-symbolist mode. As Terry Eagleton described it on its appearance, it 'is an ambitious, mythologically-oriented volume, somewhat stilted metrically speaking and a touch too verbally self-conscious', although he went on to term it scrupulous and finely crafted.[5] At times it seems as if heterogeneous words and images are being yoked together on the off-chance that they might generate some striking new meaning. Of the three extended pieces in the book, the sequence 'The Geometry of the Bull' and the two long poems, 'Solo for Stranger' and 'Look at the Moon', only the last named has a sustainable idea at its centre. This comes from its concentration on family history.

> My grandfather was of one tribe,
> my father of some other one.
> Only he had a fountain at will in his throat
> that he could sprinkle down from the little bridge to the little water.
> I was of the tribe of my grandfather
> so my most famous ancestor might be myself.
> So when the three were together
> as they were in a colourless time (*TRT*, p.43).

The elaborate organization of *The Rhetorical Town* is the extreme example cross-linking in his poetry, with the poems linked in sequences and set out in sections with titles and motifs that cross refer to each other. The final long poem in that volume, 'The Room of Rhetoric' is so closely related to his anthologising in *The Inherited Boundaries* that it reads like an alternative introduction to it, name-checking a number of the poets whom he includes in that collection alongside classical figures such as Propertius and Catullus, and modern poets such as Pound, Cavafy and Neruda. It also indicates just where the boundary lines are to be drawn, as he identifies poets:

> who sing our inventories,
> I mean in the South of Ireland,
>
> the North being as much
> a foreign country to some of us
> or at least to me
>
> as Patagonia
> or perhaps Ithaca … (*TRT*, p.66).

In his foreword to *The Inherited Boundaries*, Barry indicates that he sees John Montague as the significant forerunner for his generation – specifically, for poets from the south of Ireland born in the 1950s. The identification of Montague as exemplary figure for his generation suggests that the elder poet had a particular significance for Barry himself. He does not set out very clearly the reasons for seeing Montague as pre-eminent, other than by commenting that that his 'cross-border work' escapes the boundaries of the Northern Irish sensibility and 'belongs somehow to the Republic, or is an aspect of it'. The attempt, in the anthology and its accompanying introduction, to demarcate a new and specifically southern Irish poetic generation was a sally in the 'anthology wars' of the 1980s. It was not a sustainable intervention, and soon received short shrift in an article by Terence Brown.[6] But the appeal to Montague as exemplar is revealing for a number of reasons. One can detect a number of poetic affinities. In part, *The Inherited Boundaries*, which was among the last publications from the Dolmen Press, can be seen as an imitation of one of its earliest: the 1962 *The Dolmen Miscellany of Irish Writing* edited by Montague (with Thomas Kinsella as poetry editor). In Montague's own poetry, the return to a landscape known in childhood is a dominant subject, and that motif is used prominently in Barry's poetry as well. This casts an additional light, self-deprecating and ironic, on Johnny Silvester's comment as he reads over his autobiographical writings at the beginning of *Hinterland*: 'To think Seamus Heaney turned his Derry childhood into the stuff of a Nobel Prize'. More centrally, the reaching back to the previous generation that is a constant underlying concern of Montague's work, and in particular his upbringing by his aunt, strikes a particular chord with Barry's various returns to the life of Annie Dunne and its Wicklow setting.

There is one poem in *The Rhetorical Town* that stands apart from the others. 'The Widow of Bath' speaks strongly through a created character and conjures up a life of experience. In its evocation and investigation of character, this poem follows on from 'A Seasonal Aunt' in *The Water-Colourist*; more importantly, it anticipates the manner of the poems in *Fanny Hawke Goes to the Mainland Forever*, in which experiences are narrated through the voice of a persona. *Fanny Hawke Goes to the Mainland Forever* is the most accomplished of Sebastian Barry's four books of poetry. The language, style and form of this book exhibit a marked change from the earlier poems, and the matter anticipates the character and situations of subsequent work in drama and fiction. Even in an author who habitually mines personal and familial history to revisit remembered incidents and recounted histories, the anticipation of material later used in other works is here evident to a remarkable degree. But *Fanny Hawke Goes to the Mainland Forever* does not need cross-reference to the plays and fiction to assert its value. There is the emergence of a plain style, and a much greater appeal to narrative than is to be found in the two earlier collections, while the poems stand as individual works without being marshalled into sections or thematic clusters (although one of the poems, 'Kelsha Yard, 1959' is itself a grouping of twenty short sections). These features give the book a strength that differentiates it from the others, and there is the presence of a real poetic voice.

An appeal to narrative is apparent in the very titling of a number of the poems. The title of 'The Only True History of Lizzie Finn, by Herself' foregrounds a history, names a character and a narrator, and replicates a formulaic titling style while making a truth-claim for the story that differentiates it from any other putative versions. In 'The Life by Burning of Bridget Cleary', the word 'life' suggests the standard narrative form of biography, and also returns to the notion of life seen as a construction of the self as in the poem 'Self' (*TWC*), but here with the effective addition of a voice. This poem centres on a notorious incident in Ireland of the 1890s, when a young wife was suspected by her husband of being a witch. It is the subject of a recent book by Angela Bourke.[7] The mention of 'burning' in Barry's title figuratively suggests vitality and, more particularly, the sexual and emotional passion that emerges as driving the speaker of the poem. The narrator and the focus of the poem is not Bridget Cleary herself, but her husband, who speaks about Bridget and, at the end, invokes her in the second person. The poem 'Mary Donnelan, Seamstress of the Mad' is written entirely in the second person and is addressed to her. The title names a character and her occupation, and hints at a situation in the conjunction between the stereotypically gendered occupation of 'seamstress' and the unsettling closeness of the mad. 'Trooper O'Hara at the Indian Wars' is a similarly structured title, giving a proper name, a military occupation, and an involvement in an episode of history. And, as with 'seamstress of the mad', there is a striking conjunction, here between the evidently Irish name and the wars abroad, which creates a tension between the familiarity of home and the exoticism of abroad. An additional inter-textual tension might arise from the coincidence that the eponymous protagonist of Kipling's *Kim* is the son of a soldier named O'Hara, and so the mention of 'Indian wars' might initially be understood as referring to actions on the subcontinent.

At the very least, these titles suggest conflict, and the potential for friction. The absolute claims made by the phrasing of the title 'The Only True History of Lizzie Finn, by Herself' implicitly take a stand against, and reject, all other possible stories. As Anne Ferry writes:

> Grammatically the title of a poem acts as a statement, comment, observation, or signal about the poem that is inseparable from the reader's experience of the whole without being contained in the text.[8]

Barry's unusually full titles stand alone as labels, and are in themselves implicit with a situation or narrative that acts as an opening challenge to the poem that follows. The text may either fulfil the promise of the title by elaborating upon it, or depart from it by diverging from or enlarging upon what is implied. The poem that follows under 'The Only True History of Lizzie Finn, by Herself' is a fulfilment of that title, once the fictional convention is accepted and passed over; this is not told by herself, but imagined by the author. The poem's story gives us something of Lizzie's background. Transported from the music-halls of Brighton and other coastal towns by one Robert Gibson, she is taken westward through Wales. A sea-crossing and a mention of Christ Church indicate arrival in Ireland. The last of the four stanzas shows us Lizzie 'by herself', dancing freely in a tower room at night:

> There in the best light, with my candle shadows,
> I hitched my Belfast linens, English and Indian silks,
> and showed my starry crotch to the stiff-backed toys
> and danced for all ye who carry my whoring pride (*FH*, p.15).

The notion of display and the turn to the second person form in 'ye' conjure an audience that witnesses and participates in the performance. Within the world of the poem, the idea of performance in its final lines looks back to Lizzie's earlier life on stage; beyond the world of the poem, they foreshadow the story's subsequent transposition into theatre. The related play, *The Only True History of Lizzie Finn,* fleshes out the story by expanding on Lizzie's life in Robert Gibson's family home above Inch Beach in Kerry. The play's text is anchored with place names local to that part of Kerry: Ventry, Castlemaine, Caherconree. The house name, Red House, seems to refer to the Red Cliff which drops to the waters of Dingle Bay at Inch. (There is an actual Red Cliff House in the locality; it belonged for a time to Bishop Eamon Casey when he was Bishop of Kerry.) The expansion of the story from poem into play also entails a diversion. The poem ends with Lizzie dancing alone for an implied audience; at the end of the play she is in the arms of Robert. Poem and play present different versions of the 'only true history'. The play contains its own comment on the form of the title, where Lizzie talks about a book Robert has brought for her:

> **Lizzie:** It's called *The Only True History of Frank James, by Himself.* It's a mighty book about an outlaw in America, penned mightily by the man himself … Robert, who is a scholar, says Frank James never did write any book and it only says he did to make you believe it's the plain truth. I believe Robert, and I believe the book (*LF*, p.54).

There is an inter-textual game going on here. The claim made in the title of the poem to reject all other stories of Lizzie Finn is undermined by the subsequent production by the same author's work of another true story of Lizzie Finn. The book Robert brings to Lizzie, with its appended 'by Himself' is more closely aligned with the title of the poem than with that of the play. But one can, as Lizzie suggests, accept two versions: 'I believe Robert, and I believe the book'.

Four of the poems in *Fanny Hawke Goes to the Mainland Forever* were published in *Krino* in 1986, together with a fifth which was not republished. This last was entitled 'True Relation of the Islands Voyage, 1597', and it alludes to a little-known account of a voyage to the West Indies in which Raleigh and Essex participated, written by Sir Arthur Gorges and published as part of *Hakluytus Posthumus, or, Purchas his Pilgrimes* in 1625. The titling formula of 'True History' or 'True Relation' was a familiar one from the seventeenth century. There is a double reference in Barry's use of it, to truth on the one hand, and to an authenticating text that parallels the events of the poem on the other. These authenticating texts may quite simply be the originals that provide the starting point for translations, as in 'Cassibus Impositis Venor' (*TWC*), while 'Lines Discovered under the Foundations of Dublin in a Language neither Irish nor English' is, according to a subtitle, a version of 'a Medieval Latin Song' (*FH*). Many of the poems in *Fanny Hawke Goes to the Mainland Forever* have a narrative base, and have in addition an identifiable link with subsequent plays by Barry. For instance, apart from the Lizzie Finn poem's obvious relation to the similarly titled play, 'The Good Night' and 'At The Back of the Small Fields' are reprised in 'Boss Grady's Boys', the title-poem is at the core of *Prayers of Sherkin*, and 'Trooper O'Hara at the Indian Wars' is linked to *White Woman Street*. 'Kelsha Yard, 1959' is a sequence of twenty short pieces, closely linked to the story of the novel *Annie Dunne*, and also to the background of *The Steward of Christendom*. This is set in the south-western part of Wicklow, on the slopes below Keadeen mountain above Baltinglass. 'The Light Brigade' draws on a nineteenth-century mass death recounted in James Berry's *Tales of the West of Ireland*, a book published by Dolmen Press in 1966.[9] It is in effect a poetic paraphrase of Berry's account, leaning especially on the proper names of places and persons mentioned in Berry's account. The appeal to a correlative text features from the earliest poems. In the poem 'Introduction to Rhetoric' (*TWC*) there is a mention of the 'forest/Conrad's fate showed him', apparently an allusion to *Heart of Darkness*.

This use of an *auctor* is an incidental rhetorical feature that continues in Barry's poetry through the 1980s, even as his emphasis moves from the verbal and formal foregrounding of the rhetorical impulse in the first two collections to the simpler narrative constructions of the third. It is in the emergence of narrative and in the development of a speaking voice that the poems anticipate the later work in other genres during the 1990s. The poetry stands as a proving ground and test bed. It may be that Barry's dramas owe their success in some measure to a poetic quality in their language, but it is clear that his poems became more accomplished as he discovered and developed a dramatic voice in them.

3 | Transcending Genre: Sebastian Barry's Juvenile Fiction

Éilís Ní Dhuibhne

There is a tendency to regard all fiction for children or young people as a single homogenous genre – like detective fiction, 'chick lit', and other so-called 'genre fiction'. Within the genre loosely described, mainly for marketing purposes, as 'children's literature', a perplexing stylistic and formal range occurs, with the Narnia novels of C.S. Lewis at one end of the spectrum, for instance, the novels of Enid Blyton somewhere else. All are loosely connected by having a target audience in mind: young people, very young or not so young, very literate or of limited reading ability, very literary or otherwise.

There is also another type of 'children's literature' which is not necessarily self-defined by having an exclusively juvenile audience in mind. The novels of Tolkien are the most celebrated examples of such fiction; other recent books in this category which have enjoyed great success are the novels of Philip Pullman, or Mark Haddon's *The Curious Incident of the Dog in the Night-time.* The latter was even marketed in two formats, one directed at children and one at adults.

Sebastian Barry has published two books which could be classified as young people's literature. Both fall into the final category, of literature which could be happily read by people of any age. *Elsewhere: The Adventures of Belemus*, is the only work by

Barry which is unambiguously written for children; but stylistically and thematically it has much to interest adults as well. *Macker's Garden*, on the other hand, is a novel about young people written 'for' adults, insofar as a work of literature is written 'for' any type of reader. Secondarily it is a book which would be accessible to and of interest to younger readers.

Barry's novels, and of some of his plays, are given titles, which resonate with youthfulness. *Macker's Garden* and *The Adventures of Belemus* offer the promise of mystery and excitement, and both are works concerned, in one way or another, with young people. *The Engine of Owl-Light, Strappado Square*, even *The Whereabouts of Eneas McNulty*, or *The Only True History of Lizzie Finn*, reverberate with a similar sense of adventure although none of them is a work for juveniles. The pattern indicated in the choice of titles reflects the scope and direction of Barry's imagination, the core of his creativity: He is both a serious and a playful writer, a writer who is at home in the realm of the fantastic, refracted in adult works sometimes through the medium of history, myth, or literary classics, and in his juvenile work through the mirror of pure fantasy.

Macker's Garden was Sebastian Barry's first book. It was published in 1982 by the Irish Writer's Co-Op,[10] but he wrote it when he was twenty-one, and, one might suggest, little more than a child himself.[11] It is a short work, 122 pages, about 45,000 words – an average length for a young person's book. It is divided into two main sections – 'The Bicycle' and 'The Girl-Friend'. These two sections are then subdivided into thirty-two very short chapters, a compositional strategy which suits the content of the novel but co-incidentally means that the book is constructed in the normative format of a juvenile novel.

The novel is realistic and concerns a group, or gang, of teenage boys. Their ages are not specified except in one instance – Synnott, possibly the oldest, is fourteen.[12] We are given certain hints as to the age of the others:

> 'He didn't shave' said Clarkie. 'He's a baby face.'
> Everyone around him was a baby-face too, so no-one spoke for a moment (*MG*, p.96).

They are adolescents, in secondary school, on the cusp of pubescence, not shaving but hoping to do so very soon – probably ranging in age from thirteen to fourteen or fifteen. Clarkie, Nessie, Dill, Synnott, and Macker, are the names they call one another; at home their parents address them by their Christian names, Glenn, Paul, Dillon, Annesley. A more or less middle-class group, they live in Monkstown, in places clearly identified: Longford Terrace and Brighton Terrace are named. Macker's garden is a derelict garden on the seaward side of Longford Terrace (now the site of the Salthill DART station) where the gang congregates after school and in the evenings to chat, plot adventures, and 'mess'.

Macker has appropriated the garden, and it is he who is most interested in maintaining it and the gang. He does not otherwise emerge as a ringleader but he is introduced in the first pages as someone who is mature enough to have an insight into the character of every boy in the gang:

> If they all got bicycles, that would be something. Perhaps in summer. They were easy to find – it was a matter of being brave enough. Clarkie would do it first, though his father would kill him if he found a stolen bike near the house – Clarkie's father being a policeman. Dill would do it last … Nessie would have to have a bike got for him (*MG*, pp.8-9).

Macker seems to need the garden, symbol of wildness, childhood, shelter, retreat, more than the others. But it is not really clear why this is so. Although he has the potential to be developed as a major character, within the confines of a short novel, in which no one character is the focus of attention for long, such development cannot occur. A glimpse of his home life is granted, and he seems to be less well-off than his friends, living in a rented flat. His father repairs washing machines and the like for a living and his mother is the friendliest of the novel's mothers. He seems to enjoy a happy home life and he is not escaping from any unpleasant situation. His family life, however, like that of the other characters, is minimally depicted, since the novel, like an Enid Blyton novel about the Famous

Five or the Secret Seven, focuses on the world of children without adults.

Nessie receives more attention than any other character, and would seem to be the one with whom the author most closely identifies – his life at home, with his parents, sister and eccentric grandfather, is revealed in more detail than that of anyone else.[13] A few sections of the novel also deal with his experiences in school, whereas no attention is devoted to the school life of the others. Like Macker, Nessie is potentially a central protagonist but again the structure of the book, and its concern with all five characters, militates against his development. The hero of the novel is, in a way, the entire gang, rather than any one of them.

The plot is minimal but diverting, and turns on the robbing of a bicycle by Clarkie. He uses the bicycle to cycle to Wicklow and establish a relationship with his distant cousin, Sara, 'The Girlfriend' of section two. By the end of the novel, Sara, an Eve-figure, representative of the greater world of the older teenager as well as of her gender, has been invited into the garden and introduces the boys to smoking and cider drinking as well as romance. The bicycle, and Sara, thus wheels the boys out of childhood and into a more grown-up world.

Towards the end of the novel, Clarkie's theft is discovered and he is banished to Tralee for seven weeks by his irate policeman father (clearly very misguided about the potential of Tralee as a penitential location, as anyone will testify who has had the pleasure of hearing the Dun Laoghaire Librarian, Muiris O'Raghail – a man with a thorough knowledge of both locales in the book – describing his home town in Kerry in the fifties and sixties). Sara breaks off their budding romance and begins a new friendship with Nessie. The round table of the gang is shattered. The garden is no longer a hideaway for the cosy, wild, loyal band of boys, although Macker clings to the hope that all will be restored. At the close of the novel, in the summer when most of the boys have dispersed on their holidays, he is left alone in the garden, hacking at brambles and hoping that as soon as they all return from the country the life of the garden will be restored. We know that this is a forlorn hope. What he has lost, and longs to retrieve, is his own childhood and that of his friends. He wants time to stand still. As he hacks at the brambles he is experiencing one of the tragedies of the human condition: transience and mutability.

While the novel, which is after all the work of a very gifted, but also very young and inexperienced writer, might have benefited from a greater focus on a single one of the characters, its great strength possibly derives from the youth of its author and his proximity to the world he is describing. The exposition of the psychology of the young boys is entirely convincing. Their mindset, emotions, their behaviour and speech, are all brilliantly depicted and their point of view beautifully maintained throughout. In the company of their peers they are competitive, teasing, and protective of self-image. They never admit to ignorance:

> He's bringing his daughter with him, Clarkie says she's a piece. It doesn't matter, you know, because she's not his first, or even his second, cousin.

'How do you mean?' Dill said, becoming perplexed by Synnott's innuendo. He knew something special was meant, something conspiratorial. He narrowed his eyes to match Synnott's. 'I see', he said. 'When're they coming?' (*MG*, p.28)

The boys address one another in rough language, are always competing and terrified of losing face, but on the other hand they cover for each other when they are in trouble, and aid and abet one another constantly in their greatest challenge – which is how to escape from homework and the watchful eyes of their parents after tea every evening.

In the company of Nessie, we encounter a few representatives of the world of school, none of them very endearing. The most menacing is the dean of discipline, Father Heaney. There is a definite suggestion that he is more intimate with the students than is strictly ethical:

> If he liked you he let you off … You could talk with him in his study. He gave you coffee. The other priests drank tea.
> 'It's lonely in this profession, Annesley, lonely for a man like me.'

> 'How do you mean, Father?'
> 'I mean in the ordinary way. Lonely for things I might have done. Not had mind you, because I did with women long ago. I had a girl when I was twenty. Always in the evening when I got home I'd feel dissatisfied, as if there were something just out of reach' (*MG*, p.47).

The effectiveness of the description of this encounter is precisely in its lack of an overt adult perspective. Like everything in the novel, it is presented strictly from the point of view of the young boy, who accepts almost every kind of adult behaviour. One is reminded of the power of Joyce's story of paedophilia, 'An Encounter', which derives most of its effectiveness from the innocence of the point of view of boys who are much the same age as those in this novel. (That the twenty-one year old Barry had the skill to present this scene with such restraint is evidence of remarkable literary talent.)

Just as 'An Encounter' is a story about young boys, but not for young boys, episodes like the one just mentioned highlight the ambiguity of intention in this novel, indicating that it was not intended only as a story for children or adolescents.

Another clear indication of the adult nature of the novel is the restrained but unambiguous reference to homosexuality therein.[14] In an intentionally abrupt scene, the novel alludes to sexual relations between two of the boys in the gang, Dill and Synnott (the latter being the most sexually knowing of all the boys): 'Synnot sulked. The ache in his trousers would not die down.'

> 'You're not sorry we left, are you?' he said. 'You don't not like it, do you'?
> Dill did not seem to want to answer. He did not mind being rubbed against sometimes though. Synnott pressed his knees together and looked about the ruined tennis club in despair.
> 'Listen, you weren't thinking of saying anything?' (*MG*, p.84)

Dill tells him he won't see him much any more, using the original and disingenuous excuse of having joined the sea-scouts – a good example of one of the humorous, tender contrasts of innocence and knowingness with which the novel abounds.

Although this would seem to be a very significant aspect of the characterization of the boys – Synnott is perhaps really gay, covering it up with smutty jokes about girls, while Dill is probably simply experimenting or in the throes of an adolescent attraction from which he is now ready to move on (into the sea scouts!). It is not expanded upon, in accordance with the general trend in the novel, which is to reveal to the reader only as much of each character as he is prepared to reveal to the boys in the gang.

The style and register of the novel support the view that *Macker's Garden* is not directed exclusively or primarily at young people. Stylistically it is considerably more sophisticated than is usual in juvenile literature. Symbolism – the garden, the bicycle, the girl in the garden – contributes to the meaning of the work as much as characterization or content. The dialect – middle-class Dublin, punctuated with teenage slang of the period and place – is faithfully rendered. The descriptive passages of the novel are written in lyrical prose typical of Barry at his best:

> Nessie followed the ridge path. The black-stone beach lay below him, and the stubble of the seafield stretched beside him. He flinched at the memory of dinner – his grandfather's teeth, and his father's voice, and the accents his mother put on to amuse him.
>
> His feet slipped in the mud.
>
> False teeth slipping and sucking beside him! (*MG*, p.31)

Although there is no reason why it should not be directed at children, this style of writing is usually reserved for adult audiences. *Macker's Garden* is a coming of age novel which depicts with considerable insight and skill the psychology of boys on the brink of young adulthood – baby faces about to shave. But its readers, I would contend, could be of any age from ten to a hundred.

Elsewhere: The Adventures of Belemus, like much of the best children's literature, is also a book which adults, especially literary adults, could read with pleasure, but it is much less ambiguous in intent than *Macker's Garden.* Definitely a book for children, as the imprint, Brogeen Books, implies (referring to the leprechaun Brogeen, a character in a series of children's books by Patricia Lynch), it was published three years after *Macker's Garden*, in 1985.[15] Slightly longer than *Macker's Garden*, it contains about 50,000 words. The book is enhanced by twelve fine drawings by Raymond Mullan.

The protagonist is a schoolboy with the curious and unlikely name of Belemus Duck. We are not left in doubt as to his age: he is twelve for the duration of the book, and it closes on his thirteenth birthday. Like Macker and his gang, Belemus lives on the south Dublin coast, in an unspecified suburb but one which could easily be Monkstown, and like Nessie, he goes to school in Leeson Street. But by contrast with Nessie or anyone in *Macker's Garden*, Belemus is a loner. Macker's gang create for themselves an alternative world to the adult world, but one which is communal, intensely realistic, and full of plausible adventures, such as stealing a bicycle or smoking a cigarette or climbing a tree. Belemus is a compulsive daydreamer whose otherworld exists inside his head.

The book takes the form of eleven separate episodes. In most of these, Belemus leaves home for school in the morning, and before he has gone very far encounters an extraordinary character with whom he engages in conversation. These characters range from a fairytale character called The Big Master in the first chapter to a science fiction Dr Who-like character in the last.

The fantasies are drawn from several sub-genres of fiction, especially but perhaps not exclusively, children's fiction. The fairytale seems to be the source for not only The Big Master but also for the MOKs, in Chapter One. (The MOKS are The Big Master's term, a misunderstanding of the word 'monks', and these mysterious figures do appear on horseback.) Other episodes include a cowboy and Indian story; a story of cave dwellers, set in Booterstown Marsh; a Dickensian tale in which Belemus plays the role of a child chimney sweep and rescues a monkey from a chimney in a big Dublin house; a story of Eskimos; an adventure in a sailing ship in which he is a cabin boy and experiences being wrecked by a tidal wave; a Holmesian detective story in which he is employed as an assistant to a private investigator, and so on. The book, then, is an exploration of the various kinds of fiction available to a schoolboy, and of his total immersion in these stories.

The frames surrounding these fantasy adventures are by contrast with their sensational content intensely realistic. In them, the landscape to which we were introduced in *Macker's Garden*, and in addition that of south central Dublin around Leeson Street, the Grand Canal, and Stephen's Green, are vividly evoked in what may be for many the most appealing aspect of this novel.

Belemus takes a lot of detours to allow him to visit various parts of Dublin. For instance, in Chapter Eight, 'The Roundabout Way', he goes through the grounds of Trinity:

> I was walking through Trinity College. It's a roundabout way to school but I wanted to see if any flowers were up.They have trees in the grounds, and at a certain corner of the cricket pitch there's a place where the gardeners have lain down daffodils and crocuses. I passed among maples, searching the cut grass for the green tips. There wasn't one. It was the first day of spring (*EAB*, p.77).

In Chapter Ten he is making his way to school *via* Merrion Square:

> As I plodded to school the following morning the sun turned traditional and came out. It crept into Merrion Square. I could see through a tangle of bushes a flow of grass, and wooded mounds, private in the locked square. I passed the traffic lights and was walking in a desert (*EAB*, p.104).

The descriptions of these Dublin places is delightful evidence of Sebastian Barry's intense love of and fascination with place, but they usually serve a definite narrative purpose and provide convincing gateways to the adventure narrated in their chapters. For instance, the Merrion Square episode is a cowboy and Indian story; and although Merrion Square is clearly not the Wild West its relative spaciousness and loneliness render it a suitable enough locus for this kind of adventure. The Booterstown marsh setting, ancient and wild in the context of the Dublin suburbs, is appropriate for the tale of Neanderthal man which the sight of it inspires for Belemus. A maths class and a difficult problem lead us to the world of the private investigator, while the grounds of Trinity College inspire one of the most interesting chapters in the book, a Joycean odyssey, with nods to James Stephens and Flann O'Brien, and probably Lewis Carroll, through Grafton Street, Stephen's Green, and the general territory of *The Charwoman's Daughter,* a probable source of inspiration for this chapter:

> I met a fellow at the corner of the road. He was dancing in the middle of Dawson Street, without a care in the world. He was doing his dance for the White Church. His eyes ran over the façade, and he leaped and whirled and paused in celebration … 'If you be my friend,' he said, 'I'll teach you how to fly.' 'Oh well . . .' I said, a bit overcome. 'Of course I'll be your friend'(*EAB*, pp.82-83).

This use of specific, named places as gateways to the world of the imagination for Belemus Duck provides us with an insight into one of the ways in which Barry's literary creativity works. Place is a source of inspiration for him in many of his later works, just as it is for the eponymous hero of this children's book.

Belemus is engaging stylistically and makes certain concessions to a youthful readership.It is narrated in the first person, lending it an intimacy of tone. Sentences are short and so are the chapters. But Belemus is an articulate and imaginative narrator which means that, like *Macker's Garden*, the work is stylistically quite sophisticated.

Occasionally, he expresses himself using the startling similes, the free association, which are typical of a stage of linguistic development and of imaginative schoolboys[16] – 'The air was thinner than a little biscuit – it made me feel awake as an otter' (*EAB*, p.23).

Figurative language is not used consistently throughout the narrative, reflecting a reality, in which boys are occasionally, rather than constantly, inspired. More often, Belemus' powers of description blend adult with childlike modes of expression:

> I shrugged my shoulders at the silent city. I sat on a bollard by the gates and watched a sea-gull floating in the sky. You know

> the way they do. They catch a wave of wind and ride on it till they get fed up and slide off. The bird swooped around. The pavement under me was dimpled and cold. There was a thin sun and the morning was older (*EAB*, p.79).

Joyce's seagulls in *Portrait of the Artist* may influence the style here, and throughout the novel Belemus' personal style is blended with that of the literary genres into which he has escaped.

The novel succeeds at the level of children's adventure story, with its delineation of the character of a bright, charming, daydreaming boy, and at a much more adult level as a journey into many sub-genres of children's fiction. As one would expect, Barry is sensitive to form, style, and register within these genres, and not simply to content, as a less literary writer might be.

In both *Macker's Garden* and in *Belemus*, Sebastian Barry produces works in which generic boundaries distinguishing children's from other fiction are blurred or transcended. The first might have been written 'for adults', the second 'for children', but one suspects that he is not a writer who composes with an audience in mind. In any event, like Macker, he simply ignores the locks on the garden gate, and so succeeds in remaining true to his own voice and concerns as a writer no matter what label is pinned on the books subsequently.

Both books are important in that they were written so early in the author's career. They provide fascinating insight into Barry's creative method, and foreshadow techniques and themes which recur in his later work. Key components of his overall *oeuvre*, and thus essential material for any scholar engaged in research on Barry, these books also stand on their own merits as original, humorous and lyrically written stories. *Macker's Garden* is unusual for its sensitive portrayal of middle-class Dublin schoolboys in the late 1960s; while *Belemus* is an imaginative *tour de force* and an example of a book written just at the beginning of the period which saw the flowering of children's literature in Ireland. [17]

As a final note – bibliographically, *Macker's Garden* is a shabby badly-printed product of the heroic Irish Writers'

Co-Op, while Belemus is a handsome, illustrated Dolmen Press volume. No matter. It is regrettable that both books are now collector's items, available now only to readers in the rare books sections of great libraries, and not in all of them. There is a new generation of young readers since these books were published, and their appeal would be as fresh now as it was when Sebastian Barry began his writing career.

4 | 'To have a father is always big news': Theme and Structure in *The Engine of Owl-Light*

Bruce Stewart

Of three well-known Irish novelists born in 1955, Colm Tóibín, Patrick McCabe and Sebastian Barry, the last-named is the only one to have entered the Irish literary annals in the first year of his life. In his autobiography *The Kick* (2002), Richard Murphy depicts one Francis Barry, the father of the writer, lying 'supine on a bed like a king on a tomb' when Murphy and his wife Patricia Avis arrived with Richard Selig and Mary O'Hara for a late-night party in the Thomas Kinsella's flat in Baggot Street. Presumably the Abbey actress Joan O'Hara, mother of the novelist-to-be, stayed at home with her nursling on the night in question. Even had he been present to hear his maternal aunt Mary sing in Irish about the battle of Aughrim to a harp accompaniment later on, it would be difficult to infer how the cultural forces gathered round the child 'of future fame' (as Murphy calls him) would shape the newborn writer. It is no surprise, however, to find that his first novel is a remarkable embodiment of the idea of 'the divided mind' which the evening's host, the poet Kinsella, would later identify with 'special mutilations which are a part of the Irish experience'.[18] Such 'mutilations' are often seen today as shaping elements in the form of literary modernism variously practised by James

Joyce, Samuel Beckett and Flann O'Brien. Sebastian Barry, as author of *The Engine of Owl-Light* (1988), a much underrated Irish novel, consciously takes these writers as his precursors.

It is entirely apposite (if no more than co-incidental) that the markedly delinquent father makes his entrance in the similarly recumbent position:

> The island across the channel had a Martello tower on it, like a hat resting on a snoring man's chest. My father slept with his back to the waves, and the late fishermen passed him gradually in their squashed boats.[19]

The image is reprised later on in a magic-realist scene that revolves around the accidental hooking of a seagull by a fisherman whose own head is in line-of-sight with Dalkey Island so that it seems -

> … he might swallow the island, which at my angle began on the sea just after the fellow's mouth. The island would have a hook in it, the emotion of my father, and drag the man's stomach out, as the baited hook was doing to the exhausted seagull (p.213).

In tandem with the plaint of *pater absconditus*, Barry's novel enacts an oedipal tale complete with affecting shows of attachment to the very present mother but also an account of the ultimate and inevitable process of detachment on which the protagonist-narrator's own identity is necessarily founded. Barry's strand-entwining narrative also embraces a series of disparate episodes concerning the narrator's experiences at a more autonomous stage of life when he test-drives his adult sexuality in continental Europe and America. Part Rousseau-esque confession and part American road-movie, the episodes in question showcase an appreciably 'hip' awareness of the wider world into which the modern Irish insert themselves as neo-peregrines with an equal appetite for literary exile and global culture. Meanwhile a concurrent strand takes the very different shape of an Irish medieval romance ingeniously narrated by means of an invented language – basically Hiberno-English as spoken by a Sligo workhouse orphan spiced with orthographical improbabilities from Anglo-Saxon and Middle

English to suit the historical period in question. The latter is the most overtly sophomoric element in a novel that can at times come perilously close to callowness in temper and in treatment. Finally, the novel documents the life and times of Batty Moran, that Sligo orphan turned British soldier in a colonial war in Africa, and incidentally reveals in him an unmistakeable model for the later Barry protagonist, Aeneas McNulty, along with others of the lyrically articulate but mentally limited characters of Barry's later works whose characteristic language exploits Hiberno-English in a uniquely expressive manner.

There are, in fact, six clearly distinguishable narrative strands in *The Engine of Owl-Light*, each advancing in alternating sections of the text. What holds them together is hardly more than the title itself and a nexus of motifs involved in its devising – to which we will return in due course. But first it is necessary to examine each narrative strand more closely and, in so doing, to add reflections on its distinctive psychic and linguistic energies, as each is centred on a given character and executed in the corresponding style – a very Joycean procedure. The novel has a highly formal structure and is arranged in twenty major parts named 'sixfoils' instead of 'chapters'. This is perfectly logical, yet distinctly pseudo-archaic - a bibliographic neologism.The episodes that make up successive sections in each sixfoil invariably fall in the same order and pertain to the same narrator/character. Notwithstanding differences of style, however, the 'sixfoil' schema is not without its frustrations and, for much of the time, it is tempting to rearrange the sections mentally (if not actually to reorder them on paper) so as to produce a series of uninterrupted narratives. Indeed, until the technically admirable final chapters start to assert the semiotic harmony of the whole, the reader might be forgiven for supposing that what is being offered is an arbitrary complication of a set of very simple narratives which, in a more conventional literary ambience, could have appeared as a volume of short stories. Viewed from this perspective, *The Engine of Owl-Light* seems like a rather provisional solution to the very old problem: how to make a novel from an ill-assorted collection of shorter fiction writings. Yet that is not, in fact, the genesis of this book, nor is it a worthy solution to the problem of interpretation that it poses to the reader. For, just as the text calls for some hard thinking on the reader's part and much marginal notation, the effort is rewarded since the structure is far more cohesive than its initial chaotic impression suggests. Here is evidence of a remarkably large and coherent act of imagination, albeit the ultimate success of the novel *qua* novel may depend on ordinary literary laws which will not be suspended for the 'divided mind' or any other special pleading of the Irish literary tradition.

In each of the twenty 'sixfoils', the medieval legend always forms the first section. This concerns an Irish chieftain and his Gaelic poet at loggerheads with his ambitious Queen and a Roman cleric who jointly effect his overthrow. These events might be notionally placed at about the time of the Norman invasion (allowing for some interference from the era of St. Patrick), while many of the literary allusions pertain to the classical and renaissance periods also. This is followed by a section of first-person autobiography in an acutely imaginative style that owes much to the early chapters of Joyce's *Portrait* as regards the actualization of the mind of the child. Here the narrator is, if not the author himself, closely enough related to him to make that identification unavoidable (a case that can be made for Stephen Dedalus). What finally brackets this narrative as 'fictive' is the very late confession that 'I made up my father and my sister not being there as a child, when they all too really were there all the time' (p.378). After this comes a section dealing with the entanglement of the same character now grown to manhood with a Swiss girl called Xenia, first in Paris and afterwards in Lucerne where they engage in an erotically overheated but emotionally arid relationship before he reclaims his own identity and escapes, as he arrived, by train. This too is rendered in the first-person, as is the next strand which deals with the experiences of a young Irishman travelling from New York to Key West with Sue, an insouciant young American of 'pretty face and slim naked look' (p.15), and with the owner of a stolen car called Chicken, since his real name is unknown. As matters subsequently unfold, Chicken's anonymity is tragically significant when Sue ends up dead in a motel for reasons connected with events in a town called Dublin, Virginia, which they pass through on the way.

It is here that the identification of the narrator becomes very tricky. The penultimate section in each 'sixfoil' concerns a similar young man's adventures in Key West involving friendships with a Rastafarian called Ali and a stripper called Susan, and leading finally to the robbery of a house at the behest of its owner Stephen. The aim of the robbery, it emerges, is to take a manuscript that bears the title of the novel we are reading: *The Engine of Owl-Light.* This sort of Escherian infolding of literary signifiers suggests meta-narrative and the factual confusion it creates is equalled by a latent ambiguity as to the identity of the narrator-protagonist of the strand in question. In the simplest view he is the author himself, sitting in Key West at the conclusion of all the events which have so far transpired recalling even-handedly both those that involve him personally and those which, as a writer, he has imagined and which concern Batty Moran and the characters in the medieval Irish legend. If so, he has thrust the sad fate of Sue at the hands of Chicken from his mind before submitting to an attraction for Susan by whom he is finally rejected - as he is by Ali, in the upshot of his knack for unthinking betrayal ('Hey Mon … don't give your friendship to anyone', he said. 'A good man can live without dat' [p.375].)

Yet this is not the explanation, since the narrator of the strand explicitly lays claim to the identity of Moran, whose distinct and unmistakeable experience is conveyed in the third person in the final strand of each 'sixfoil' in the novel. Indeed, when Ali says to him, 'Hey Moran … What you do? What's your own trade, mon?' the narrator replies, 'I was working a little in Africa, not a lot' (p.72), thus revealing that he shares a past experience with the Sligo orphan. For the common reader, this is an undeniable problem.

The matter is both clarified and confused early in the novel when, in Sixfoil Two, the narrator writes: 'Batty Moran, and I, lay on the sack and examined the distant ceiling. When very young he forgot the ceiling as often as he looked at it, but after a few years he began to foster a memory, and the ceiling was his memory' (p.38). Passing over a possible allusion to *The Third Policeman*, we see here an adumbration of the theme of memory which dominates the work. At the same time the narrator has interpolated himself in a scene where he does not properly or even plausibly belong except in so far as Batty Moran is the creature of his own imagination – a conjunction that tends to make the ideas of memory and imagination collapse into one. This is to jump from the realm of suspended disbelief where Moran has a life of his own to that of meta-narrative where he is little more than the correlate of thoughts and feelings pertaining to the author. It is, of course, in the middle zone between these two positions that magic realism subsists, and it is there that Barry manages for the most part to sustain the momentum of his interwoven narratives. In this case, however, that interpolated 'I' – both shocking and prohibited in ordinary novelistic terms – comes as a chancy afterthought between its unnecessary commas. But, in reality, the novelist is entirely serious. On the one hand Moran is himself, a representative of Barry's interest in the pariahs and underdogs and untouchables of Irish society; on the other, he is *Moran redivivus*, a version of the same who has entered into a kind of symbiosis with the autobiographical narrator of the American sequences of the novel. Given a temporal interval of seventy years and more between his experiences in Africa and Key West, this amounts to an argument for the transmigration of souls, though in *The Engine of Owl-Light* the rejuvenation has been effected by the commonplace elixir of modern air-travel. Behind this lies a definite idea about the permanence of forms which answers to the Biblical saw 'no new thing under the sun'; and this, in turn, is brilliantly epitomized in the epigraph from Sir Thomas Browne which should be the first and the last thing that the reader glosses in treating of this novel.

In the last analysis everything depends upon the metamorphic identity of Moran and, not surprisingly, a good deal of attention is given to this question in the final pages where we learn that, '[h]aving been a largely extra citizen of Ireland, Africa, Europe and America, Moran went back to Sligo with fifty pounds and an unshakeable wish to be left alone' (p.387). In his new-found solitude, he bears the general aspect of a Syngean tramp or a discarded *seanachie* maundering at the fireside to the equally redundant female called Moll who is never actually seen but who nevertheless serves from the first page as the silent interlocutor to whom both the tale of medieval Conn and the tale of Moran at Key West are narrated. Ergo, they are narrated by the same person notwithstanding the fact that one is told in the third person and another in the first. Clearly Moran is the narrator on both occasions. Here is Moran, on the first page of the novel, telling Moll the legend of Oliver Conn:

> Conny. Oliver Conn. Man of his tribes and tributes, eh? I was sore in love with him. No I were not. Wree did I learn English? Sure it was di army, you know dat place. Listen, *Moll*, drag up.Here's a one. Long time ago, maybe. Mebbe not. Scittish? Not at all. notatall, he was of the West, a man in his black boots ... Yas, yas, he was a rum one, last of his linegage, went into the gutter of histyre shortly after, and no place for a soldier-boy, I think (p.7).

And here, to illustrate the difference between Moran's modern-day adventures and his Gaelic patrimony, are further examples of each from the body of the novel:

> The miniature plane thunders tinily through the minutes on its way to the end of America, a raising sinking through flour. I was on my way there, *Moll*, because the army had almost done with me. The end of some place will suit me fine. So let it be the end of this place. The bottom of England, the bottom of Ireland, the bottom of Europe, all would have attracted me equally (p.17).

> And the queen lifted her clothes, and the Conn remembered why he liked her ... because she had a solid circular bottom that was his delight. So they hove into the bed straight off, *Moll*, and the Conn, lord Olive, dogged her as she desired. And he loved the great smell from her, and hated it also (p.25). [Italics mine in both cases.]

It is only in the last pages that the identity of Moll is much elucidated, on the one hand by Moran himself in his character as narrator of the medieval saga and, on the other, by the narrator charged with telling Moran's story and who now distances himself from the *style moyen indirect* to sound his own 'I' where it has only once been heard before. In the absence of a better hypothesis, one must conclude that this 'I' is an evolution of the child and man of the Irish, European and American first-person narratives and hence, in a conjecture that no one need quarrel over long, a persona of the author of the novel. First this, from Moran confiding to Moll that Conn and his queen are figments of his own imagination – as she is too, according to his remorselessly solipsistic version of the matter:

> Moll, dese two creturz onlee livv in mee, as yoo doo too. Ande soo I haff toldt moi childishe storee ta a womin dat hass nivver bene, an yatt Oi lovt herr (p.387).

And then this from the autobiographical narrator, Moran and Moll together, and mapping onto the former disclosure without any contradiction:

> He spent a great deal of his mornings talking to a woman he called Moll, and often I used to pretend that I was she. This shouldn't be taken as a sign of weakness on my part, but actually a type of generosity. I found it light enough to assume the character of a patient interested woman, and as he never knew anything about it, it hurt no one (p.388).

Squaring these two depositions and drawing the only possible conclusion, it is safe to say that Moran is likewise an invention of the autobiographical narrator – though this is a trump which he holds close to his chest just as the author of *At Swim-Two-Birds* holds his own. It is to Flann O'Brien, of course, that Barry owes the idea of a novel with several different openings, each 'entirely dissimilar and interrelated only in the prescience of the author'.[20]

If invented, there is no reason why Moran should not be as metamorphic as the author likes, spanning different periods and assuming different characters, sensibilities, experiences, capacities and responses. Yet a problem of stylistic dissonance remains for the reader since, allowing for all such changes, the two narrative strands in the 'sixfoil' schema have a good deal *less* in common than the road-movie and the Key West strands, while these involve similar mental and perceptual horizons as well as the same general characteristics of age, gender, physique and social outlook characteristic of the 'green card' Irish male footloose in America in the early 1980s. If proof is sought that the child Oliver grown older is the character who ends up at Key West, it may be found in the remarkable interrogation sequence in Sixfoil Ten which includes the opening question, 'How do you like Key West in comparison to, say, Highgate?' (p.172) – since Highgate is one of the places where the boy has lived with his father. The reality is that Moran's identity has been rather notionally superimposed onto a set of circumstances that patently belong to another one of the author's alter egos, if not in fact himself as autobiographical subject of the whole caboodle at a slightly later phase than the discrete narratives located in Europe and on the road in America. The artistic gain in doing so is to effect a convergence between the character Moran and the first-person narrator; the no-less obvious cost consists in the damage done to probability or, more precisely, an enhanced sense that wilful methods of composition are being permitted to overshadow non-negotiable differences of time and place upon which the ordinary reader depends for satisfaction in or out of magic realism.

At numerous points the novelist introduces artful confusions as to the name of the characters involved, all tending to the suspicion that, in some ontological sense, they are at bottom the self-same person. Moran is Moran – a name evocative of Beckett's trilogy – in both the first and third-person narratives devoted to his doings. By contrast the hero of his Irish legend is called Conn or Oliver. Likewise the child whose narrative forms the second strand in each sixfoil has 'Oliver' as his given name, as when the anonymous interrogator says, 'Come on, Oliver, you remember' (p.173) – or when his mother calls: 'Oliver! ... Oh there you are!', in a later recreation of a childhood summer idyll (p.383). The protagonist of the road-movie calls him 'Oliver' ('Don't be such a cowbell, Oliver honey' [p.319]), although 'Owl' more often ('Whatever you wanted, Owl', she said [p.320]). Xenia, the aptly-dubbed Swiss girlfriend, sticks relentlessly to 'Oliver' too, perhaps for want of practice with the English nickname system: 'You are not very much, are you, Oliver?' (p.338). No reader will repudiate the obvious inference that, since the protagonist of all the many episodes set in Ireland, Paris, Switzerland and America share the same name, he is nothing other than a younger or an older version of the same person. Yet what to make of the fact that the Irish chieftain in Moran's medieval saga is called 'Conn, lord Olive' (p.25) - a strange collision of the Gaelic patronymic of the kings of Connaught with the Lord Protector of the English Commonwealth who famously equated that Irish province with Gahenna (i.e. 'hell or Connacht')? Or that Oliver is, in its historical associations the name of a martyred Irish bishop and saint (Oliver Plunkett) and a maker of Catholic martyrs (Oliver Cromwell). Indeed, when Oliver falls into conversation with a taxi-driver in Key West he skirts around the 'where-from' question: '"England", I said, "I'm from England"', explaining to the reader: 'I didn't want to risk Ireland, in case it encouraged him … I felt as if I were denying my religion to Cromwell' (p.372). Only to discover that the driver's grandfather had been Irish: 'he came over in one of them coffin ships. I bet he was pretty shook up when he got off' (p.372). Personal names, no less than nationalities, are politically loaded. Finally, to confuse the issue further (unless the personage in question has the answer), one Oliver Reynolds, 'true relater', is named in the dedication page of the novel.

One of the special effects for which Joyce's *Ulysses* is known is the trick of conjured detail. Words or facts properly known to one character turn up in the interior monologue of another. (The phrase 'retrospective arrangement' circulates in the novel in ways only partly explicable in terms of its original employment by one derided character.) It is a device that confirms the utter authenticity of the text by hinting at the limits of literary realism; pushed any further, however, the authenticity would crumble. It is to this procedure that we may ascribe the remarkable slippage of identities which brings about a sudden convergence between Moran of Sligo and the eponymous Oliver on the basis of an apparent error perpetrated by the overtly literary character Stephen whose stolen manuscript may well be the very novel we are reading. That the episode involved is narrated by Moran and not Oliver is apparent from the opening: 'Well, Moll, you may never have seen such a place' (p.282). What follows is a bar-room conversation, Ali, redneck sheriff Ron, Moran and Stephen participating, with the last-named offering this specimen of Wildean sagacity to his new Irish acquaintance:

> 'What I've always liked about this town', said Stephen to me, or me as an audience, he wasn't particular, 'is the democratic vulgarity of its insults. Do you find that, as a new arrival here, Oliver?' (p.286)

Next we hear:

> I stared at him as if he was going to shoot me. I didn't dare risk a laugh or a word of agreement or denial. If I'd breathed I was sure on my slight drunkenness he would have bitten me with some polite fang. That he'd mistaken my name was no protection (p.286).

This narrator, once again, is Batty Moran not Oliver (whose surname is never, in fact, given); yet the interloper Stephen clearly confuses him with the protagonist-narrator of a narrative strand in which he himself has no existence. If there is any link between Oliver and Moran on the naturalistic plane of the novel's events it is very thin indeed though gamely the novelist has a stab at suturing up the virtual rent in the veil of realist illusion by supplying Moran with a motive for his migration to America at the time in question: 'Something had happened to me in the so-called dark continent, and it confused me, and was the why I got out of the army' (p.71), we are told, by way of explaining how he took the King's shilling in 1902 and subsequently rolled up at Key West in early manhood in the 1980s.

Naturalistic probability is not the ruling principle of the narrative, which is more like the stuff of verbal association – a recurring resource of magic realism. Rather more than that, the question of naming and identity is subsumed in the wider or more significant one of symbolic association. Here the enabling detail is that Oliver is nicknamed 'Owl', as we have seen. This amiable monicker crops up at sundry points in the road-movie narrative. Now, when we turn to the medieval narrative, we find that the Irish chieftain's poet– an *ollamh* in the original 'Galluc' – is variously known as 'meester Owl' (p.23), 'maister Owle' (p.386), and so forth, depending on the orthographical spirit of the moment. Inevitably some ornithological changes are rung, not least in the title of the novel. This appears to be a definite adherence to the autobiographical protagonist's imaginative landscape insofar as his method of self-checking is to listen 'to the owls or the owl and I asked everyone I knew in my head how things were with me' (p.16). That is hardly surprising since his name is Oliver and since his mental habits are mythopoeic rather than strictly rational, as with all the protagonists of Barry's fiction.

Although Moran does not bear the name of 'Oliver' or 'Owl' in his own person except insofar as he transmogrifies into the autobiographical narrator of the novel, his share in *owl-ness* is nonetheless assured inasmuch as he possesses a stated 'preference' for the avian species which 'no one ever saw, or rarely, and only when the owl chose it' (p.389). Falling as it does virtually at the end of the novel when all the semiotic business of beginning and middle are being wrapped up, the ensuing sentence leads us quickly on to the rationale of the title:

> He thought of owls in the plural sometimes although he only ever heard one, but he heard it for so many years, in so many places, that he could calculate there would have to be more than one such engine (p.389).

If the words 'owl' and 'engine' are effectively conjoined in this, so are 'owl' and 'moon' superimposed on one another in what follows: 'The best nights indeed were the ones when the sky opened, and the moon got in … and the owl thrummed in its machinery' (p.389). Of the moon there is a great deal said in various parts of the novel including an adroit reference to Philip Sidney's famous line, parodied in one of the Swiss sections: 'with how sad steps, O moon, thou climbest the skies, with how sad steps … O foolish-either-way Oliver, thou abandonest thy bag in Lucerne station' (p.355). But it is in his extended dialogue-in-absentia with his mother that Oliver, newly grown to manhood, actually divulges to the reader what is the dominant trope of the novel – a journey outwards from and ultimately back towards to the mother, though transformed by an acquired selfhood that was not to be discovered in her shadow:

> Mother, cotton child, it's a long walk from you, in that it doesn't curve back like walks used to, and had to, or they were not walks (p.354).

'Trains, I suppose', the autobiographical narrator tells us in a Swiss episode, 'are true journeys' (p.177), and the trains that run on front of the childhood home at Longford Terrace in Monkstown are certainly part of the living landscape which leads to this conclusion. Those living on the modern DART line can still appreciate what it meant to see the old steam trains flowing north and south from the balconies of the grander houses along Dargan's railway line.

> … how I see a gull now is how I saw it then: a dark broken noise coming slantwise down the sky, from the brown gloom of the church roof. The church roof which was truly the whole outside the edge of the planet. And the balconies of the houses carried trains in the night-time, big silent travellers in them (p.10).

And then a little later, after some introspection on 'the owl-train stilled by the yeared distance it has to travel' (p.354), we hear the signature-phrase from the title given intact in its most important context:

> Good god [*sic*], it was a long walk after all. I just made it, mother, look at the silver air cutting into the silver water. This is owl-light, mother. The owls made this (p.355).

It is perhaps admissible to infer that the semantic equivalence of 'owl-light' and 'moonlight' implied in such a passage, together with the proximity of allusions to 'engine' derives from some moment of parental fantasy and childish receptivity in the enchanted, mother-son relationship of the author's childhood. It is a moment when the maleness of train and the femaleness of moon combine to describe a real world created by imagination.

An indispensable key to the reality thus defined is to be found in the epigraph from Sir Thomas Browne's *Christian Morals* (1716):

> He who hath thus considered the World, as also how therein things long past have been answered by things present, how matters in one age have been acted, over in another, and how there is nothing new under the sun, may conceive himself in some manner to have lived from the beginning, and to be as old as the World; and if he should still live on, 'twould be but the same thing. [21]

Apart from echoing the book of Ecclesiastes or the Preacher in the Old Testament (' … no new thing under the sun' – Eccl. 1:9), this informs us that lives lived in different times and places are fundamentally the same, thus affording a philosophical rubric for the practice of identity-swopping and thematic mirroring which supplies the basic logic for the stranding method of Barry's first novel. What it does not afford at all is an insight into the postcolonial sensibility of a writer who has been more than once aspersed for failing to participate whole-heartedly in the Irish nationalist project, a feature of *The Engine of Owl-Light* that deserves serious consideration in view of both its striking force and the relatively early date at which it was written. Some remarks of the successive strands will, I hope, bring out both these points.

Moran's saga of Conn Oliver and his unfaithful Queen is a satirical variation of the story of the Leinster king Dermot MacMurrough and Dervorgilla, the couple whose adulterous affair brought the Normans to Ireland. In it Conn plays the part of the O'Rourke while a Roman bishop takes the part of MacMurrough, adding a zest of anti-clericalism to the tale of the broken Gaelic nation. 'It was in the West', says Moran, 'I well remember, before the last and final conflict, that did put the kibosh on the nation, that did hurt it sore and ever' (p.7). He even has a historical tag for the event in question: 'If I may call it the Catholik revolving, the King of Rame's work, an excellent man, none of ours, and wanted none of us' (p.7). Conn, it seems, is suspended between two cultures, his mind divided between druidic and Christian power: 'A christian man, a catoolic by law, bit by natoor he wasint but a pagan, with his poetic priest and his odder catoolic bishop from the modern times.' (p.9) Disaffected from the bishop, the people have still to be won over they 'loved the hoary poete [and] knew his songs and is songs of family before' (p.41). It is obvious from this that king and poet are about to be overthrown and the manner of their demise is brutal in keeping with the character that the bishop, a sadist and a hypocrite, privately reveals. After a solitary procession through his kingdom in the time-honoured manner of his forebears, Conn is left to die suspended from ropes attached to the battlements of his own castle. As for his poet Master Owl, his death ensues, but only after his cheeks are torn off by hounds when he courageously cuts the cords that keep his master hanging on the wall. Conn survives to hide away with a village of faithful subjects while the Queen and Bishop Laurent or Laurentoo (cf. Laurence O'Toole) prosper, she becoming famed for sanctity in the end.

Of Conn or Oliver the poet has this to say: 'Olieve is not man abov all man/but makes ee ech man abuv himself' [59]. Of the Celtic realm he rules, this: 'We hav no countroo inta empir, /we have no godde leden al. / Coon is no springer frum godes hed, / no bluty emprer oot a Rame' (p.59). In his final exchange with the bishop, Owl professes a polytheistic credo 'I havee manee manee gots, batter an mur poerful den yours. Bat I wil nat boste dem to yoo' (p.292), soon to be supplanted by the new monotheistic dispensation. The advent of Christianity, in *The Engine of Owl-Light*, is therefore a form of imperialist conquest – much as it was, in fact, for James Joyce. In Barry's treatment of the matter there is a distinct suggestion of Joyce, not only in the resort of a 'new language', but also in the array of forces and characters which comprise his near-burlesque treatment of the subject. The 'Colloquy of Balkelly the Archdruid and St. Patrick' in *Finnegans Wake* (Bk. IV) provides a perfectly plausible model for the episode. This does not make a Joycean scholar of Sebastian Barry, but it is interesting to note that his contribution to Dermot Bolger's edited collection *Invisible City* (1991), is a story in which a 'Joycean scholar' is said to occupy a room beneath the narrator in a former Georgian mansion turned Dublin tenement turned student squat on Mountjoy Square where Barry actually resided for a time in the late 1970s.[22] This was not quite yet a period of Irish social history when the following idea, ascribed to Conn, became the common stock of advanced opinion: 'My owel house is full uf praistliness, an it is nat kinde' (p.98).

The brutality meted out to Moran in the workhouse where he is reared is an exemplary instance of the patriarchal and matriarchal crimes committed at Letterfrack and the Magdalene laundries of Ireland. His being booted off to join the British Army, then fighting in South Africa, opens the window on an extraordinary series of scenes in which Barry tellingly depicts both the carnage of empire and the development of human dignity through anti-colonial resistance. Two remarkable characters appear in this strand: Henry Grant, the Earl of Tanzania, who is a curious proto-type of Nelson Mandela, and the Irish officer whom Moran serves as batman, Captain Collins, whose position, name and personal outlook as a Catholic in a Protestant world ('You want to watch out for stuffy people in this wide world, Moran' [p.227]) provide an early glimpse of the dynamics that went into the making of *The Steward of Christendom.* (He is also an antecedent of Captain Pasley in *A Long Long Way* as Moran is an earlier version of Willie Dunne.) Grant's oration to the Africans, who are later shot down by the British Army in an episode that bears comparison with the depiction of the 1919 Amritsar Massacre by General Dyer's forces in Salman Rushdie's *Midnight's Children*, triggers an intense reaction in Moran, by then a Sweeney-like figure stravaguing in the war-torn Transvaal:

> Henry Grant and the audience had left all odious fragmentary language behind, and their new notes were whole and destructive. Moran didn't know where he was crying from, but wherever it was, the huge song was inside there, turning the handles and taking off stops. It climbed down into his engine of

> happiness, and worked it till its valves were threatening an explosion … He was changed into a man (p.328).

In numerous Irish and transatlantic episodes of the novel, the history of colonialism and slavery are glanced at, often in pithily satirical ways as when Oliver considers that his remaining on in America might make him seem like 'the original item, more American than the Indians themselves' (p.203). Yet Ali, though Jamaican, has had 'no Romantic notions about American Indians' (p.302).

The account of child-Oliver's relationship with his mother is a thing of great vitality and charm, enlivened by a comical treatment of the delinquent father is 'to be remembered merely for the Herrick-like roll-call of his necessary mistresses and monstresses' (p.118). In translating their disappointment at the inadequate crucifixion lavished on Charles Haughey, putative model for the central figure in *Hinterland* (2002), the Irish critics failed to grasp that the essentially vacuous nature of the character was based on a conception of the father first articulated in this novel. Something touching and significant is achieved in the passages where the sheer absence of the father is represented as a form of painful presence, as when the boy first goes to school in Ireland and finds that his 'father was at my school in spirit. He lay in the lines of the catechism I couldn't read, and smiled at me, godishly. He was the painting competitions I wasn't accurate and colourful enough to win.' (p.193) Two scenes of exceptional comic brio involving visits by policemen to his mother's door in Dalkey culminate in the news that the father will return no more. The mother voice trails off: '"Even so", she said, "never to see someone again is."' And the boy's takes over: 'There was little point telling me he wouldn't be back. He had been hanging from a rope all morning in my bedroom' (p.315).

It is possibly trite to say that the young man's quest for love from other women is an attempt to substitute for the lost love of his mother, yet the intensity of that primal love is a singular mark of this novel: 'It didn't matter about my father because she had me, and it didn't matter about my father because I had her … We both felt half-murdered by him, but we had a grand time together away from him' (p.273). Maturity dictates that the grown man should develop 'a hatred, or maybe a dread, of old sons still clinging to their even more ancient mothers' (p.273), but the original attachment is beautifully commemorated and perhaps even – if the term applies – exorcized in the novel. The protagonists' other relationships with women can be seen as variants on the first yet that does not preclude some daring and effective writing when it comes to capturing the erotic temper of those younger women. Sex with the voracious, controlling and ultimately unfeeling Xenia is an athletic business:

> Her tossed head would turn and glare at me with dribbling rabid growling. Her lean danced buttocks bucked up at me so that my distant phallus, more faithful to her than to me, would delve her smell and her belching cunt – like a child's hand trying to scoop a sandy hole at the tide's overactive edge (p.255).

Sex with American Sue is a gentler affair:

> The way her bottom raised against my stomach long minutes after new time, was a newer version of being born, a wakeful ticking observed version. She birthed me with the silence and the heat that would make me believe in the attraction of being alive (p.160).

As an introduction to the world it was ideal.

Ironically, it is on meeting Xenia's ladylike grandmother that Oliver finds himself 'troubled by how happy being valued again made [him]', leading to the reflection: 'Here was the material of my crudest and most constructive notion of romance' (p.318). Further explorations on the margins of actually-existing human sexuality include a series of coruscating descriptions of the *modus operandi* of the topless bar in which Moran's sojourn in Key West is chiefly anchored, and a perceptive descent into the hell of porn in a Lucerne movie-house. In an encounter with a 'gift-gerl' on his travels, Conn finds her 'a cretur as silvree as snowe in cloodlite, but too yung tak kisse and fondel' [p.210]), thus setting a marker for decency and self-control. He later finds out that he underestimated her age and later still he marries her, living on to share in 'a loif wass dificelt and colde, and ther woreld wass a musik of deseez an owels' (p.386). More generally, and in keeping with Merleau-Ponty's brilliant assertion that 'sex is never entirely absent nor entirely present', the prose of *The Engine of Owl-Light* is infused with sensuality as a form of constant simmering awareness that informs the luminance and colours of perception. Violence too has its moment, as when a drug-dealer is shot dead in the middle-distance on the beach at Key West: 'There would be blood st[r]eaming from the wound, feathering in a widening invisible shape, and dyeing into his light summer clothes. He might be panting a final morsel of air. The sky light be unbearable, and exaggerated to a furnace in his shocked unable pupils. But more certainly none of these things could be unfolded, at such a distance – nothing could be real so far away and stagelike' (p.242).

In all the passages so far quoted it will be apparent that language, and particularly the Hiberno-English language, has always been a highly plastic medium in Sebastian Barry's hands and one which he has forged into a dialect and grammar with rules of expression very much his own. In *The Engine of Owl-Light* more than in the other prose writings (fiction and drama), there is a constant barrage of venturous and not always successful phrasing: 'the unusual clouds ... the complicated grass' (p.219); 'bleeding unimportantly into the water' (p.243); 'the frightened bar' (p.256); 'over to his vague left' (p.265). Words like 'geometry', 'pattern', 'diagram' have a curious quasi-structuralist life in Barry's prose, as if revealing an architectonic of experience of almost skeletal severity awaiting the flesh of more emotive terms. In practice, however, all such moments speak of anxiety and a consciousness of threat in new environments. It may be impossible to count the number of times in this novel that the word 'important' is drawn into a conjunction, e.g., 'I want Sue's important skin to be medicine to mine' (p.124). It is certainly strange to contemplate such writing without reflecting on the way that the Irish literary tradition has been shaped by the combination of creative translation and poeticism which finds its *locus classicus* in the plays of J.M. Synge. Indeed, it might almost be taken as a conscious homage to the

Anglo-Irish playwright that the word 'lonesome' creeps into the first sentence of *Aeneas McNulty*, while renowned Barry phrases such as 'loved, loved … and greatly' at the close of *The Steward of Christendom* can comfortably be linked to antecedents such as 'innocent, and greatly innocent' in Beckett's stylistically seminal *Molloy*. There is, of course, a politics of literary style, and the stylistics of postcolonial novels is notoriously treacherous: take, for instance, the studiously inept English of Hasina's letters from Bangladesh in Monica Ali's *Brick Lane* – for some a poignant medium for the naively-related horrors but for others a slight to Bangladeshi culture and intelligence.

One of the more interesting veins of discourse in *The Engine of Owl-Light* is the more or less continual reflection on questions of language, dialect, style and tone. The more otiose versions of the language wars are readily dismissed, and the novel contains an effectual debunking of humourless, puritanical Irish-language revivalism in the person of a *gaelgoir* school-teacher which really should not be missed: 'He was certainly from Cork, as he claimed, and he loved an extraordinarily unusual language called Theirish.' [322]. The episode concludes with the boy's release from school after he has truthfully drawn his mother complete with what the teacher calls 'boozams': 'The master named me the filthiest little boy he had ever come across, the ruins of a good Irish lad after my English education, and expelled me for a week. He had done something wonderful for me at last. Agus amen' [335]. The Catholic Eucharist and the 'Catkism' gets a swipe too when the boy's reactions to the religious ethos of his school are expressed in this form: 'Everyone was mad, with their rotted bodies and their unplayful languages' [334]. Aside from the thin element of philosophical criticism embedded in these phrases there is a large element of social discrimination, a matter which can, as the Irish experience shows, operate equally effectively both ways. Barry's autobiographical characters are members of a distinct class, as Oliver's embarrassment at a Swiss dinner-table eminently shows:

> I felt divorced excessively from my own family, and what culture they might represent at home. And as they suspected me as an example of vagabond Irishman, I began to feel like one, if there is any such a thing (p.198).

Issues of class inevitably pervade the dialect strategies of the novel, and apologies are registered more than once for attempting to transcribe the strange locutions of a Moran:

> In bringing Moran's life to light by means of a poor and uncooperative language, I am staining that river further, and more than I should. Whether there is some punishment set out for this case will be of some interest to me in the future. For the moment I am content with the interest I seem to retain in Moran (p.73).

or an Ali:

> I'm still not certain if I can truly tell you how my old friend Ali spoke. It was very complicated and sometimes I didn't even follow him, because though he was using something like English, and probably better, he had a lot of new words for his own private and national use. But I'm translating him here, because it's the best I can do and anyway I don't really remember exactly what I said either, and in that respect I'm translating myself also (p.71).

These embarrassments are staunchly countered by a series of reflections on the place of accent in the realm of existence: is it essential or inessential?

> Memory has no accent, like one of those people whose origins are vague and called neutral – but it also has all accents when it has been them all. A pervasive liquid traveller, who is as comfortable in third class as first, or uncomfortable. Neither tyrant nor guardian, something to fear and love – which reminds me of something, but of course I don't know what (p.232).

It can hardly be said that this ambiguous account resolves the issue. Indeed, it does little more than to reveal an anxiety which subsequent practice as a dialect writer ultimately dispelled. At the same time it places the emphasis where it properly belongs, not on the issue of social sensitivities which so often – albeit under the guise of national consciousness – frequently dominates the question of postcolonial language. The proper emphasis is memory, and memory is, indeed, the pervasive and the most vital theme in the novel – a theme gracefully captured (though not without a final quake of writerly self-consciousness) in the following sentences, which themselves describe the nature of the kind of activity that *The Engine of Owl-Light* undertakes and the goals that it very creditably achieves:

> Sue and the wrong roads we are learning to love, will never be so again, not in the generosity of my own particular memory. It allows a mere shadow, a slight frame of what happens, to persist without glory and without true muddle into the sections of the future that are set aside for the hunting of the past. Et cetera (p.138).

In writing of the role of memory *The Engine of Owl-Light* takes language on a journey of discovery that serves to identify its author as a true writer – a veritable *homme plume.* In this sense if no other it is a bildungsroman narrating the process by which the protagonist becomes an artist drawing upon the energies of self and society, history and adventure, in order to assert the possibility of writing and its purpose. This as an outcome is foreseen in the childhood section of the novel where (after the manner of Stephen Dedalus) the writer-to-be discovers the power of the new medium: 'In that room of cold ocean I wrote out my name for the first time, servant of letters at last and … was happy, and felt cruel and wicked at the same time' (p.155).

Illustration 1: Alison Deegan and Brendan Gleeson in *Prayers of Sherkin.* Abbey 1990

Illustration 2: Alison Deegan and Alan Barry in *Prayers of Sherkin.* Abbey, 1990

5 | 'Everyman's story is the whisper of God': Sacred and Secular in Barry's Dramaturgy

David Cregan

The first experience the reader of a Sebastian Barry play encounters is the affective and evocative language used in his stage directions. Using language as a broad and somewhat abstract canvas, Barry paints a literary picture which transports the reader to a place which is viscerally familiar, and yet imaginatively uncommon: theatrical landscapes which defy the rational project of dramatic realism or naturalism in their poetic structure, and conveyed in the style of literary prose. His stage directions serve as a stylistic prelude, setting the tone for a dramaturgical technique which favours beauty over function. For example, the first sentence of *Boss Grady's Boys* (1988) offers the reader a description of the character of Mick sitting on the stage '*with a large purple sweep of light as of a mountain*'[23] for a backdrop. His play about a religious sect living off the southern coast of Ireland, *Prayers of Sherkin* (1990), embarks on an historic journey of religious fervour tempered by domestic simplicity through unadorned language, '*Curtain. A shadowy stage ... Dusty late sunlight through a high window. Ten candles hanging from their rack, partly formed by ladling*'.[24] The style is prose, but the organization of the language suggests a type of poetry which artistically defies the rational expectation of a literary drama and offers, alternatively, a heightened composition rich in theatrical imagination. This inventive and seductive method of introducing his plays transports by visual mood and excites by the promise of heightened theatrical aspiration.

It is the captivating nature of Barry's dramaturgical strategy combined with the otherworldly quality of his theatrical imagination that this essay will explore. Focusing primarily on his plays, *Whistling Psyche* (2004), *Prayers of Sherkin*, and *Fred and Jane* (2002), this study seeks to identify and describe the transcendental yearning at the centre of his work which elicits a type of pathos scarcely matched in the Irish dramatic tradition. It will attempt to identify the existential constituent of his creativity, all the while locating that 'spiritual' component of his creative desire within the context of the metaphysical project or genre which we call the theatre.

Sebastian Barry's choice to work as a playwright, within all of the practices and principles of the theatre, is an artistic decision which invites query. It is a textual project which desires to go beyond its own limitations, ultimately seeking embodiment. As theatrical dramaturgy is incomplete in its literary form, and only one in a series of aesthetics which participates in the phenomenological experience of production, theatrical writing serves as a medium through which the elements of the theatrical production merge with the literary project of authorship to create live theatre. The text is always reaching toward something which is both its own set of constructs and something more than its own limitations. And yet in the analysis of theatre, a language to describe this tension between the achievement of text and its consequent expectation of production is only beginning to emerge. It is therefore necessary for the purpose of this study to examine the interstices in which Barry's production aspirations affect pathos, the quality of his work which infuses his dramaturgy with an emotional empathy unrivalled by most Irish playwrights.

In the search for the critical tools and the consequent professional language necessary for a concise and illustrative analysis of the multidimensional structures of drama many theatre scholars are stumped by the prospect of articulating a non-opinion based perspective of the numinous aesthetics of the theatre. Denying the feasibility of taste and defying the limitations of 'feelings', scholars are often dependent on the traditional theories of analysis tried and tested by the academy. Systematized theories such as psychoanalysis, or power-based theories of gender identity and marginalization provide invaluable perspectives which more than adequately illuminate the possibility of subliminal meaning, or articulate cultural and textual bias, yet, the ever-elusive task of documenting what otherwise might insufficiently be described as the 'magic' of the theatre simultaneously perplexes and seduces those of us who make a profession based on performance analysis. Sebastian Barry's writing could, and certainly is, interpreted through these various critical lenses, and yet, these perspectives hardly articulate the more affective qualities of yearning so powerfully illuminating the interior of his plays.

Acknowledging the limitations of endorsed systems for dramatic analysis is not to reduce or eliminate them, but rather to press for an investigation of the devices required by the objective of writing for the theatre. In his dramaturgical method, Barry strives, by means of the creative rationalist project of language, to achieve the temporally conditional moments of the overall theatrical experience, moments which in actuality define the art form of the stage. The rituals of theatrical practice seek to move beyond the informational creativity of literature and into the live encounter with aesthetic. Barry's skill as a writer is certainly centred in his ability to be descriptive, but what is arguably most distinctive in his material is his aspirational language and his purposeful attempts to structure beauty in his drama. For the purposes of reaching beyond the cognitively descriptive we will cross the linguistic threshold of the 'secular', venturing into the language of the 'sacred' in order to articulate the attraction to the pathos of the stage. The words 'sacred' and 'secular' are purposely placed in inverted commas to indicate that the intent is not to make this analysis religious, in the institutional sense of the word, but rather spiritual in the ethereal or elusive sense of that which defies rational cognition and structured classification, in search of beauty and truth. This is the language of ritual, of existentialism, and with the highest of aspirations, the language of beauty and transcendence, all of which are found in the luminous plays of Sebastian Barry.

The task then is to bridge the modern division between the function of secular theatre and notions of the spiritual. In his book *Great Reckonings in Little Rooms*, Bert O. States, using the language of philosophical theology, describes non-naturalistic theatre like Barry's as 'a closed circuit of metaphysical feeling induced by the interplay of visual and aural images'.[25] This interplay of the visual and the aural highlights the essential connection and energy between what is seen and unseen, a common correlation in both religious and theatrical experience. The relationship between audience and artist – be it playwright, actor, designer or musician – is dependent on the artist's creative ability to generate verbal and representational metaphors which allow the audience to experience empathy. States describes this correlation thus:

> Isn't empathy the force that keeps us in our theatre seats? In short, a sort of sensory self-projection, or willingness to vibrate in tune with the work, with whatever the work may be up to. On this level empathy disappears only when beauty disappears, when the play makes a mistake, when the acting is bad, or when an accident occurs on stage, and we come back, prematurely to ourselves.[26]

Through the purposeful and particular formation of his stage directions Barry creates a means by which his plays can be embodied, beginning them by setting a tone in both image and language.

In the opening stage direction of *Boss Grady's Boys*, cited earlier, Barry structures his sentences to privilege the theatrical over the grammatical – '*with a large purple sweep of light as of a mountain*' (*BGB*, p.5). In the initial directions for *Prayers of Sherkin*, he textures the language so as to move beyond stage instruction into the sensation of atmosphere. Evidence of the same type of heightened language and creative structure is also found in the stage directions for both *Whistling Psyche* and *Fred and Jane*.

Whistling Psyche, produced at the Almeida Theatre in London and directed by Robert Delamere, is set in the waiting room of a Victorian railway station. It is a two character play in one act which brings together two British historical figures involved in nineteenth-century medical reform – Florence Nightingale and Dr. James Miranda Barry. Barry weaves together the lives of these apparent strangers as they endure a purgatorial experience and their painfully repetitious memory. The stage directions evoke an antique atmosphere in structure and metaphor, willing into existence a time and place other than here: '*There is a quietness as ill befits a railway station, and music runs along like confident rats*'.[27]

Fred and Jane, produced at the Bewley's Café Theatre in Dublin and directed by Caroline Fitzgerald, is also a one-act, two character piece. The play traces the story of an abiding friendship between two nuns: Anna, who is in her thirties, and Beatrice, who is in her sixties. This play about the intensity of relationship also begins by imagining the setting: '*The ante-room of a convent. Slow milling of sunlight. Rich polish of wood. Sense of care*'.[28] Barry goes beyond the descriptive to create a combination of sensation and image which is nearly olfactory and tactile.

Barry's linguistic metaphor here conjures perception and emotion. Yet these words are never intended to be expressed to an audience, but instead are for the edification of the reader, the designer, the actor or the director. The nature of these directions differs from trends in modern Irish dramatic practice. They have a literary quality reminiscent of George Bernard Shaw or Sean O'Casey in their detail, but are much more poetic than narrative. A somewhat closer comparison to compare Barry's stage directions can be made with those of Frank McGuinness and Marina Carr, contemporary playwrights who, like Barry, work outside the parameters of realism.

McGuinness's stage directions are general, leaving broad room for artistic interpretation, such as this in Part Three of *Observe the Sons of Ulster Marching Towards the Somme*: '**Moore** *takes another step on the bridge. Lights fade on the bridge*';[29] or that found at the end of Act One of Marina Carr's *On Raftery's Hill* where the playwright describes the unfolding action between father and daughter: '***Red** continues cutting the clothes off her.* ***Sorrell** gesticulates and struggles pathetically ...* '[30]

Both these authors use the stage direction to advance the narrative through action; McGuinness to negotiate the relationship between actor and set, and Carr to electrify the tension between actors in much more practical ways than Barry employs. There is a functional nature to these directions which much more clearly serves the technical requirements necessary for production and direction: in short, they are far less aspirational than Barry's atmospheric directions.

It is thus important to distinguish Barry's dramaturgy from that of the tradition in which he writes, and from the styles of his contemporaries, in order to highlight the need for a unique form of analytical language to apply to his material. What is distinctive about his stage directions suggests that his authorial intention is not focused on detailed accuracy of place or instruction for actors and designers. It is, rather, inclined towards mood, atmosphere, and sensation, essential elements in the quest for beauty, the search for meaning, and for the means to elicit the empathy necessary for an artist to create pathos in an audience.

Having established a preliminary access into the metaphysical element of Barry's dramatic style, it now becomes necessary to prove this thesis by mapping his 'transcendental' method of creativity in the plays identified earlier for analysis. In order to do so, an application of more specifically spiritual paradigms such as those of ritual, pilgrimage, and liminality, will provide a suitable vocabulary through which to examine the overall experience of the theatre. Both disciplines compel practice, and both the theological and the theatrical necessitate a language of analysis that attempts to give shape to abstractions such as experience and beauty. Consequently, the principle of the imagination will be the mutual objective in both the creative and spiritual realms which will connect the theatre of Sebastian Barry with notions of the sacred.

As a theatrical artist Barry uses imagination to transform identifiable human experience into dramatic pathos. His theatrical strategy in *Whistling Psyche* relies on divergence. Although the actors respectively playing Florence Nightingale and Dr. Barry occupy the same space on stage, they are otherwise worlds apart. Dr Barry is clearly the protagonist of the piece as he bemoans his story of stolen youth and tormented adulthood. Eventually he exposes the source of his angst, revealing that he is in fact a woman, disguised as a boy to enable her to study medicine in a misogynistic society. Against all odds, Dr. Barry became a doctor in the British army, famous for his work with lepers and the mentally ill. His tortured memories of a life in disguise, an inauthentic life despite his career success, infect the play with the type of circular desperation necessary to imply a version of tortured purgatory.

On the other hand, Nightingale remembers her past with pride. As mid-Victorian medical crusader for the then revolutionary concept of hospital hygiene for saving the lives of British soldiers, she nostalgically recalls the difficulties of her task. As a woman she undertook the reformation of practices for treatment of soldiers in military hospitals following the Crimean War, but her dramatic function within the play is primarily as listener, eavesdropping on the private hell of Dr Barry's persistent memories. She speaks empathetically to him, offering words of consolation, but is given no assurance that he can even hear her expressions of sympathy. Eventually, overwhelmed by the frustration of the impassibility of their mutual isolation, she cries out in a scene in which anxiety and alienation dominate the stage:

> **Miss Nightingale:** I begin to be anxious about the great silence of this place. There is a lack of anyone attending to us, no? I think there would be an ease of the mind if you would speak to me … I grow afraid, and am not suited to it (*WP*, p.47).

The words of Florence Nightingale express an existential anxiety, one which poses the question 'Are we alone in all of this?' or in broader terms 'Does God exist?' This is the existentialist emphasis on human experience in the face of an uncaring and unresponsive universe; a universe in which the human being is solely responsible for self. In *Existentialism and Human Emotions*, Jean-Paul Sartre describes it in these terms:

> Thus, there is no human nature, since there is no God to conceive it. Not only is man what he conceives himself to be, but he also is only what he wills himself to be after this thrust toward existence. Man is nothing else but what he makes of himself … Thus, existentialism's first move is to make everyman aware of what he is and to make the full responsibility of his existence rest on him.[31]

Atheism, or the denial of the existence of God, is an essential component of this philosophy, and it finds obvious reference in *Whistling Psyche*. Dr Barry describes this isolation and disbelief in his own lived experience:

> **Dr Barry:** And so, though I long to go, I cannot go for there is no approbation, no love of monarch or mortal to release me. Here I abide as the mourner of myself, as the rememberer of my own heart, waiting in this waiting room, even the desperate celebrator of an imprisoned soul (*WP*, p.57).

The play reflects the isolation of the human condition in its repetition of the individual story, as well as in the monologic form of its structure. Each character has long sections of descriptive dialogue addressed to the audience, rather than to each other, as they remember themselves as they had lived.

Considering Sebastian Barry's creative positioning in line with the questions of existentialist constructs it would appear that this play uses imagination with the opposite intent of reconciliation or healing. Instead, the playwright intentionally probes the depths of human experience to emphasize our alienation from ourselves and others; a secular struggle for meaning but nonetheless infused with the search for significance tied to the notion of the human spirit. Just when it might appear that Sebastian Barry is ready to admit the meaninglessness of life he allows Dr. Barry to speak these final words of hope and faith:

> **Dr. Barry:** … This is why humanity itself is but a laughable storm of leaves and ash. This is why everyman's story is the whisper of God. This why we are redeemed at last, because nothing else can be done for us. Worn out, erased, breathless and distained by the merriments of tomorrow we will cry out for forgiveness and be forgiven, for God takes each and everyone and makes him new, returns him to the crisp clear lines of the original mould, relieves him of his heavy sins, and in His wise mercy let him go into the strange eternity where there is not earthly story and no human song. To that mercy now my heart calls out. I pray, I pray for that (*WP*, p.60).

Sebastian Barry diverts from Sartre's existentialism and asserts the hope of a divine redemption of human experience. Dr. Barry's words ceremonially impel the play towards its ending in a final prayer. The language is liturgical in its choice, and playwright Barry leaves the reader with holistic imagery that unites and heals in a play about brokenness and pain:

> *Leak of dawnlight from above, like a sacred painting. Light from behind binds them … A whole music, a rescuing music … a strange marriage, an unexpected couple* (*WP*, pp.60-1).

As the lights fade on *Whistling Psyche* Barry creates an equally ceremonial ending by drawing the two characters together physically, and referring to this resolution of character division as '*a strange marriage, an unexpected couple*' (*WP*, p.61). The symbolic action of the performed piece combines with the language of the stage directions to form a representation of understanding, forgiveness, and redemption in the two characters who seemed throughout the play to be irreconcilably divided. As '*Light from behind binds them*', both audience and reader are left with the sense of a greater force than the flawed individuals embody as they are saved from the purgatory of endless repetition and isolation. In a moment such as this it is clear how the theatre has the power to extend the representation of text by relying on the visual reference to symbols of unity and reconciliation. It is here that the action of the theatre, the presence of audience and actor, and the energy and pathos upon which this communion is dependent, defy the simplicity of a criticism which is merely cognitive, demanding instead an expression which touches on the mystical communion of shared experience and emotion.

Experience is the defining reality of the practices and principles of the theatre; the shared reality between the conventions of stagecraft and the perceptions, both emotional and cognitive, of the audience. Through the perspective advocated by authorship, and further enhanced by production, audience and practitioner unite through a shared identification with the dramatic symbols implemented and by the language used. In the most effective theatrical events, audiences recognize their own actual experience in the fictional semiotics of the production, and share in the moment of dramatic pathos. This connection between the theatre and the existential realm, with all its implied philosophical ideas of secular sacredness, demands a discussion of the more practical aspects of the theatre of Sebastian Barry as they embody the notion of encountering transcendence through beauty. Such a discussion is necessary in order to make the transition from the ideas of literature to the experience of theatre. Theoretical paradigms associated with the power of ritual as the embodiment of sacred ideas transformed into the tactile realm of common experience and collective affect prove useful for this project.

Ritual itself is defined as a series of actions which subscribes to religious or cultural norms. Jerzy Grotowski, the great twentieth-century Polish director and theatre theorist, asserted notions of the 'sacred', in very secular ways, as the source of inspiration for the practice and achievement of theatre. He describes what he identifies as a problem with the theatre's inability to recognize or tap into the power of its sacred affiliations:

> I do not think that the crisis in the theatre can be separated from certain other crisis processes in contemporary culture. One of its essential elements – namely, the disappearance of the sacred and its ritual function in the theatre – is a result of the obvious and probably inevitable decline of religion. What we are talking about here is the possibility of creating secular *sacrum* in the theatre.[32]

These words serve as a call to the theatre to identify and acknowledge its vital energy for social transformation at a time of vast secularization.

Barry's plays go beyond the mere identification of the decline of organized religious sentiment in modern Ireland towards creating a theatrical ritual of longing, reconciliation, and transformation long associated with sacred faith and religious practice. As argued, Barry provides a text which artistically advocates the expression of the intangible in a context – the theatre – which not only encourages imagination but requires it. With the increasing cultural distance in contemporary Ireland from the communal experience of ritual through organized religion, the theatre has become a rare conflation of collective energies. Just as institutional religious ritual requires a communal belief in that which is tacit, the theatre invites a co-operative assent to imagination, creating a secular space for re-imagining cultural possibility. Thus, the theatre becomes a sanctuary representing and celebrating that which has yet to be actualized in human experience – hope.

In his book *From Ritual to Theatre: The Human Seriousness of Play*, Victor Turner asserts that performance is the appropriate expression of human experience. Throughout Barry's work he represents the types of alienation and harmony, separation and unity, life and death, experienced in a world which has lost much of its faith in organized religion. In many ways his plays are performing the experience of secularising modernity. In so doing he draws on contemporary values. His is the modern search for principles and paradigms of living, in order to represent the human experience of the here and now. Although, as is the case with *Whistling Psyche* or *Prayers of Sherkin*, his subject may be the past, his object is the present. In this way he does not simply reflect modern experience but uses history to refract that experience. His is not a documentary representation of history, but rather an investigative one. Turner highlights the analytical nature of theatre itself which encourages analysis:

> Theatre is, indeed, a hypertrophy, an exaggeration, of jural and ritual processes; it is not simply a replication of the 'natural' total processual pattern of the social drama. There is, therefore, in theatre something of the investigative, judgmental and even punitive character of the law-in-action, and something of the sacred, mythic numinous, even 'supernatural' character of religious action ... [33]

In this explanation Turner, like Grotowski, validates the 'supernatural' vocation of the theatre, but extends that association into the idea of action. This allows for the creative space between common cultural experiences which audiences recognize and with which they are in sympathy. The playwright organizes those experiences into the ritual action that is the performance of the play. In the introduction to *Irish Writers and Religion*, Robert Welch highlights the significance of the writer's task as cultural translator: 'But what is there to the eyes everyday becomes filmed over with the dust of familiarity, so we need ritual, poetry and art to awaken us to the 'charge' that holds things together in form in the most common everyday things'.[34]

How then does Sebastian Barry create drama which interrogate experience while relying on commonly recognized cultural symbols and rituals to elicit empathy and pathos? The space between cultural information and artistic renegotiation of collective experience is well served by notions of the *liminal* as described in the work of Victor Turner. Turner suggests that this in-between space is the area in which culture creates and redefines meaning. He writes, 'Liminality is a temporal interface whose properties partially invert those of the already consolidated order which constitutes any specific cultural "cosmos"'.[35] *Prayers of Sherkin* embodies Turner's philosophy, employing ideas of the liminal in its treatment of cultural transition and change.

Prayers of Sherkin was first produced on the stage of the Peacock at the National Theatre in Dublin in 1990, directed by Caroline Fitzgerald. The play is set in 1890 and depicts the story of a family who travelled as part of a small group from Manchester for religious reasons, settling on an island off the southwest coast of Cork. The family, now in its third generation, is in decline, with no one left to marry from within the community and a prohibition to marry outside it. As they struggle with issues of religious destiny the eldest daughter, Fanny, decides to marry a Catholic Irishman. This deeply poetic text explores the death of a traditional way of life, which ultimately means the end of the family's existence on Sherkin, and Fanny's hope for a future through exogamous marriage.

Setting the play on a small island, Barry explores the joys and the struggles of isolation. The presence of the sea dominates the action of the play. Through his use of one of the oldest salvation tropes in literature, he employs the idea of passage by sea as a spiritual, temporal, and ideological metaphor which extends from the original mission which sailed from Manchester to Sherkin, through to the family's regular journeys back and forth from the island to the mainland. In Act One we are introduced to the ghost of the founding father of the mission, the original visionary who led a group of three families away from England, Matt Purdy. Matt can only be seen by the audience, functioning as a type of historical narrator. He describes the idea of the passage in vivid language:

> **Matt Purdy:** We embarked from the dark port of England and sailed to Cork in the whitest ship.There were storms in the purple sea and there were fruitful fishes, and the three families clung to the rail and found their haven … And I, Matt Purdy, had my vision that was like unto the vision of John of Patmos, and it came to me in my dreams to go to Ireland for to find an island where we could abide. And we sailed out of the city of suffering to Cork, and found out this little island of Sherkin where we could wait for the city of light (*PS*, p.54).

The story is nearly biblical in the dramatization of a journey intent on religious salvation. The transformative power of the purple sea and the sustaining quality of the fish within it consecrate their pilgrimage. The reference to John of Patmos provides a complimentary eschatological connection, uniting the Book of Revelation and the Sherkin sect.

Matt Purdy disappears as quickly as he emerges and the action of the play picks up with the present reality of the last remaining inhabitants of Sherkin, the Hawke family. John Hawke is the widowed patriarch, living on the island with his children Fanny and Jesse, his sister Hannah, and his wife's sister Sarah. The family sustains itself by making candles and engaging in other cottage industries which allow for the continuation of their separate lives, but which simultaneously requires them to interact commercially with the mainland. In the following scene the family discusses at dinner the prospect of crossing over to sell some honeysuckle and butter to the people of the town:

> **Sarah:** I do not like to cross without a purpose.
> **Hannah:** Flowers is purpose enough.
> **Fanny:** And we would love to come, me and Jesse.
> **John:** (*to* ***Sarah***) Now.
> **Sarah:** Well. The wicked thing this is I love to cross. I dream of crossing. I am too attached to the town. I dream about that material in Pearse's. Wicked (*PS*, p.56).

Sarah's language is noteworthy in that it suggests an immoral aspect to the desire for this passage. Whereas the trip from Manchester was considered redemptive and eschatological, the family's prospective journey to the Irish mainland could be considered potentially corrupting because of the material temptation inherent in the town's ethos. In these moments Barry sets in motion the concepts of the inevitability of movement and the fear of change in the play. In some unmarked territory, on the sea, between island and town, a danger is suggested. The geography of the sea becomes the liminal space in which two worlds prepare to collide, perhaps eventually to invert one or the other. Using the religiously prophetic language of vision and dream, Barry gently prepares his audience for the destiny of community transformation by linking the past with the present. Sarah evokes the past to validate her desire for passage:

> **Sarah:** (*simply*) Matt Purdy saw five angels on the bridge crossing the great river. He saw them walking among the crowd of mortals, plain bright people with feathered wings.
> **John:** (*as a fact*) I never did see one (*PS*, p.57).

In Sarah's description the number of angels crossing into the town and walking among the people matches the number of family members left on the island, and thus foreshadows the events to follow.

The crossing of water in *Prayers of Sherkin* functions as a rite of passage through which life is changed; the sea is the liminal territory where major life changes begin. In their book *Image and Pilgrimage in Christian Culture*, Victor and Edith Turner extend the notion of the liminal: 'It has become clear to us that liminality is not only *transition* but also *potentiality*, not only "going to be" but also "what may be" …'[36] This 'potentiality' is inherent throughout the play, highlighting the hope that runs above and below the storyline, but is also the moment when theatre enters the sacred realm of secular transformation.

In *Sherkin* Barry writes a play of vast metaphoric intimation and biblical analogy, drawing together a variety of natural references from birds to sea to trees and associating them with religious vocation by grounding the play in nonconformist notions of destiny. In many ways the family's journey from the island to the town represents a journey from nature to culture, and the 'divinity' of the plain religious way of life is threatened by the commercial draw of the town and the secular values it represents. Fanny is the character who embodies the hope of the dying family, but as she crosses the water one last time, leaving her community and family behind, just as in *Whistling Psyche*, light is the symbol of anticipation and a rejection of the darkness of death. Once again to the luminous language of Barry's final stage directions for *Sherkin* conveys the import of her decision:

> *Out on the water.* ***Fanny*** *in the stern seat, her sea box held firmly.* ***Eoghan*** *rows. The darkening sea spreads all around. Plash of oars in still air. The lamp shedding light. A quiet moon, above. In his own bright light,* ***John*** *comes to the end of the pier.* ***Eoghan*** *rows,* ***John****'s light diminished plash by plash. He can barely see his daughter. He gives a slight wave to her. His light extinguishes. Slowly, the other side, from the darkest shadow, on the wharf at* Baltimore, *light grows on* ***Patrick****, looking out, worriedly waiting. Plash by plash his light increases* (*PS*, pp.118-9).

The diminishing and increasing light during Fanny's crossing symbolizes transition, leaving the audience with a sense of potentiality and the inherent hope of what may yet be. Fanny's transition is a hopeful move away from the religious community and towards the secular needs of the individual; a movement which can also be traced in the cultural patterns of modernization in contemporary Ireland as it sheds its national religious identity in favour of a cosmopolitan individualism

The beauty of Barry's prose in this play is undeniable, and the poetic metaphors are clearly sacred in their reference, but it is essential in arguing for the concept of secular sacredness in the type of modern theatrical practice which Barry espouses to distinguish between traditional religiosity and the type of secular *sacrum* suggested earlier in the quotation from Jerzy Grotowski. In order to do this one must return to the investigative nature of theatre as suggested by Victor Turner, a theatre which seeks to ritualize experience in order to analyse or critique it.

How does the theatre itself become a site for the representation of potentiality within Irish culture? *Fred and Jane* is another of Barry's character studies of individuals grappling within the complicated and redemptive depths of interpersonal relationships within community. Formal Catholic religious or vowed life is the context in which these two women, Beatrice and Anna, have formulated their unique bond of friendship. And yet, traditional notions of Catholicism, or modern Irish assumptions about nuns, play no role in the human – as opposed to institutional – story Barry tells through these women. Instead of relying on cultural polemics which seek to erase the Irish past by the subversion of religious identity, Barry co-opts the language of faith with a postmodern twist. Both women have film stars as their idols rather than saints; for Anna it is Jane Fonda, for Beatrice, Fred Astaire. Beatrice describes her fascination with Hollywood stars:

> **Beatrice:** I used to wake up when I was a novice and see Fred standing in the corner of the room, smiling very nicely. I must say he always did smile very nicely. At the back of my mind I wanted Gary Cooper to turn up, just once for the effect. Or Henry Fonda (*FJ*, p.73).

Anna also describes her fascination with Jane Fonda, declaring her desire to become this icon of film and fitness videos.

Herein lies the key to understanding the sacred nature of Barry's secular plays. In *Fred and Jane* Barry refuses the polemics of the popular Irish national discourse on the church which marginalizes and accuses religious life. He does so in two interrelated methods of dramaturgy: firstly by choosing the context of religious life for the exploration of modern Irish struggles with identity and relationship, and secondly by employing comedy as the primary genre in the piece.

It would be a gross oversight to ignore in this play the choice of portraying Anna and Beatrice as nuns. As Ireland becomes progressively less dogmatic in its approach to notions of the spiritual, Barry appears to be exploring one of the most restrictively dogmatic styles of living in order to address existential concepts similar to those raised in *Whistling Psyche* – loneliness, authenticity, vocation, and individual responsibility for self and others. As questions of national identity in Ireland fragment the alleged homogeneity of the past, disassembling traditional structures of community and belonging, *Fred and Jane* poses the question 'to whom do I belong?' The play, or perhaps more accurately, the culture in which we view the play, voyeuristically encourages us to desire that the relationship between these two women is sexual. This fits our contemporary preconceptions of the nature of such an intensely bonded love between two individuals. But Barry does not fulfil this desire, allowing the women to remain true to their vocations while simultaneously allowing them to explore the platonic connection of abiding companionship. Anna describes what happened after she was ordered to go to England by her community, and her consequent separation from Beatrice:

> **Anna:** My whole system went out of kilter. It was like a menopause and a pregnancy rolled into one. I ate so much bad food I couldn't think for calories. My hair began to thin out – to fall out, for heaven's sake. I had more aches than a soccer player. The doctor thought I was an hysterical young nun and gave me barbiturates ... Beatrice started to come apart like an

> over-boiled onion. Not that she ever told me. I thought she was doing fine, aside from mere grief (*FJ*, p.81).

Logic would inhibit an Irish author from setting a play, written with the hope of eliciting audience empathy through characterization, within the context of modern Irish religious life. But here is the dramaturgical genius of the piece: Barry rejects reason in favour of imagination. For him imagination is inextricably associated with the deepest of human experiences: love, friendship, understanding and mutual ideas of responsibility. His aesthetic vision represents the same principles on which faith is established: possibility, hope, reconciliation, and the essential element of doubt – all striving towards meaning and connection. Because these notions are difficult to systematize, the natural consequence of Barry's artistic vision is that he rejects the rationalist project of realism which depends on temporality, and reaches towards that which is atemporal.

Diverting from the characteristic intensity of political and emotional subjects and language which appear in virtually all of his plays, Barry uses humour to address complicated subjects in *Fred and Jane*. He does so not to ignore these important issues, but to investigate them, within the safeguards of laughter. Barry explores the vital and shifting spaces of identity in contemporary Ireland as the nation reaches towards a modernity free from the constraints of the past. He does so through the passion of abiding, if not conventional, friendship. Beatrice and Anna are opposites in many ways, Beatrice is from the country, Anna from Dublin. There is also a thirty year difference in their ages, and yet, their spirituality, their religious vows, and their belief in God become common ground for what could be considered an otherwise incongruous relationship. Beatrice tells how their friendship began, quoting the Mother Superior who separated them in the first place:

> **Beatrice:** … She said no one knew the essence of things. Nobody, she says, can really say what represents what. What the meaning of things is, what the meaning of nuns is (*FJ*, p.86).

Admitting the unintelligibility of our human condition, Barry's dramatic language is released into the realms of imagination, symbol and analogy, exploring meaning and experience, transcending the limitations of the ordinariness of life through the extraordinary sacredness of the theatrical experience.

In conclusion, here are some of the author's own thoughts on the 'spiritual' nature of his work:

> A further thought: the spiritual dimension of the plays is obviously there, but couldn't be there if it did not arise out of the usual confusion and mess of the modern mind (mine, that is). I would not say it arises even out of doubt, because doubt presupposes real and admirable belief. When the actor Donal McCann said once to me that one of the reasons he took on *The Steward* was because I obviously believed in an afterlife (a thing that became hugely pertinent to him as he was dying of course) I did register, though did not show, a sort of inner disquiet about it, as if I might be cheating him. When we were rehearsing *Whistling Psyche*, Claire Bloom, who is Jewish, was anxious about the ending, which seems to assume a Christian God and heaven, and again, I felt like some reverse image of the Penal-law priest who had to deny his status by a double negative, 'I am not no priest" (as we were taught at school). Similarly, I am not no (sic) proper believer, but I am certainly appalled enough at the provisionality of the self (again I mean myself) to wish for some possible state of completeness, when the house is finished and the garden thriving, but ... But it is deeply deeply (sic) provisional, and of doubtful clarity and quality. Hence in part the plays. I look in at the bright room from outside in the dark yard.[37]

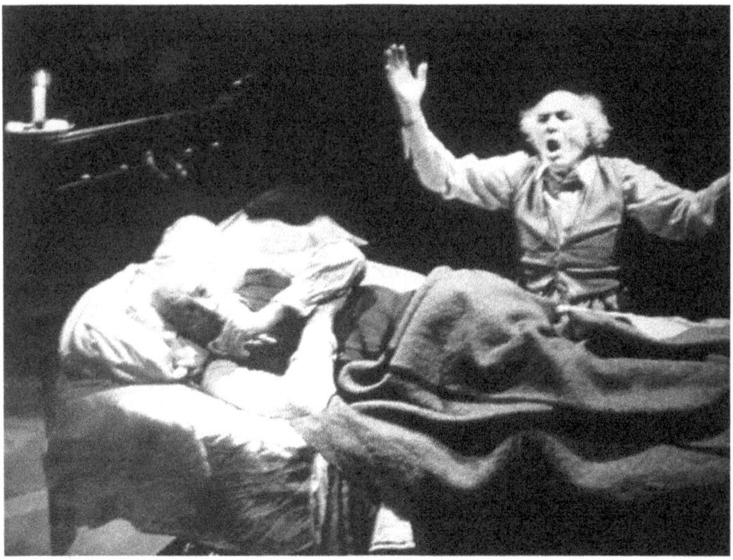

Illustration 3: Jim Norton and Eamon Kelly in *Boss Grady's Boys*. Abbey, 1998

Illustration 4: Eamon Kelly and Jim Norton in *Boss Grady's Boys*. Abbey, 1998

6 | Children of the Light amid the 'risky dancers': Barry's Naïfs and the Poetry of Humanism

Christina Hunt Mahony

Sebastian Barry's early plays, such as *Boss Grady's Boys* and *Prayers of Sherkin,* can be read as incipient stages of an ongoing dramatic project linking the vagaries of his family history with the history of the nation. Here Barry endows ordinary people with a degree of sustained innocence and a purity of soul and spirit which seems to defy any negative experience life might have dealt them. This trait is also apparent in many of Barry's later works, notably in the central characters of his novels *The Whereabouts of Eneas McNulty, Annie Dunne,* and *A Long Long Way*, and has resurfaced again recently in the representation of one of the pair of characters on the stage in *Whistling Psyche.* Barry's innocents, in their damaged or thwarted conditions, convey an astounding lack of bitterness. Despite having been born into limiting circumstances, or having to endure pain, disappointment, neglect or cruelty, they have not become downtrodden or despondent in a lasting sense. Neither have they emerged savvy as a result of ill-treatment by others much more grasping or cruel than they; instead they maintain rarified views of the world and its inhabitants not at all in keeping with what we would expect of those whose aspirations had been clipped at a young age. At times Barry's naïfs even articulate aims which are loftier and purer than those experienced by the more fortunate characters within the works. This disparity between the fictive reality of Barry's innocents and their levels of desire is poignant in its fragility and poeticism, but most especially in its shining hope. In the hands of a lesser writer the gap of sensibility could easily have seemed jarring or been found artistically unsuccessful. Even when his characters have goals which are humble enough, their voicing of the desire to achieve them and the rapture experienced in the contemplation of such desired states, make the goals themselves seem heroic or exotic. Barry's often ornately poetic language is used to cultivate a lush aural environment in which such intensity and purity can thrive, forcing audience or reader to suspend disbelief, even while it remains steadfastly at odds with the realism of Barry's historical and geographical settings.

One might expect such a luminous quality of thought and speech in a beautiful young heroine such as Fanny Hawke in *Prayers of Sherkin.* She has been brought up on an island off the coast of an island, an earthly pre-lapsarian environment in which candles, bees, honeysuckle, pigs and humans have equal claim to respect and divine love. Fanny's language reflects her youth and her innocent upbringing in a plain sect – in short, her *rara avis* status. Her growing desire is for a husband and children, for the kind of fulfilling love her father has experienced. Though she is a compliant adult child and one who is possessed of an ardent faith, for Fanny biology will trump culture in the end. The remaining members of her family will be without partners because they are forbidden to marry outside their sect, but Fanny will embark bravely on just such an exogamous match, accept the consequences and embrace the future.

Fanny's language, though pure of intention and religiously inflected, is subtly rather more employed toward the attainment of sexual and personal fulfillment than it is to any religious aim. All of her family members speak in naïve registers, but each has a circumstance to explain his or her retention of innocence. Brother Jesse may suffer from a type of mental illness. In today's parlance there is an autistic or idiot savant element to his verbal discourse and his obsessive interests, although the Sherkin sect takes the view common in older societies that he is possessed of special gifts. Sarah and Hannah, both middle-aged, are maiden ladies and possessed of nun-like purity, paralleled in the text by the Catholic nuns in the town who are regular customers of their kinsman John, a candlemaker by trade. From the play's beginning, Fanny's doting father, John, is cast in the role of saint, true disciple of their plain faith, and selfless patriarch. He is the surest adherent of their religion, but his language is devoid of zealotry.

There are six other characters in the play. With one exception they operate outside the naïvety zone of the Sherkin islanders. Meg and Stephen Pearse, a May-December couple, exchange saucy remarks, and have a level-headed and vital approach to life and love. The boatman, Mr. Moore, carries the others between Sherkin and Baltimore on the Cork mainland, and is thus a liminal presence. His poetry is not that of innocence but of wanderlust, a preoccupation throughout the play. Eoghan O'Drisceoil, a fisherman from a neighboring island, speaks the poetry of the vernacular language, a mystery to all the rest; Matt Purdy, a *deus ex machina* apparition of the Sherkin Islanders' religious founder, speaks the poetry of revelation. The town's newcomer, lithographer Patrick Kirwan, has travelled some, and lived in the city of Cork before finding himself in Baltimore. In Cork his trade required that he record multiple murders, but, despite this grim intersection with the world of crime, only Kirwan seems to approach the levels of innocent speech, indicative of purity of heart, that will make him a suitable groom for Fanny. While still negotiating their elopement he applies thus to his beloved:

> My speech, my speech … I did spend such a winter … You know why I've come out here? … I've dreamt of something … I've purchased a new premises in Cork city, it is beside the new theatre hall. If you don't mind comedians and risky dancers too much, we might stick our sign beside such light and splendour.[38]

Far from minding, Fanny has already been reading, somewhat wistfully, about can-can dancers who wear 'nothing underneath'. Despite such risky pleasures being within the pair's reach in their future together, the audience can only project a long and continuingly innocent future for them.

Such pristine yearning and its articulation is much harder to convey convincingly in the crusty bachelor brothers in *Boss Grady's Boys*, who are decades older than Fanny Hawke and Patrick Kirwan, and are largely beaten down and brutalized by harsh living conditions and the yoked isolation they have endured on a subsistence farm in pre-Celtic Tiger Ireland. Delicacy of desire is particularly difficult to insert convincingly into the speeches of a character like Josey Grady, the rather 'simple' character in this play, who may be an innocent in some sense but is not fully socialized. Josey, who cannot control biological urges he doesn't understand and who is incontinent through much of the play, requires a certain concentrated generosity on the part of the audience to retain sympathy. Mick, Josey's caregiver, though fully functional, is (understandably enough) cranky, short-tempered and at times morose. The reader of the play and the audience viewing it must get past knowledge of the reality of the shabbiness, bad smells, and impoverished surroundings which the realism of the text suggests to accept the heightened yearning and the innocence which both brothers exhibit briefly, and against great odds, and which they each express in flashes of lyricism.

Boss Grady's Boys is unusual in Barry's corpus in that it includes fantasy sequences telescoping historic time – scenes from the brothers' childhood and from the very few films they have ever seen. Most of the play is cast in a realist mode, and it is in these, not the fantasy sequences, that the language is most likely to glisten in an otherwise sombre landscape, as though in compensation. Mick Grady should be too thoroughly exhausted and defeated to dream anymore, condemned as he was by his father to be the guardian of his slow-witted brother. As the audience encounters him, Mick is in his sixties, but he can still adapt his lifelong dream to go to a 'shining city' where he would find a beautiful young wife, to being able even now to cherish a mental picture of that imaginary wife 'old now, like myself' – and *still* dream of her. It is difficult to imagine a more astounding affirmation of the resilience of the human spirit. Mick's pantheistic prayer stands in contrast with his captive state:

> Lord of the streams, the hills, the farms, of the farmers, what's wrong with us, what's amiss with us? I'm a smallish man. I would like a slightly larger acreage, with a deal of sunlight to improve the grazing. I don't actually. (*To himself*) I won't talk to glass windows any more (*BGB*, p.87).

And Josey's prayer, which appears earlier in the act, may either have inspired Mick with its simplicity, or may, like so much of his Josey's behaviour, be simply an example of his mimicking his brother:

> Bless this small house and bless me and Mick. Bless the sheep and the dog and the horse … Bless the piece of money in the bank in Killarney, if it's still there … Bless the trees and the whins, and the rowanberries and the berries on them … (*BGB*, p.82).

The brothers do not share the same levels of yearning nor of aspiration. The tragedy of the play is centered in Mick's dilemma, whereas Josey in his simplicity is content to live in part in the past, with only a slightly apprehensive awareness of the future. Still their ability to dream, to fantasize and to reminisce childhood moments of joy, despite the dire realities of their past and their present lend them a poetic status and raise them far above the meanness of their station.

Sharp-tongued, and much the same age as Mick Grady, Annie Dunne is the crippled spinster and title character of Barry's 2002 novel. She could have been written as a woman who simply gave up on life many years past. One can find prime examples in the literature without looking far. The most obvious is Kavanagh's Patrick Maguire, who had a heart and a soul and a poetry of aspiration as a young man, but who is reduced to semi-bestial sensibility combined with anger and an inability to dream as *The Great Hunger* progresses and the protagonist ages. Barry's novel, which brings Annie to the cusp of old age, is a portrait of a handicapped, childless woman who has known verbal abuse and outright neglect from family members, particularly her widowed brother-in-law whose remarriage signalled the end of Annie's direct contact with her nuclear family. Her humped back has precluded her own prospects for marriage, the only possible bulwark against her being at the mercy of others. Still she is capable of this eloquent nocturnal soliloquy:

> Under the starlight I stand, ruminating, like a creature myself, an extra thing in the plenitude of the world. I know I am nothing. My pride is not based on my own engine, but is just a lean-to built on prejudice and leaning against anger. But this is not the point. God is the architect, and I am content there, sleepless and growing old, to be friend to his fashioned things, and a shadow among shadows. More rooted and lasting will be my crab-apple tree – some day, no doubt, another heart will give allegiance to it and its bitter fruit, gathering the tiny apples and crushing them in their season with the same passion and humour, laughing at the generosity of the tree, its ease and seeming happiness, its fertility, as I do ... This is the happiness allowed to me.[39]

This passage follows immediately a physically dangerous and emotionally devastating moment in the novel in which Annie's vulnerability as a woman (especially a woman who is no longer young and who has no male provider) is made visible to all. After ignoring sound advice about not taking out an unreliable horse alone, she must be rescued by a male neighbour whom she loathes, and also sees as an interloper. Annie fears that her rescuer, Billy Kerr, might through a proposal of marriage unseat her on her cousin Sarah's farm in County Wicklow. The indignity involved forces Anne, late at night, to resuscitate consoling memories of her grandfather's status in the community – a status based on 'that sense of being separate'. These remembered shreds of distinction carry her into her solitary night thoughts which function like a prayer. As with those of the Grady brothers, however, Annie's is not a conventional prayer. This is Annie's naturalist *Magnificat,* and the God invoked in the passage is rather like the 'Kings and

Queens of England' invoked earlier in the passage, and linked with her sense of her father's and her family's status and dignity; especially the much-quoted paean to Victoria uttered by her father in the *Steward of Christendom.* Hers too is a Victorian parental God overseeing plenty, or at the very least order, and rewarding industry.

Like Fanny Hawke, under a threat of shunning, and Mick Grady, condemned to drudgery and unrelieved responsibility, Annie has not succumbed to bitterness on a subject of central importance to her, and one of the great losses of her life. Like Mick Grady, who can dream of the wife he never had without dissolving into self pity or resentment, so Annie can view another woman's children in this pure light:

> … I am buffeted, tormented even, again by this feeling I have for them. It is like the treacle in the pudding when it is first thrown down on the dough, and the spoon so slow and held back as the mixture is stirred, dragging on the muscles at the top of the working arm. And then the treacle begins to let itself be folded in, and surrenders, and imparts to the pudding that wild taste of sugar, foaming and cavorting in the mouth. Not that treacle pudding features much down here in Kelsha – that was an item of my mother's in the old kitchen in Dublin Castle in our heyday, so the memory of the weak arm is my arm as a little girl helping her mother, in the eternal security of early years (*AD*, pp.50-51).

This closing monologue of the chapter had begun with a sense of Annie's being slighted by the children's mother, moved quickly to an intensely sweet vehicle to carry the metaphor for her ersatz maternal love for the children, and ends by squaring the circle of the experience by linking it to her own happy childhood memories. In the course of this long mental monologue she never intimates jealousy or disappointment that she will have no children of her own.

Such occasional expressions of poetic purity as Annie does voice can at times seem an inherited condition. It is a speech like that of her father, Thomas Dunne, in *The Steward of Christendom,* in which we encounter Annie as a much younger woman. In *Steward*, Thomas Dunne first appears on stage in old age, dressed only in dirty long-johns and living in a madhouse. His moments of lucidity in the present of the play, and in flashbacks, indicate that his language is oddly never that of the tough, high-ranking policeman that he was. (Athough his language and behaviour are reported more brutally by Annie in both the play and in her novel, and also by Willie in *A Long Long Way).* Similarly the audience learns of the childhood injustices meted out to Thomas Dunne by *his* parents, and the great sorrows of his life – the deaths of his beloved wife in childbirth and his only son in war – in speeches which are sorrowful but accepting, and contain no recriminations for the abuse he suffered nor resentment of his rotten luck.

Barry's most recent novel, *A Long Long Way,* provides the prequel to *The Steward of Christendom* (just as *Annie Dunne* is its sequel); or rather it fills in the narrative gaps of that play as they concern one character. Willie Dunne, who appears as a ghost, both as a soldier and as a child in the play, is the central character and narrator of Barry's 2005 novel, and continues throughout most of the book in the tradition of innocence and fine feeling which marks his family. In this work, however, Barry threads a more convincing series of incidents indicative of growth and change in a character than is seen in perhaps any of his works to date. Willie's naivety going off to war is certainly not out of place historically nor in literary historical terms. The Great War began arguably more naively than any war of modern record. It was the war which would be over by Christmas, and the forces of good and evil seemed clear cut to all. Governments as well as recruits were firm in the belief of their righteousness and predestined victory. Like many of those recruits, Willie had travelled little from his home place, and is at first exhilarated by sea-travel and the foreignness of what he encounters in England and on the continent. He does not question the concept of taking orders, as he was raised a Victorian child and knew his place and was secure in that knowledge. Authority was not to be questioned, whether it was in the figure of a family elder, a government, or an army officer. Willie, like soldiers of all eras, doesn't always understand what he is doing, where he is or why he must follow particular orders; but he feels strongly that he is there to serve and to protect. His trust in institutions, hierarchies and authority figures is implicit. He enters the army at the age of eighteen, and will die at novel's end at twenty one, feeling in the course of the novel that he has become a man. He has seen incredible horrors, lost many friends, his virginity, his girlfriend, his rock-solid belief in the empire and, most tragically, he dies believing he has lost his father's love. The perspective on Willie's naivety is different in *A Long Long Way* from that found in Barry's previous works. In the rough world of young men at war, he is derided openly for his persistent innocence of thought and expression. Some of his mates find it endearing, but more are maddened by it or are merely incredulous. He is accused, roundly and falsely, of cowardice by a virulently anti-Irish major who labels him Little Willie (in a reference to the Kaiser's son); and Willie returns to his men with the major's half-hearted apology and his own response ringing in his ears: 'That's all right, sir'.

> And somehow he felt it was all right. Given the new world that held sway over things. And given that he himself, Willie Dunne, had had to kill a man. Anyway, you couldn't give an officer a box in the gob … He headed back through suffering and growing darkness to rejoin what was left of his Company. With a scalded heart to guide him, and an affrighted soul, which in these parts of the insulted earth, proved not bad lamps.[40]

On his leave from the war in Dublin Willie witnesses the 1916 Rising and the devastation in the city in its wake. He has already evinced ignorance of the political background of the factionalism, irritating both his Irish and English comrades. Because he has worked for a builder before being a soldier, he muses instead on the physical job which will be at hand in the aftermath of the war, something which he can grasp more fully:

> It would almost make an apprentice builder weep to think of the deep work gone into the making of those houses. But men would come, he supposed, to build them up again, it was no more than the towns and cities of Belgium. Dublin and Ypres were all the one. And I saw heaven opened and behold a white horse and he that sat upon him was called Faithful and True.

> That was his favourite line in the whole Bible. And he didn't suppose it meant anything at all (*LLW*, p.124).

In each case cited above, the rhythm and pacing of these musings turns on the hopeful, upbeat quality of their resolve. Heart-scalded and with his 'affrighted soul', he finds a useful lamp to help him find his way. Dublin is rebuilt in his imagination, and a heroic vision of faith and truth consoles him. It means, in each case, not 'nothing at all', but that Willie has a continuing belief in progress and in human endurance.

From Willie Dunne's practical musings on the destruction of war, one can move easily to the world of Eneas McNulty, a man who works his way through the world and much of the century, barely intuiting what motivates him, or those for whom he toils.

Eneas is Barry's truest and most extensive portrait of a naïf. His experiences in part parallel those of Willie Dunne, nearly his exact contemporary. Eneas leaves his Sligo town to join the British Merchant Navy during the Great War, although rather than seeing direct action in Europe he is sidelined onto a supply ship which plies out of Galveston Texas. This exposure to a rather exotic New World port on the Gulf of Mexico is exciting for a young man, who also like Willie has no experience of travel or life outside Ireland, but Eneas harbours a disappointment about not being more fully engaged in the war. Feeling he has taken from the experience at sea as much as he can, and eager to return to home, family and friends, Eneas leaves the merchant service after the war and returns to Sligo. But Ireland after the Easter Rising is a different country, and Eneas seems to have no place in it. His closest friend from childhood, Jonno Lynch, a character who will inform much of Eneas's future life, snubs him on the street, leaving Eneas dumbfounded. There is little excuse for the extent of Jonno's rejection, yet Eneas, told of the realities of Sligo life in the intervening years by his bookish twelve-year-old brother, muses thus:

> Still and all it's a sort of sorrow to him that Jonno Lynch will not greet him. The old going-about companion of his boyhood.

> What's left of his boy's heart is wrung by it. It's a little thing maybe, a nod or a word flung across Main Street, or even to heel up, the two of them, like two cabbage carts against the wall of Plimpton's or even God knows head into the Café Cairo for a citron lemonade and swap all the ould recent histories. But it's recent histories indeed are the damnable problem. Jack, younger though he may be, has a better grasp of these affairs. He says bright boys and wide boys and bitter-hearted older men with tribes of brats and hard wives too are milling about up on the Show-grounds of a Sunday night and under their floorboards are real guns and in their souls the foul pith of rebellion. So Jack says ... And maybe he gets a grasp now of why Jonno Lynch calls him an eejit. There's a lot of slip and tug and pulling of Tidal waters that he can't make out the pattern of. Not for want of banging his head against all the new stone walls of Sligo.[41]

Like Annie Dunne, Eneas suffers personal hurt and betrayal largely undeserved, but younger and more naïve than she, he tends to find himself lacking.

Eneas's travels take him far from Sligo time and again, trailing through life, and various countries, to end in England running a down-and-out hotel on the Island of Dogs with a black mate from a previous episode in his peripatetic life, and there dies in a final redemptive act. His situation is hardly elevated, but mirrors that of one of Barry's more illustrious protagonists.

Barry's most recent play, *Whistling Psyche*, concerns Victorian characters – one has become a household name, the other, Irish, became a neglected historical curiosity. Two extended monologues, becoming only tangentially dialogic at the play's close, take place in an Edwardian neverland of realistic impossibility which exploits its stage potential. Florence Nightingale, prim and aged, justifies her rise to imperial fame as the crusading medical reformer of the Crimean War against her upper class background of leisure and projected female limitations. James Miranda Barry, a generation older, forced into or choosing a life as a woman disguised as a man, is doctor, not nurse, and resentful of Nightingale's later female success. The historical Barry is by far the more fascinating of the two, and this is also true of his reincarnation by playwright Barry. As the embodiment of nearly ever conceivable contradiction – a woman who functions as a man, an Irishman who embodies much of the imperial directive, a world traveller whose compass-points all lead to his Irish origins – Barry is impossible to categorize. That his language can soar while relating the worst of human misery is of a piece with the character's duality. Barry passes over his own sexually irresponsible behaviour (willfully attracting a colonial governor's attention in his guise as a young man, and then bearing a stillborn child of this strange illicit union). He also exploits a devoted black servant, though mindful of the subjugation and misery of dark-skinned colonial subjects he has observed in his travels throughout the empire. These offences would seem insupportable, except for Barry's own imposed sexual ambiguity and his total unwillingness, which suggests inability, to assign blame. He does not bemoan at length the circumstances of his own impoverishment in childhood and the misguided goodwill of his mother and his guardian which caused him to lead a life of careful concealment and hideously deforming lies. He does, however, give vent to envy of Nightingale's female success, but this can only be seen, finally, as a form of denial or displacement. In these passages he mirrors the acceptance levels of both Thomas Dunne and Mick Grady, who never thoroughly berate their parents for the callous role they played in the shaping of their respective son's lives, and also Annie Dunne's refusal to condemn entirely the equally callous treatment of her family, nor to dwell upon her own infirmities. The levels of acceptance in all cases are what set playwright Barry's characters apart.

Whistling Psyche is a play outside the immediacy of Sebastian Barry's familial project in that the direct link to this forebear cannot be verified. It is part of the project, but more a period piece, to be seen appropriately as a loosely historical play. Florence Nightingale and James Miranda Barry are conceived purposefully in the spirit of the times, and thus the ending of the play is very more conventionally religious than any of Barry's other works, with prayers and supplications to an orthodox deity.

For literary historical precedents of a language such as Barry's which convey a sublimely positive view of life, and the articulation of high hopes uncluttered by the limitations of reality, it is natural to look first to playwright J.M. Synge who invests his ragtag characters with such words and notions. The outstanding examples are timid runaway Christy Mahon who pours forth spontaneous love lyrics when liberated from tyranny and enabled to foresee an unfettered future nearly within his grasp, and the wandering beggars, Martin and Mary Doul, in their convincing false aesthetic in *The Tinker's Wedding*. In Christy the movement from one locality to another brings a different perspective, particularly as he is relieved of familial determinism. Physical blindness accounts for the latter pair's naïve, lustrous world view, especially as it relates to themselves since they have not been disabused of it. Barry's characters have no such excuse. His people exist in a more modern world in which innocence is much harder to achieve and maintain. Martin and Mary Doul, after all, chose blindness again rather than deal with the reality of imperfection. Barry's characters, though sighted, remain blessedly blind to the darker motives and intentions of others. It is thus tempting to think of Barry's achievement as being solely or primarily an aesthetic one, with the sheer force of his poetry raising characters to elevated heights, and with his creation and development of the prose aria being something of a signature device – but comparison with Synge is also relevant in emphasizing both writers oblique stance in relation to religion.

There is certainly a God in Synge, a product of a fundamentalist Protestant background, but little of religious practice even given his remote locales or the outcast status of his characters. Maurya in *Riders to the Sea*, having lost most of the men in her family, and losing the remaining two during the course of the play, uses God's name in the play often, as do her daughters. But there are no orthodox prayers murmured for the dead and there is no institutional church except in reference to the offstage young priest, whose emphasized youth suggests lack of authority or relevance in the difficult lives of the islanders. In the final scenes of the play local people arrive, and holy water is sprinkled, but no priest appears. The frequent apostrophes to God in *Riders to the Sea,* like the sprinkling of holy water, bear the hallmarks of cultural custom rather than commitment to religious practice or belief.

The only plays of Synge's to feature a cleric are *The Well of the Saints* and *The Tinker's Wedding,* both comedies. In the former the priest (called 'The Saint', a wandering friar) is viewed as an otherworldly irrelevancy; in the latter he is a rather defeated force, looking for monetary recompense in an unseemly fashion. In both plays those who know better dismiss priestly importance in their lives. In the comic *Playboy* the priest is an offstage, peripheralized threat, again dismissed by all but the most comic of characters, the rejected bridegroom, Sean Keogh. Synge's priests are part of a satirical tradition of ridicule in both Irish and in English which has been a part of the literature for centuries. What began as part of the Christian/pagan dynamic of earlier eras, has continued until finally in contemporary Irish writing, (even contemporary writing set in earlier periods), priest and religious practices very much a part of Irish life until quite recently, are portrayed minimally or not at all, or even are derided openly.

Barry's work, whether set in Victorian Dublin among the Catholic lower-middle classes, or in the hierarchy of the farming classes in Wicklow, or in Sligo town among fairly upper-middle class Catholics in the 1950s, is largely devoid of religious reference, though set in times and circumstances in which institutionalized religion was much more in force. No one has rosary beads, attends a novena, invokes a saint, frets over getting to confession or attending Mass. In this Barry is not unusual among contemporary Irish writers. Few of them have attempted to convey religious practice in their plays, despite settings and time frames which seems to call for it. Brian Friel's plays set in the early twentieth century are more traditional in ethos than most, and do feature the occasional priest; but the standard devotional routine does not intrude on the lives of his small town or rural characters (and small towns, certainly, were where such practice would have been most rigourously observed, and commented upon if neglected). Tom

Murphy set *Sanctuary Lamp* in a church but does not place the play specifically in Ireland, and only one character in that play is identifiably Irish. Murphy's plays set in Ireland, in a rather timeless but decidedly modern, twentieth century time-frame such as *Bailegangaire*, do not feature religious obligation, nor does anyone suffer in any personal or social sense for non-observance. Mommo spends senile hours going over past misdeeds of her life, but none of her admissions make her seek divine or pastoral forgiveness for the grave injustices she inflicted on members of her family, nor do members of her family consider calling for the priest.

Nearly all of the people portrayed by major contemporary playwrights are Catholic, but Tom Kilroy may be unique in having his characters attend Mass at the end of the early play *The Death and Resurrection of Mr. Roche*. Kilroy also made the unusual choice of focusing uncomfortable attention on the exaggerated mystic practices of Matt Talbot in *Talbot's Box*. Here the priest poses an alternative religious perspective which, although mainstream, is portrayed as suspect, crass and lacking the superior spiritual impulse of the mystic.

Sebastian Barry, who was brought up and educated as a Catholic, and who has chosen, in the main, to retrieve Catholic forebears who were not quite in the usual mould, has few of them attending to the sacraments or observing devotional practices. Like Synge's, many of his characters instead seem to practice a form of late Victorian humanism – their faith is in themselves and others, and in the human spirit. They trust to innate goodness and are possessed of it themselves. They are often troubled and sorely tempted; they have demons with which they contend, yet none of them seeks recourse to religion in its more obvious forms. His two early plays, *Prayers of Sherkin* and *Fred and Jane*, are exceptions, as both take place with a recognizably religious community – one non-conformist and the other Catholic. In neither play, however, are the principal characters conventionally religious even within the set strictures of their own religious grouping. The Sherkin Islanders do not worship a deity so much as they deify their human founder, and the two nuns in *Fred and Jane* have taken film stars as substitute idols.

Much of Barry's work, though, is set in Victorian times or about people who were born into the Victorian era. *Prayers of Sherkin*, *The Only True History of Lizzie Finn*, *White Woman Street*, parts of *The Steward of Christendom*, *The Whereabouts of Eneas McNulty* and *Whistling Psyche* are all Victorian despite the broader sense of a twentieth-century reclamation process that emerges from Barry's corpus. There is, then, a considerable gap between the sensibility of contemporary playwrights like Barry and the world which their characters inhabit. The gap is bridged by his aesthetic language which encloses them in a bubble of innocence, but also by a very contemporary liberal humanism which suits the times in which the writer and his audiences exist while also reflecting the form of late-Victorian humanism featured in much of his work. Such an approach is at odds with traditional Irish Catholicism and certainly contrary to the prevailing ethos of the intervening century in Ireland. Barry's plays, often accused of promoting a revisionist historical agenda, posit instead a contemporary post-Catholic liberal view of the world of his forebears, which shares some characteristics with that earlier ideology. Importantly, Victorian humanism was only ever a minority strain in Irish thought and practice of the period. With its sublime poetry of belief in what is possible and most elevated in human experience – love, forgiveness and hope – Barry's reclamation process of minority figures in the Irish historical landscape, buoyed by his distinctive poetic dialect, could be described perhaps more accurately in this way than as a revisionist historical undertaking.

7 | 'All the long traditions': Loyalty and Service in Barry and Ishiguro

John Wilson Foster

Sebastian Barry's perhaps most characteristic idiom, in novel, poem and play, is a gravid lyricism, admirably suited to his most characteristic discourse – the monologue or soliloquy; his most characteristic note – the elegiac; and his most characteristic device and dimension – the flashback, recollection or vision. All are expressions of a long suspiration. There is something outmodedly unabashed in Barry's portrayals of the extended aftermath of heartbreak which is the characteristic condition of his central figures. In his play *The Steward of Christendom* (1995), surely imminent heartbreak is felt virtually, and perhaps actually, by the audience when towards the end of the play Smith reads aloud young Willie Dunne's now posthumous letter from the French front in the Great War, which he did not survive and when, at the play's end, the long dead Willie reappears to comfort his father. Willie lies down beside him, after the battle as it were, like the ghosts of enemy soldiers at the close of Wilfred Owen's affecting poem, 'Strange Meeting'.

Willie is a living ghost, but then so too is his nominally living though demented father. For in 1932, when the play's action takes place, both causes for which father and son fought – the British cause in Ireland and the Allied cause in Europe – were discountenanced and indeed virtually discredited among the new Irish. To an English audience for whom the Trench Poets and such a play as R.C. Sherriff's *Journey's End* (1929) are cultural bite and sup, the poignancy of the figure of Willie Dunne would seem close to formulaic. But not to a Catholic Irish audience, unused even by 1995 to this kind of sympathetic figure, and whose older members would no doubt have their emotional engagement edged by a frisson of disapproval, Willie Dunne being no 1916 patriot martyr or survivor, and – worse – his father an ex-member of a police force which kept order for the British.[42]

Of course, in their fundamental situation, Willie and his father Thomas are not different from the rest of Barry's central figures in his other works, whom Fintan O'Toole has deftly summarized as 'history's leftovers, men and women defeated and discarded by their times ... misfits, anomalies, outlanders'.[43] Thomas and his daughters, who unlike Willie survive the great watersheds (however incommensurate) of the Great War and Irish independence, sustain a painful loss of status, have been marginalized and superseded in Irish society, and have felt the mortification of having their values and loyalties isolated and mocked by a new generation. Even Willie, in his letter from the front, indulges in the sad irony of thinking of Ireland as the front because of the troubles there that made some Irish soldiers feel they were already marginalized by events taking place in their absence.

O'Toole claims that Barry's casualties yet have 'an amazing grace'. This is true. But we can go farther. Those Irish cultural watersheds function to rescue Thomas, Willie and his sisters from an obscurity and marginality that are irredeemable from where they live and talk, but not from where certain audience members sit. These characters' unhappy condition of isolation is less existential (though it is this, and they indeed show grace in submitting to it) than cultural. They embody a whole culture driven underground into the condition of a subculture and thence the *oubliette* of Irish history.[44] They carry with them values that are yet defensible and recuperable, at least for the purposes of elegy and regret, and of instruction and revision of our recent Irish past. These values may even prove once again viable, though the particular historical conditions have vanished forever.

Among those values is loyalty, loyalty to the past and loyalty to a soon-to-be, and then indeed discredited, *ancien régime*. Their loyalty at first glance is foolish and justifies their apparent status as time's laughingstocks. They are stripped of the support of history's (apparently) winning side and left exposed to failure and ridicule. But it is as if they are stripped to the bare essentials: literally in Thomas's case, as in King Lear's, since he performs most of the play in longjohns. Here, as in Barry's other works, clothes play a large role, as O'Toole perceptively notes. But their dignity, as we (though not their fellow characters) see it, re-clothes their nakedness in front of history. Instead of being foolish and reprehensible, their loyalty is revealed as core value and meaning emancipated from history and cause, from both loyal*ism* and its insurrectionary opposite. Their dignity serves not only to place loyalty centre stage as a virtue but also – and this requires some thought and empathy on the part of the audience – to cause us to re-evaluate the once deplored loyalty to particular features of the old regime. For without distortion or prejudice, we can allow the Dunne family in their inconvenient and sometimes awkward eloquence to represent those tens of thousands of Irish who shared their values, if not always their fate, and whose voices either fell silent or fell on deaf ears when they did leave a record of how they thought and behaved during the cataclysms of world war and national convulsion. This need not blind watchers and readers of the play to the fact that Thomas Dunne, if not Willie Dunne, might have been that less than noble figure, the dupe (or someone suffering from false consciousness, as the ideologically inclined used to say), and might even have done some reprehensible things while exercising his power. Whereas we see Thomas Dunne as a figure alone on stage with his ghosts, we need to recover the culture of which he was once a part in order to measure the magnitude of his fall, his terrifying isolation. This rich sense of history, conveyed by a kind of sustained synecdoche in the economic way of drama, is what brings *The Steward of Christendom* close to greatness.

As late as 1916, there still were in force the opposing attractions for many Irish of loyalty to Britain and the Empire (brought to crux by the Great War) and loyalty to Ireland (brought to crux by the rise of Sinn Fein and the executions of the 1916 rebels). This tension we can find depicted in several neglected Irish works, including a readable novel by Mrs Victor (Jesse Louise) Rickard of Dublin, *The Fire of Green Boughs* (1918). But Rickard's is only one among several largely neglected Irish writings of the Great War, among them memoirs, novels and essays by Patrick MacGill, Lord Dunsany, St John Ervine, Robert Lynd, Katharine Tynan and Thomas Kettle. All of these writers save MacGill represented in their work a choice between Sinn Fein physical-force activism and support for the Allies in the Great War. Sometimes it was not a clear or simple choice, as Ervine's novel *Changing Winds* (1917) shows. For one could deplore Sinn Fein militancy while remaining an Irish patriot or staunch nationalist of the constitutional or Home Rule kind. But in 1914 all of these writers, and the poet Francis Ledwidge, expressed fellowship with the Allied cause and all, including Ledwidge and excepting Tynan and Lynd, did so in the most eloquent way – by donning a British army uniform. Tynan sent her sons as proxies, as it were, while Lynd – Gaelic Leaguer and Sinn Fein supporter though he was – applied to join the army only to be rejected. It was possible of course to interpret one's enlistment as loyalty, not to England or the Empire, but to Europe and to Ireland, as Kettle and Lynd did. John Redmond, the Nationalist leader, likewise thought that Irish soldiers would be fighting for Ireland, though he also thought they would be fighting for the Empire which he hoped (at least initially) the service of the Irish soldiers would help to alter and redirect for the moral good.

One senses in these cases an overlap or more precisely a *superimposition*, of allegiances, loyalties and identities which did not demand the pain of final dissociation or peeling apart until after the War. We think of Kettle, the Irish nationalist, dying at the Somme as a British lieutenant, albeit a Dublin Fusilier. We think of Erskine Childers, who became a British naval lieutenant *after* he ran guns for the Irish Volunteers in 1914 and before he made his unilateral declaration of Irish republicanism. And of Lynd, the republican, proud of the Irish soldier's record of bravery, and proud especially of his record in the Great War. Lynd's pride was expressed in his 1919 book entitled *Ireland a Nation*. I would suggest that there is only the appearance but not the reality of irony here, not just because Lynd used the Irish record in the Great War as evidence of Ireland's nationality, but because the nation of Lynd's republicanism historically accommodated the virtue of fighting for the Crown and for Empire. That long tradition was not to be easily repudiated by anyone historically aware and generous in his patriotism.

The superimposition of loyalties ran down through Irish society in the early months of the Great War and was intersected by an array of positions and organizations. It is set out for us with clever hilarity at street level in a vigorous but little-known book by Gerald Griffin: *The Dead March Past: A Semi-Autobiographical Saga*, published in 1937 and easily bearing comparison with Oliver St John Gogarty's much more famous *As I Was Going Down Sackville Street*, published the same year and which at times it resembles.[45] The saga opens in the early weeks of the Great War with an enthusiastically received street oration in favour of the Allies by Reverend Dr. Doherty, administrator of the Pro-Cathedral, while Lord and Lady Aberdeen's vice-regal cavalcade clatters past to clamorous ovation, and the Irish Volunteers, the National Volunteers and the Citizen Army – each opposed to the others – parade about, not to speak of G-men and giant specimens of the Dublin Metropolitan Police (DMP). This ideological smorgasbord on offer is depicted by Griffin with tempestuous humour as he remembers (or invents) pavement conversations with Augustine Birrell, Chief Secretary of Ireland; Rev. John Mahaffy, Provost of Trinity College; Tom Kettle and Francis Sheehy Skeffington. Griffin has Dr. Doherty inform the crowd that the Citizen Army has threatened to prevent Prime Minister Asquith from getting to the Mansion House that night for a recruiting drive, but that 'some of the good women of Dublin whose husbands and sons are fighting the Huns at this moment, have threatened to box the ears of these tin soldiers ... and to throw them into the Liffey'. 'All the Irish', Griffin recalled, 'were at present war-mad. Ninety-five percent of them wanted to fight Germany, and five per cent wanted to fight England' (p.42).

We know that, for one reason or another, those percentages shifted as the War continued, Sinn Fein strengthened and the chief Easter rebels were executed. For a while, the sentiment of Ireland was in flux and something of a lottery. This unstable Ireland torn between loyalty and rebellion is caught without fanfare in the often humorous and poignant *Irish Vignettes*, published in 1928 and written in the early 1920s, by the now unknown Ella MacMahon, born in Dublin and domiciled in London.[46] These nineteen vignettes exist suitably midway between short stories and essays. There are references to both the Zeppelin air raids on London and Easter 1916. The characters are suspended between 'a bygone day' and a 'new Ireland' of the period 1914 to1918; Sinn Fein is on the rise but the Troubles have not begun. Among the 'peasants' (her word) whom MacMahon writes of in the guise of a travelled and cultivated Irishwoman there is a new 'impidence' (as one of the country cast calls it); there is an increasing dislike of England and a discernible pro-Germanism. The rural Irish are caught between 'purely feudal predilections' and 'modern democratic opinions' but the latter could themselves – though this is only implied – favour either Sinn Fein populism or continued unionism. The author herself seems similarly suspended in sympathy and opinion between two Irelands but retains an observant ironic detachment. It seems fitting that MacMahon seems to have begun life as a Protestant and ended as a Catholic.

In time the tide of opinion turned against loyalty, and those like Thomas Dunne and his family are amidst the debris left by the receding waters. The Troubles have begun in a realistic piece that appeared in *Blackwood's Magazine* in 1920, 'The Terror by Night', by 'An Irishwoman' (unidentified). In it a young country man who joined the British Army and fought with distinction returns to find a very different Ireland in which Sinn Fein is a power. He is subjected to a persistent and relentless persecution, boycotted and then his farm is sabotaged. In his room he displays a portrait of King George V topped with a Union Jack. He is told by masked gunmen it must go; he removes it and bears his wife and child off to England in disgust. The author claims 'similar cases occur continually all over the country'.[47] And not just involving ex-British soldiers. The narrator, whose car breaks down at night, makes her way to the police barracks only to find dereliction and a message written in pebbles: 'DEATH TO THE R.I.C.' (p.29). After the setting up of the Free State, Irish soldiers of the British Army and members of the RIC and the DMP as sympathetic or even acceptable elements were largely written out of the story of Ireland and lodged hostilely in the popular memory.

It is, in part, a vacancy in the narrative of Irish history and the popular memory that accounts for the heterodoxy and surprising success of *The Steward of Christendom*. It is the vacancy where Irishmen loyal to the Crown or loyal simply to the Army or police (and to the long traditions of service in them) should be. Barry rescues from near literary oblivion the loyal Irishman as hero, but in no clear-cut or agenda-driven way. The central character is Thomas Dunne, ex-chief superintendent of the DMP, in a position of responsibility in Dublin Castle during the official change of regimes. 'I had risen', he recalls, 'as high as Catholic could in the Dublin Metropolitan Police'.[48] But now, in 1932, he is lodged, near where he was born, in the county home in Baltinglass, County Wicklow, in his seventies and prey to memories and visions. In his 'Notes on the Play', Barry acknowledges that the choice of his great-grandfather as the play's hero was 'worrying', especially since Dunne had taken part in the suppression of labour activists during the Dublin lock-out of 1913.

But this is an acutely moving play even on the page, and Dunne an acutely sympathetic figure; and the play ends with Dunne's vision of his dead son, killed in 1917 in the trenches as a soldier of the Dublin Rifles, appearing in his room to affect a posthumous exchange of love between father and son. Had he lived Willie would no doubt have suffered the minor hostilities addressed in Ireland to ex-soldiers. In a flashback, Dunne's daughter's friend is assaulted in 1922 by a woman for having seen off the Tommies as they departed Ireland for good, and the bus conductor who intervenes and tells the woman that he too had served in the War as a National Volunteer is glared at by the woman 'as if he were a viper, or a traitor' (p.29). Dunne himself recalls being spat at in the street 'by some brave boy' in 1922. The break up of the Irish units after the Treaty fills the aged Dunne with sad indignation:

> ... all the proud regiments gone, the Dublin Rifles and the Dublin Fusiliers. All the lovely uniforms. All the long traditions, broken up and flung out, like so many morning eggs on to the dung heap (p.27).

An elementary point I would wish to make is that loyalty could be under the circumstances a complex fate, a difficult state of mind that was often betrayed through the cruel necessity of choice of action into the appearance of simplicity. And so in Willie's unbearably moving letter to his father from the trenches, the son reports that 'we have been told of the ruckus at home, and some of the country men are as much upset by that as they would be by their present emergency. I know you are in the front line there, Papa, so keep yourself safe for my return ... this is a strange war and a strange time, and my whole wish is to be home with you all in Dublin ... ' (p.57). The triumph of the play is its sympathetic understanding of the complexity of loyalty which at first glance – and with the grotesquely unfair view of Irish posterity – can seem like the mere puppetry of betrayal at worst, delusion at best.

The terrible temptation to simplify, to turn the legitimacy of doubleness into the illicitness of duplicity, a temptation which few Irish have resisted for eighty years or more, is what Barry seemingly wishes to resist in *The Steward of Christendom.* The risk taken in front of an Irish audience lies in Dunne's easy, even natural, partnering of love of Ireland and love of the monarchy. Speaking of the unarmed DMP, Dunne recalls:

> We were mostly country men, and Catholics to boot, and we loved our King and we loved our country. They never put those

> Black and Tans among us, because we were a force that belonged to Dublin and her streets (p.9).

Dunne remembers King Edward praising his wife's hair when they were presented in 1903: 'All the ladies loved him. Of course, he was old in that time. But a true king' (p.25). But it was Queen Victoria whom Dunne loved most deeply, and even if Barry means the elder Dunne to be extravagant in his nostalgic half-dotage, and perhaps Barry disapproves (though I reckon he doesn't), it is still a moving testament of love:

> I loved her for as long as she lived, I loved her as much as I loved Cissy my wife, and maybe more, or differently … The great world that she owned was shipshape as a ship. All the harbours of the earth were trim with their granite piers, the ships were shining and strong … And men like me were there to make everything peaceable, to keep order in her kingdoms. She was our pride. Among her emblems was the gold harp, the same harp we wore on our helmets (p.14).

Dunne's love for Victoria can seem bizarre to us, but history suggests that it would have seemed less so in the early and middle portions of her reign. Assuredly we might condemn Dunne for anachronism though even that is movingly expressed in his broken soliloquies:

> Dear Lord, put the recruits back in their barracks in Fitzgibbon Street, put the stout hearts back into Christendom's Castle, and troop the colours once more for Princess and Prince, for Queen and for King, for Chief Secretary and Lord Lieutenant, for Viceroy and Commander-in-Chief. But you cannot. Put the song back in the mouth of the beggar, the tune back in the pennywhistle, the rat-tat-tat of the tattoo back in the parade ground, stirring up our hearts. But you cannot. Gone (p.37).

But we cannot condemn Dunne for *bizarrerie*. Although James H. Murphy entitles his 2001 book on Nationalism and Monarchy in Victorian Ireland *Abject Loyalty*, his own analysis of the period is no study in abjection:

> It is presumed that Irish nationalists were hostile to the British monarchy. And, indeed, by the time of Irish independence in 1922, there was an official and settled antipathy toward the monarchy both among the new governing class and among

> large portions of the Irish population [the Catholic portions he must mean].The route to such antipathy, however, is long and tangled ... The perhaps startling reality is that the British monarchy, inasmuch as it was perceived as a threat by nationalists in nineteenth-century Ireland, was not a threat because it had any political power but *because it was popular in Ireland and because it was seen to symbolize a future for Ireland as a contented part of the United Kingdom that was anathema to nationalists.*[49] [My italics.]

Even nationalists sometimes argued that Victoria was still the queen of the kingdom of Ireland. Indeed, 'Most Irish nationalists were monarchists', writes Murphy, 'of either the enthusiastic or the grudging but realistic varieties ... Monarchy seemed the natural form of government and it had the blessing of the Catholic Church ... Republicanism was the preference of only a minority in Ireland' (pp.xix, xxi).

Certainly these observations provide a context for Dunne's memories and visions that qualify their apparent dotage or falsity of consciousness. He need not even have been wrong-footed by history, which unexpressed claim is the underlying thrust of his aggrieved and unforsworn loyalty. 'The failure or rather the defeat of monarchy in nationalist Ireland', says Murphy, 'has been so great as to seem inevitable in retrospect. Yet this was not so. Monarchy might have succeeded in Ireland had circumstances been different' (p.xxxiv).

The Steward of Christendom is on one level a political tragedy, the tragedy of a man marooned in his opinions and allegiances by the changing tide of Irish history. The source of this tragedy is Dunne's resistance to the idea of changing sides, declining to accept fully the new Ireland and preferring to remain in heart with the old dispensation, that being the nobler choice. For he recalls that when Dublin Castle was signed over to Michael Collins (to whom he was in fact drawn), most of the men in his division of the DMP would have gladly transferred their loyalty to the Big Fella: 'And for an instant ... I felt the shadow of that loyalty pass across my heart. But I closed my heart instantly against it' (p.50). Loyalty puts honour and principle over feeling and pragmatism.

On another level, *The Steward of Christendom* is a domestic tragedy – in the way *King Lear* is a domestic tragedy – about a widower with three daughters and who in the end goes mad with the weight of authority, the weight of historical change and the thanklessness of loyalty, the weight of the years. Of these daughters it is Annie who is most incensed at how the DMP and loyalists were treated after 1922 (and to whom Barry gives a novel to herself – a sustained coherent recollection like a soliloquy – some years later).[50] Dunne himself feels aggrieved too but not bitterly:

> We did our best and followed our orders. Go out to Mount Jerome some day, in the city of Dublin, and see the old monument to the DMP men killed in the line of duty. Just ordinary country men keen to do well. And when the new government came in, they treated us badly. Our pensions were in disarray. Some said we had been traitors to Ireland (p.9). Annie goes further, thinking her father humiliated by Collins, in her eyes the true renegade: she has become a bitter loyalist (of the kind we in Ulster know well), but Dunne on the day of transfer of power deems himself content: 'I served that King, Annie, and that will suffice me … I don't grieve' (p.42).

Above all, Barry's play is a moral tragedy about a man whose relationship with society, with the world, is undermined and transvalued by circumstances over which he has no control. At the heart of Dunne's relationship with society and the world is the notion of *service*. When Annie calls him a king, he demurs: 'That is the whole crux of the matter. I am not a king. I am the servant of a king. I am only one of the stewards of his Irish city' (p.42). This theme of Barry's play associates it with *Othello* in which the tragic hero, Shakespeare's soldier, 'invests himself in the ideology of service and obedience'.[51] Like Othello, Dunne could say, *does* in his own words say, 'I have done the state some service and they know't'. But in Dunne's case they do not know it and do not wish to know it because the state has undergone a seachange.

So politicized are we in Ireland that Irish readers have to work hard today to see virtue in Dunne's rambling self-justifications; he and the DMP followed orders and cleared

O'Connell Street of strikers in 1913 and several men died; and we know today what we think of those who follow orders at all costs. Professional duty and professional obedience can appear almost by definition nowadays as vices not virtues. But Barry puts accountings of service into Dunne's mouth and mind in sophistication far beyond these ideas, complex though these can be. It can only be adjudged by situation when a cause feeds back to de-legitimize or undermine obedience, duty, service. Moreover, as Murphy has indicated, the historical record shows the nationalist spectrum of attitude in Ireland ranging from revolutionary republicanism through to loyal – even when tactically loyal – monarchism. Republican nationalism, indeed physical-force republican nationalism, may seem to have triumphed as the purest form of nationalism in Ireland in the twentieth century – largely because we have conceded that triumph to it – but the legitimacy of other forms of nationalism, let alone unionism, clears a space for a reconsideration of *service.* I am aware that service to revolution or subversion could appear to benefit from what I write here. It was, after all, with deliberate irony that Maud Gonne the republican entitled her memoir *A Servant of the Queen* (1938),[52] but there are often crucial disqualifiers at work – not the least of them on occasions, on terrible occasions, moral disqualifiers – which I will not have space to explore or even summarize.

Dunne hopes he guarded the monarchs' possessions well, for he has interpreted his service as stewardship.He was named for his great-great-grandfather who was the first steward of Humewood, a Big House and estate, a position in the family which his own father filled. Despite the solipsism of his dementia, he senses the Christian echo in stewardship: 'My father was the steward of Humewood, and I was the steward of Christendom' (p.37). He calls Victoria with the misshapenness of delirium 'the very flower and perfecter of Christendom' (p.14). Yet there is a coherent if outdated vision of society in his broken mind: 'The world was a wedding of loyalty, of steward to Queen' (p.14). And it is a vision of family too, for just as Dunne lost his queen so he lost his wife, and he tried and failed to prevent the aftermath: the 'savagery and ruin' (p.50) in

Ireland that followed the Treaty and that broke his heart, and the 'mire of this wasteland' (p.57) that Willie calls the front and that also breaks Dunne's heart.[53] Part of Dunne's delusion is his vague sense of responsibility as a steward who ultimately failed, and this is his tragic, Othello-like stature. But at times he realized success, in society and also at home, moments 'When you see that God himself is in your wife and in your children, and they hold in trust for you your own measure of goodness' (p.38). Stewardship is contained in loyalty, and loyalty seems like adherence to a cause or person or principle beyond the call of duty or requirement of obedience, a surplus space occupied by love and faith. Clearly loyalty can err on the side of complicity in a bad cause, person or principle, it can exhibit blindness and even abjection; but in Barry's play the loyalty in question is noble even if many readers or audience members would regard it as mistaken.

Dunne's idea of service was once no dementia, as is clear from the work of the Shakespearian scholar, Michael Neill. While discussing service in *Othello* and *King Lear*, Neill identifies its roots in sacred ritual (we speak of 'divine service'), and reminds us that the early moderns saw Christ taking upon himself 'the forme of a servaunt'. 'The faithful servant's fulfilment of his office' could be seen as 'an expression of Christian duty'. It was arguable that the Bible and *The Book of Common Prayer* alike saw all service as belonging to God and the servant as, paradoxically, 'the Lord's freeman', as St Paul insisted.[54] Neill claims Othello 'imagines his service to the state (in a secular version of the Christian paradox) as the very ground of his "free condition"' (p.22). Of course, Neill's point is that the sacralization of service was contested in the early modern period as is demonstrated in these two Shakespeare plays. Anabaptists saw service as subjection and could quote St Paul's 'be ye not the servants of men' (p.14). My own point would be that we in Ireland have sacrificed so vigorously the personal and the professional, indeed even the sacred, to the political, that we have been unjust and one-eyed in the matter of service performed by Irish men and women, and that Barry's play is a rare and powerful demurral. The warped nature of

Ireland's political experience has skewed our perception of virtue and vice. We have settled for simplistic rather than rich stories of Ireland, simplistic stories of villains and heroes, traducers and champions in which service is servility and slavery even when freely tendered. These stories firmly exclude the notions of service explored in *The Steward of Christendom*, and have excluded them sometimes at the point of a gun or the blast of a bomb.

Service and loyalty are explored at greater length in Kazuo Ishiguro's *The Remains of the Day*, a superlative 1989 novel that shares with Barry's play a deliberately outmoded hero and set of values and a gathering poignancy that dangerously skirts sentimentality. Each is a prolonged heartbreak behind its own denial. Ishiguro's entire novel is the account by Stevens, Lord Darlington's butler, of his holiday through the west of England in 1956, an account dominated by, first, his recollections of his master's growing involvement after the Great War in friendship with, and later appeasement of, Nazi Germany, and, secondly, his developing thoughts on the perfect butler. Stevens's ponderous, if beautifully expressed, ideas skirt unintended humour, since his language, though precise, is dated, as he himself is (like the Dunne of 1932) – an old-fashioned figure dressed in a 1931 suit and consulting a 1930s guide book.

Both Stevens and Dunne are servants who reflect on the nature and virtue of ideal service. Both exist for us at first glance midway between folly and nobility. Just as Stevens has a bizarre notion of his audience – he addresses us as though we knew and cared about the minutiae of butling and its history – so Dunne's often elevated and poetic, if confused, monologues are addressed to the vulgar orderly Smith (who embodies the crass condescension of Irish posterity) and the home's sympathetic seamstress, when they are not addressed to shades and visions. This serves in both cases to render at first the respective ideas of service and loyalty anachronistic. In each case the hero is a dubious one who belongs to a previous era; moreover, both are loyal to the end to discredited causes – in one case British administration and monarchy in Ireland, in the other the appeasement of Hitler and reluctance to confront

Nazism. Stevens and Dunne could even be regarded respectively, and to their chagrin, as anti-English and anti-Irish.

Stevens takes his symbolic trip through the changed heart of England in the year of the Suez crisis (though it is unmentioned) that is often cited as that which signified the end of global British power. The present in Barry's play is 1932, the year Eamon de Valera came to power and the beginning of the end of those vestiges of British power in Ireland, of the Ireland of Thomas Dunne that lingered on after 1922. Stevens has been the faithful steward of Darlington Hall, guarding it through the difficult passage from Lord Darlington's ownership to that of a rich American (reflecting the transfer of global power from Europe to America); and in his own way, though sane, rational and alert, he is as mired in the past and oblivious to the present as ex-Chief Superintendent Dunne. Ishiguro's poignantly conveyed sense of an ending, the evocation of evening, the remains of Stevens's day (which gives the novel its title), has its equally poignant counterpart in the candlelight that softly illuminates Dunne's most emotional memories. Both works reverse our expectations. A play which makes an ex-DMP member a sympathetic hero is not what we expect, while *The Remains of the Day* has downstairs in the stately home rather than upstairs as the foreground, though as the novel proceeds what is going on upstairs, seen only through a butler's eyes, grows steadily more intrusive. In a wonderful counterpoint, Stevens's genuine concern for duty, service and loyalty is in mute, but increasing, contrast with Lord Darlington's apparent disloyalty to, and aristocratic disrespect for, the will of the British people and the opinions of their elected representatives. There is an evocative similarity in the way in which the deepening nobility of Dunne's loyalty must cast at least a degree of shadow over those who created the circumstances in which that loyalty was no longer a virtue; Annie calls Michael Collins and the IRA 'renegades' (p.48) and in the novel that Barry gives her in which to expand her views, she remembers Collins and De Valera as 'fierce gunmen … savage killers'.[55]

Moreover, Stevens's almost surrealistic sense of professionalism is, we steadily come to realize, in contrast to his master's well-intentioned but – in the opinion of an American senator and Darlington's journalist godson – dangerous amateurish meddling in international politics. *The Remains of the Day* is a secular account of loyalty, duty and service whereas Barry offers a sacralized account. A cardinal feature of service for Stevens is professionalism, though like Dunne his service extended into loyalty, another cardinal feature. Stevens reflects in a kind of conceptual *reductio ad absurdum* on the components of true professionalism: restraint, ability to plan, expertise, experience, insistence on high standards, and above all, dignity (a third cardinal feature), loyalty and the ability to truly inhabit the role. These, explicitly the last three, are readily applicable to Dunne of the DMP. So too is Stevens's knowledge of the tradition of his service which, whether or not Ishiguro has made it up, is fascinating and borders on the comic. We witness with Stevens, as with Dunne, a stripping away until loyalty and dignity are seen to be independent of professional livery and uniform; these are virtues humanized when man and professional role become indistinguishable.

In each work, the professional stands over against the gentleman and the amateur, yet, despite the fact that 'amateur' derives from 'lover', it is love that is hand in glove with professionalism, gainsaying our usual association. The love is repressed in Stevens's case, expressed in Dunne's. One difference between Stevens and Dunne is that the butler is utterly compos mentis, seemingly scrupulous in his recollections (even emending them on second thoughts), punctilious in his words and thoughts and apparently arid of heart; a far cry from Dunne's senescent confusion and unbuttoned displays of emotion. But we infer that Dunne has been undone, as it were, by the turn of historical events, that he suffers a kind of post-traumatic stress. Stevens too has been let down by history, marooned like the Irishman in an uncongenial time and place. His obsession with professionalism and tradition – which Dunne exhibits too – may in his case be a sublimation of unfulfilled affection, love and sexuality. The vent of his feelings has been capped by these obsessions and by his Englishness, and now by his middle age and membership of a generation receding into history. In any case, his rationality is something of a carapace and underneath there is a Dunne-like disturbance he manfully keeps at bay while Dunne indulges it.

As even Dunne's life illustrates, professionalism must on occasion sacrifice the personal and familial. Dunne's domestic life has borne the brunt of his profession and his earnest, even sacralized, perception of that profession. (His son and his daughters are casualties of his career and values, and Annie the most wounded and resentful of them.) No wonder both Dunne and Stevens are tragic figures, and ones which can be found in real life, though for its part Irish literature since independence has tended to be narrow in its choice of heroes and protagonists and has exhibited something of what we might now call Irish political correctness. Few businessmen, few engineers, few modern aristocrats, few Irish soldiers, few professors, few scientists, few policemen – few Thomas Dunnes – in its pages. It is as if Seán O'Faoláin in his 1947 book, *The Irish*, set (or followed) the agenda and exhausted Irish society with his shrunken roster of six kinds of Irish for contemplation – priests, writers, new peasants, rebels, politicians, and Anglo-Irish.

Stevens and Dunne are not without faults, and it is debatable to what extent both have been unwittingly (or even wittingly) complicit in an undemocratic system. Just as it is possible that Dunne is whitewashing in memory his role in the breaking of the strikers in 1913, so Stevens might know, and have known, more than he professes about what was going on in Darlington Hall in the run-up to the Second World War; it remains unclear to what extent each is a reliable recounter of the past. But the sheer poignancy and eloquence (however different in kind) of these two characters surely endorse the nobility of their idea of service, even if the world could, and can, no longer accept it. We, especially in Ireland, should at least acknowledge, as Barry and Ishiguro compassionately do, its previous existence.

It is the nobility that seems to count in both works. It is true that Stevens surrenders himself – like a good servant – to a perception and valuation of the world that he himself is prevented from embodying. On his travels, driving his

American master's extravagant Ford, he is mistaken by villagers for a gentleman and encourages the mistake by allowing his acquaintances to believe that he had been immersed in international affairs, like the unmentioned (and apparently unmentionable) Lord Darlington. Since he has twice already denied working for Lord Darlington, one is tempted to hear the cock crow a third time. He does not come clean until forced, while claiming that dignity is the essence of gentlemanliness. He thereby appears to betray his own belief in dignity as the essence of the great butler. But he is no Judas; it is with relief he confesses his true status to the perceptive Dr. Carlisle. His imposture is oblique loyalty on the part of a man who has been induced to impersonate his 'betters' (his employer insisted he take the Ford). Indeed, the dignity he has aspired to all his life requires him courteously not to disappoint the expectations of others even if that necessitates deception. When one of Lord Darlington's cronies questions Stevens about current affairs in order to show through the butler's ignorance the absurdity of universal franchise, it is uncertain Stevens is not humouring his interrogator in order to provide another instance of immaculately professional service: the servant assuming himself required to affect lack of knowledge even when he possesses it.

Yet all is not well, and Stevens's trip is an attempt to redeem the past. He does this literally by proposing to rehire a woman who had been housekeeper at Darlington Hall and his feelings for whom Stevens had, it seems, foolishly repressed out of loyalty to his profession and master. His apparently casual itinerary increasingly becomes an embassy in order to retrieve love before it is too late, though he masks it from himself as professional necessity. He also attempts to redeem the past metaphorically by justifying Lord Darlington, and indirectly himself, in the light of posterity's condemnation. In this wonderfully layered novel, the more prismatic Stevens's reflections become, the more we sense certainty of the wisdom and innocence of Lord Darlington draining from him. Thomas Dunne might be regarded as engaged upon the same kind of attempted redemption of the past, even in his half-dotage, during which he too is engaging once again in the mimicry of his 'betters' yet without losing our respect.

These are not unblemished heroes, and their vision of the world is not ours, but it surely commands our respect. Dunne's vision of a world wedded by loyalties and stewardships, at the centre or top of which stood the monarch, a world now broken in Ireland in 1932, has its more elaborate counterpart in the image to which Stevens returns again and again: the great house as a hub:

> Butlers of my father's generation, I would say [by which Stevens means before the Great War], tended to see the world in terms of a ladder – the houses of royalty, dukes and the lords from the oldest families placed at the top, those of 'new money' lower down and so on, until one reached a point below which the hierarchy was determined simply by wealth – or the lack of it. Any butler with ambition simply did his best to climb as high up this ladder as possible … *our* generation, I believe it is accurate to say, viewed the world not as a ladder, but more as a *wheel*.[56]

Stevens clearly thinks the wheel no less undemocratic than the ladder, and he is complicit with the aristocratic disdain for democracy and Lord Darlington's preference for policy arrived at in the privacy of the great houses, as Lord Darlington seeks to do. There is comic and even distasteful fantasy in his image of the wheel, and yet it is Shakespearian. 'To us … the world was a wheel, revolving with these great houses at the hub, their mighty decisions emanating out to all else, rich and poor, who revolved around them' (p.115). We might recall Rosencrantz's words in *Hamlet*:

> The cess of majesty
> Dies not alone; but, like a gulf, doth draw
> What's near in with it: it is a massy wheel,
> Fix'd on the summit of the highest mount,
> To whose huge spokes ten thousand lesser things
> Are mortis'd and adjoined; which, when it falls,
> Each small annexment, petty consequence,
> Attends the boisterous ruin.

Stevens, like Dunne, is one of the doomed small annexations of the once sturdy aristocratic wheel. The wheel is an image far older than the ladder where power and status are involved, and positively Yeatsian in its neo-feudalism or neo-medievalism, though Yeats wanted the hub of the wheel to be the great houses of the 'native' Anglo-Irishry instead of the palaces of a monarch or vice-regal lodge. Dunne preferred the latter, and his daughter Annie in the later novel recalls:

> My father's country had first a queen to rule it, and then a king, and then another king. It was a more scholarly, a more Shakespearean world, it was more like a story.[57]

Stevens remains loyal to the memory of Lord Darlington and the idea of the great house, as Dunne remains loyal to the memory of Queen Victoria and imperial Ireland. If play and novel tacitly question the limits and wisdom of loyalty and service, each nevertheless seems to ennoble those who practiced them and even those who received them. Stevens is prepared to admit that 'the passage of time has shown that Lord Darlington's efforts were misguided, even foolish' (p.201), but rejects the corollary that he should retrospectively disown his master and annul his years of loyalty. Loyalty, it seems, is in this case larger than the cause that first invited it and here includes self-esteem, even self-identity. Besides, Stevens thinks of Lord Darlington as a man of great moral stature. The young journalist, Mr. Cardinal's, assessment of him as an amateur bungler and gentlemanly naïf is closer to the mark, and Stevens may be indulging in indirect self-justification when he defends Lord Darlington; moreover, the enormity of what was at stake with the rise of Nazi Germany may be emphasized by Ishiguro's very consignment of it 'offstage' to the novel's sub-plot. Nevertheless, and by the same token, Stevens's own dignity, should we grant it, acts to dignify the figure of Lord Darlington by association, the lord being served in this ironic but most loyal way by the servant. There is even a sense in which Stevens bears away from the house and on his back his master's sins, like a scapegoat.

I would be tempted to argue in similar vein that the essential nobility and dignity of Thomas Dunne in *The Steward of Christendom* – any folly or misguided priorities to the contrary – retrospectively dignify appropriate cases of Irish servants of the state in pre-independent Ireland. Moreover, I would gingerly suggest that the play, apart from its intrinsic excellence and its fresh illumination of the years of the first Troubles, is a welcome contribution to the literature of our own recent and unlamented Troubles.

Illustration 5: Donal McCann in *The Steward of Christendom*.
Out of Joint Theatre Co./Royal Court Theatre 1995

8 | Colonial Policing: *The Steward of Christendom* and *The Whereabouts of Eneas McNulty*

Elizabeth Butler Cullingford

In his play *The Steward of Christendom* (1995)[58] and his novel *The Whereabouts of Eneas McNulty* (1998)[59] Sebastian Barry has attempted to do for the Dublin Metropolitan Police and the Royal Irish Constabulary what Frank McGuinness did for the Ulster Division at the Somme: explain and justify Irish loyalty to the British Crown.[60] In each work Barry gives centre stage to an Irish policeman who served an Empire that could no longer reward or protect him once Michael Collins had taken over Dublin Castle. Thomas Dunne and Eneas McNulty are loosely based on members of Barry's own family, whose fragmentary history left their descendant free to re-imagine their lives. The decline of the Anglo-Irish Ascendancy is by now a well-worn literary trope, but Barry examines the demise of a less fashionable group, the Catholic Loyalists. In the nineteen-eighties Barry was ashamed to admit that his great-grandfather was the last Catholic Superintendent of the Dublin Metropolitan Police, because he was 'a figure to bring you literary ruin. What price my credentials as a real Irish writer?'[61] Nevertheless, by the time he wrote *The Steward of Christendom* in the mid-nineties, Barry was ready to exorcize the 'demon', to 'wrench a life from the dead grip of history and disgrace' and proclaim his blood kinship with that 'disgraceful man' (*Papers*).

Similarly, the original of Eneas McNulty was 'my great uncle who did something ... terrible by joining the RIC', and therefore belongs to 'a censored past ... and a country whose history is erased'.[62] Barry borrows the rhetoric of silencing from radical critics and appropriates it for conservative ends: his desire to give voice to the historically occluded native collaborator is a literary extension of the project of historical revisionism. Both the play and the novel represent the internal or literal exile of former policemen who find themselves without a place or a narrative of identity in the post-colonial Ireland of de Valera. Are they traitors to their country? Was their service to law and order an instrument of colonial oppression, a genuine ideological commitment to Empire, or simply a means of economic survival?

The Steward of Christendom, which achieved international success and gave Donal McCann a major stage triumph, is a memory play set in 1932. The central character, Thomas Dunne, now confined in the county home in Baltinglass, County Wicklow, recalls incidents from his childhood, his family life, and his professional career as a policeman. Unable to distinguish between past and present, Dunne is visited by the ghost of his dead son Willie, who served in the British Army and died in the First World War, and by the younger selves of his three daughters, with whom he has always had a troubled relationship. According to Barry:

> This play is about his own true journey to freedom, many years after the Irish freedom which he rejected, an old man in extremis, a Royalist, a loyalist, a Castle Catholic, a father, a grandfather, a bare forked man, the steward of a lost Christendom, a hidden Christendom, Catholic Unionist Ireland of long ago (*Papers*).

Here Barry alludes to King Lear's characterization of man as 'a poor, bare, fork'd animal',[63] while in the play Dunne's resemblance to Lear (emphasized by his having three daughters) positions him as a flawed tragic hero who reveals through his insanity the truth about the human condition. When we first meet him he has given away his expensive tailored suit to a fellow madman who thinks he is a dog, and is dressed only in his undergarments. Like Lear he seems to be rejecting the trappings of his privileged condition: 'Off, off, you lendings!'[64] But Lear strips himself during the storm in recognition of his kinship with 'houseless poverty', whereas Thomas Dunne, a member of the comfortable middle-class, seems motivated primarily by his quirky and thematically central affection for dogs. It is not his policeman's uniform that he has cast off: indeed he begs for gold thread in his new suit to remind him of his past official role. Thomas's resemblance to Lear, the most powerful creation of England's most canonical author, seems designed to shore up his human dignity and emphasize his political ancestry.

Until 1916 the vast majority of Irish people were constitutional nationalists, if they were nationalists at all, and Crown employment was a fact of life rather than a cause for patriotic self-doubt. Numerous poor Catholic men also took the Saxon Shilling: until the beginning of the twentieth century the British Army was disproportionately Irish, and numerous Irish people 'helped conquer, govern, and evangelize imperial possessions overseas'.[65] Barry's imaginative recreation of Southern Irish Unionism, therefore, rests on a secure factual basis. Yet his comments on the politics of the play often sound defensive or disingenuous: 'People said that *Steward* was a play about Dublin Loyalism, but I was writing about what it means to be a father'.[66] Barry's hero Thomas Dunne certainly insists that he regrets his cruelty towards his daughter Annie rather than his public role in Irish history (*SC*, p.246), but the play gives more than equal time to the question of Dublin Loyalism. Moreover, Barry professes himself an innocent when it comes to precise information: 'I am in fear as a playwright of facts and dates, and I will never make an historian' (*SC*, p.xv). Again and again he has claimed to be inventing rather than recording the lives of his own family members. Yet the substance of the story is always the same: his Southern Unionist ancestors are 'discarded and forgotten' men and women because, as middle-class Catholic servants of the British Empire, they failed to conform to the hegemonic narrative of Irish resistance. What Barry calls 'the heavy weight of Nationalist history' has 'demonized' them (*Papers*). In positing a monolithic nationalism associated with what he calls 'the suffocating joylessness of de Valera's regime',[67] and attempting to resurrect the ghosts of those native Catholics who approved of the colonial connection, or who did not perceive it as colonial, Barry aligns himself with the ideology of revisionism.[68] Indeed, he claims that Roy Foster's history writing 'can have the same effect on the hairs on the back of the neck as poetry' (*SC*, p.xv).

Drafts of *The Steward of Christendom* in the Harry Ransom Center at The University of Texas demonstrate that a play with a central event which must be understood in terms of class politics was subtly altered to privilege the problematic question of national allegiance. Chief Superintendent Thomas Dunne (his name was really John), is remembered in Barry's family for ordering the vicious baton charge that dispersed a largely peaceable crowd of strikers in what was then Sackville Street during the Dublin Lockout of 1913:

> In the folklore of Dublin working class life and Trades Union history he hardly holds an enviable place. He was the man with responsibility for Dublin Castle, the very heart of British rule in Ireland' (*Papers*). In fact John Dunne was only one of several Police Superintendents on the scene, and no one had sole responsibility for what happened.[69]

The Dublin Lockout pitted the Irish General Workers Trade Union, headed by labour organizer Jim Larkin, against the Dublin Tramway Company, owned by the businessman and newspaper magnate William Martin Murphy. In August 1913, Murphy 'locked out' all the men who belonged to Larkin's Union, and the workers retaliated by attacking trams run by scabs. Because of the disorder in the city, a mass meeting called by Larkin for Sunday August 21st was proscribed. Although he was wanted by the police, Larkin was determined to speak. Borrowing the makeup expertise of the Abbey actress Helena Moloney, who supplied him with a false beard, and the formal wardrobe of Countess Markievicz's husband Casimir, who lent him a top hat, Larkin disguised himself as a respectable old gentleman, reserved a room in William Martin Murphy's own Imperial Hotel, and briefly addressed the Sackville Street crowd from the hotel balcony before being arrested by Superintendent Dunne and several other policemen.[70] According to Padraig Yeates's account of the Lockout, this comic foray into politics as performance art swiftly turned sour:

> The officers in charge of Larkin – Superintendents Murphy, Kiernan, and Dunne -seem to have mistaken the people recoiling from the police batons at Prince's Street for a mob trying to rescue Larkin ... Superintendent Murphy ordered the arrest party to make its way over O'Connell Bridge to College Street station and ordered every other policeman in earshot to drive the crowd back.[71]

In the resulting baton charges, which lasted less than five minutes, between four and six hundred civilians were injured, 'the credibility of the DMP was severely tarnished',[72] and the force earned itself the lasting hatred of the Dublin working class.

This incident originally occupied the most dramatically privileged moment of *The Steward of Christendom*: in several early drafts the play begins with a *son et lumière* evocation of the riot: 'The mill and ruckus of people running suggested by pools and hurrying rags of light, shouts of protest and pain, the ghost of Nelson's pillar upstage like a lost lighthouse over this vanished history' (*Papers*). Nelson's pillar, blown up by the IRA on the fiftieth anniversary of the Easter Rising, is an ideological ghost: it reveals the contemporary anti-Republican politics that inform Barry's evocation of August 1913 and its 'vanished history'.

Barry experimented with several beginnings, but kept returning to the image of his great-grandfather directing the baton charge against the strikers from the back of a rearing horse, and to a monologue spoken in 1932 by the ageing Dunne. The latest corrected typescript begins:

> I send my constables charging forth into the black crowd of simple men. It is my proper duty, as chief superintendent of B division. Their batons are rising and falling. There on the

> balcony of the Imperial Hotel rises that dangerous man. He wears a fake moustache, like an actor. The working men have come out to honour him, and the thugs of Dublin to enjoy the mischief, and he has his arms raised, and his voice is drowned. There was a proclamation posted the week before. It is my proper duty to clear the thoroughfare. I am the guardian, the steward of B division. The order must come from my mouth. Larkin wears his moustache. My heart is sore suddenly. There is a sense of a sea of sheep, and slaughter. Four minutes. We lead him away, the crowd goes up like a November bonfire. Larkin has said his piece, but his world is over. The great appear great because we are on our knees, let us rise. For him never again will there be rising, never again. My men strike down the strikers. For four months I work dawn to midnight for the same pay. Guarding the city. It is my proper duty. There is nothing else to say about it. I was a policeman (*Papers, Spiral notebook*).

Somewhere between that corrected typescript and the published text, this monologue was cut, although the baton charge still figures prominently in the dialogue. Indeed, the nationalist orderly Smith accuses Dunne of responsibility for the deaths of four men on 21 August 1913, abusing him as 'A big loyal Catholic gobshite killing poor hungry Irishmen' (*SC*, p.243). Dunne defends himself on professional, not political grounds: 'I'd like to see them clear Sackville Street of an illegal gathering without breaking a few heads … There was no one killed that day that I know of' (*SC*, p.246). When Smith later attempts to control the raving old man, his so-called 'pacifier' resembles a police baton: the nationalist takes symbolic revenge on the Unionist 'traitor'. But the loss of the striking opening speech alters the symbolic pattern and dramatic balance of the work. For example, towards the end of the play, Dunne says 'humorously' to the ghost of his soldier son Willie, 'The great appear great because we are on our knees. Let us rise' (*SC*, p.299). Larkin's words, inscribed on his statue in O'Connell street, may be familiar to an Irish audience, but since they no longer echo the opening monologue much of their effect is lost: nor is it clear whether Barry intends them to indicate Dunne's political change of heart.

More importantly, Dunne's original image of 'a sea of sheep, and slaughter' finds a poignant echo in his closing monologue, in which he recalls how his favourite sheepdog attacked one of his father's sheep: 'I found our dog there with the carcass of a ewe well-eaten, only the hindquarters remaining. I saw my father's blue sign on the wool and knew the worst. For a dog that would kill a sheep would die himself.' The child loves his dog too much to bring it back to the farm for execution, and his parents imagine that he is lost. When he finally returns he is terrified: 'And I knew then that the dog and me were for slaughter.' His autocratic and abusive father, however, cares more about his child's safety than the dog's transgression, and both are forgiven: 'And the dog's crime was never spoken of, but that he lived till he died' (*SC*, pp.300-1). The deleted opening monologue suggests that the crime for which Dunne is symbolically forgiven at the end of the play is the betrayal of public trust involved in the police charge in Sackville Street, when the police, the guardians and stewards of the people, turned on them savagely: when, metaphorically, the sheepdog slaughtered the sheep. Without the opening monologue, however, Dunne's identification of himself with the errant dog now refers to a personal rather than a political crime: his cruel treatment of his daughter Annie: 'You were not civil to your daughter, no, you were not. You were ranting, you were raving, and so they put you where you were safe. Like a dog that won't work without using his teeth, like a dog under sentence' (*SC*, p.240).

The direct political exposition provided by the Larkin soliloquy has been replaced by Dunne's memories of infancy:

> Da Da, Ma Ma, Ba Ba, Ba Ba. Clover, clover in my mouth, clover-honey smelling, clover smelling of Ma Ma's neck, and Ma Ma's soft breast when she opens her floating blouse … (*SC*, p.239).

This babbling pastoral, with its obvious debts to Freud and to Joyce's Baby Tuckoo, lacks the dramatic strength of the closing monologue about the dog, and thus changes the rhythm and balance of the play: the emphasis is now on personal rather than political redemption. Moreover, without the historical information provided by the Larkin speech Barry's subsequent allusions to the baton charge are more difficult to decode. The loss of the monologue also throws greater dramatic weight onto the most problematic moment in the work: the speech in which Dunne attempts to create out of the figure of Queen Victoria a female icon of Empire to rival Kathleen ni Houlihan.

The quarrel between Larkin's union and the Dublin employers was a local labor and class dispute that had little to do with Irish loyalty to the Crown. The 'Victoria' speech, on the other hand, moves directly into nationalist territory, in order to appropriate and reverse its most hallowed trope: that of Ireland as a beloved woman. In response to Smith's evocation of the martyrdom of Robert Emmet, Dunne recreates the sensation of Irish loyalty to the Empire in terms of heterosexual desire:

> I loved her for as long as she lived, I loved her as much as I loved Cissy my wife, and maybe more, or differently. When she died it was difficult to go from her to the men that came after her, Edward and George, they were good men but it was not the same. When I was a young recruit it used to frighten me how much I loved her. Because she had built everything up and made it strong, and made it shipshape. The great world she owned was shipshape as a ship. All the harbours of the earth were trim with their granite piers, the ships were shining and strong. The trains went sleekly through the fields, and her mark was everywhere, Ireland, Africa, the Canadas, every blessed place. And men like me were there to make everything peaceable, to keep order in her kingdoms ... She loved her Prince. I loved my wife. The world was a wedding of loyalty, of steward to Queen, she was the very flower and perfecter of Christendom. Even as the simple man I was I could love her fiercely. Victoria (*SC*, p.250).

The complicity between heterosexual domesticity and imperialism is not satirized: on the contrary, it is affirmed. The line, 'When I was a young recruit it used to frighten me how much I loved her', seems exaggerated: the dumpy black-clad figure of Victoria as she was in 1877, when Dunne joined the DMP, makes an implausible object of passionate desire. The inestimable advantage of Kathleen ni Houlihan was that no-one had ever seen her. The 'Victoria' speech, inserted in later drafts of the play, is a set piece contrived to produce dramatic surprise: 'she', the object of desire, is not named as Victoria until the last word. This device is designed to expose the anti-imperial assumptions of a postcolonial audience: it demonstrates how the 'weight of Nationalist history' has made such a paean almost unthinkable on the Irish stage.

Both in history and in the original drafts of Barry's play, the socialist Jim Larkin complicated the usual opposition between nationalists and loyalists. Larkin's chief opponent, the capitalist William Martin Murphy, was a nationalist, and Irish-Irelanders like Arthur Griffith and D.P. Moran also attacked the labour movement: despite Connolly and Markievicz. Social revolution in Ireland was never neatly aligned with national revolution. Barry's excision of the opening monologue lessens the impact of Larkin and highlights the old quarrel between Sinn Feiners and Castle Catholics. The historical Dunne's service during the Lockout clearly impressed his superiors: he was awarded the King's Police Medal in 1913 (possibly for his role in the arrest of Larkin), and promoted to chief superintendent in October 1914. But the unarmed DMP was taken off the streets of Dublin during the Easter Rising, and Dunne retired on his sixty-fifth birthday, 1 January 1919,[73] three weeks before the beginning of the War of Independence. He therefore played no part in the struggle to retain Ireland for the Crown.

Barry may not have known the dates of Dunne's career, but family 'folklore' concerns his confrontation with Larkin, not with the nationalists. The playwright's counter-factual decision to keep Dunne on the beat from 1919 to 1922 allows him to engage with current political and historical controversies by introducing Michael Collins and his nemesis Eamon de Valera, who has just come to power in 1932, the year in which the play is set. One of the fictional Dunne's recurring memories is of 16 January 1922, the day he handed over Dublin Castle to Collins. Although Annie rails against Collins, a criminal with 'a tally of carnage, intrigue and disloyalty that would shame a tinker' (*SC*, p.278), Dunne finds himself drawn to the enemy of Empire, and pays him the ultimate compliment:

> He would have made a tremendous policeman in other days … I would have been proud to have him as my son … I thought too as I looked at him of my father, as if Collins could have been my son and could have been my father (*SC*, pp.285-6).

Collins is thus inserted into the heart of a play that, despite the importance of Dunne's three daughters, turns ultimately on the familiar Irish trope of misunderstanding and reconciliation between fathers and sons. Dunne is aware that his attraction to this charismatic rebel is shared by his own police force:

> I knew that by then most of the men in my division were for Collins, that they would have followed him wherever he wished, if he had called them. And for an instant, as the Castle was signed over to him, I felt a shadow of that loyalty pass across my heart. But I closed my heart instantly against it (*SC*, p.286).

Like Neil Jordan's movie *Michael Collins*, which was released in 1996, a year after *The Steward of Christendom* was first produced, Barry's play uses Ireland's lost leader to discredit his rival, Eamon de Valera, and by implication the whole of the subsequent Republican tradition, including the contemporary IRA.[74] De Valera's suppression of the IRA in the mid-thirties is, as usual, conveniently forgotten. Barry writes that:

> De Valera it seems to me wanted a history of Ireland written that expunged the lights and lucks of Collins and embodied his own hopes and deeds (*Papers*).

This, de Valera's version of history, is what Barry seeks to revise. Dunne recalls the day in August 1922 when he wept to learn of the assassination of the Big Fella, and his last order to his policemen: 'to be sure and salute Mr. Collins's coffin as it went by' (*SC*, p.299). A play that once began with the defeat of Big Jim Larkin adopts a different trajectory, one that leads towards Beal na mBlath and the subsequent ascendancy of the despised 'King De Valera' (*SC*, p.262). Although this play says nothing about the conflict in the North of Ireland, it is, like Brian Friel's *Translations*, a history play about the future.

The Whereabouts of Eneas McNulty is governed by a similar desire to discredit the contemporary IRA. Although they do not appear until the end of the novel, the Provos are presented as the diabolical inheritors of twentieth-century Irish history, as seen through the eyes of Eneas, born in 1900 and violently deceased in 1970. Barry's family again inspired the work:

> The origin of this novel lies in the scant echoes of a lost great-uncle of mine, who, as far as I could gather, got himself into grave trouble because of something that happened to him in the nineteen twenties in Ireland during the war of independence. He disappeared from view, from hearts, from history, and after the early sixties, when he briefly resurfaced, was heard of no more. And I was attracted to him not only because I thought that was a sad fate, but because there were but two facts to rub together to make a spark to make a story, and great swathes of time that no one knew about, so that one could build a novel and imagine a world for him freely (*Papers*).

This powerful novel sympathetically recreates the psyche of a man who 'disappeared from view, from hearts, from history', and confirms the value of the things he has lost: home, family, friendship.It is indeed a sad story, a study of the psychic damage caused by political exile. On one of his doomed attempts to reclaim his place in Sligo, Eneas sees his brother, Jack, reading to his daughter:

> … and he is distressed at the empty rooms of his own progress in the world. No children, no wife, no picture house where human actions unfold and are warmly enacted … Here before him is the achievement of Jack, despite whatever trouble was upon him, here is the child and the father and the book, here is the living scene more holy and sacred than any official ceremony, for which all wars are declared and every peace manufactured (*WEM*, p.195).

Although Eneas grows used to his 'bare' life, he never ceases to regret his lack of human connections, and one of the finest achievements of the book is its evocation of loneliness, waste, and loss. The novel's affective power, however, is diminished by the single-mindedness of its anti-nationalist allegory. To advance the historically defensible argument that decolonization was a disaster for some native collaborators, Barry offers a complementary but less legitimate generalization: all nationalists, with the inevitable exception of Michael Collins, are killers and crooks, and freedom itself is the disaster.

Although his frustrated desire to return home to Sligo aligns him more closely with the Greek Odysseus than with the Roman Aeneas, the protagonist's name, which was changed in succeeding drafts of the novel from Charles O'Hara to Charles McNulty to Eneas McNulty, comes to symbolize his alignment with the British Empire. Aeneas, the Trojan founder of the Roman Empire, was the grandfather of Brutus, the legendary founder of Britain, who called his capital Troynovant after the city from which his grandfather had been forced to flee. The commonplace analogy between the Roman and British Empires has frequently led anti-imperialist Irish writers to rediscover their supposedly Carthaginian origins.[75] In embracing the story of Aeneas instead, Barry is metaphorically swimming against the nationalist tide. Eneas McNulty, after a lifetime of wandering from Sligo to Texas, Grimsby, France and Nigeria, never returns to his native place: he finally settles down with his African friend Harcourt in London – Troynovant – running a sailor's hotel on the Isle of Dogs.

Eneas's wanderings are initially voluntary: at the age of sixteen he goes to fight in the First World War rather than join the Irish rebels. He insists, accurately, that thousands of Irishmen have enlisted in the British Army, but his own motives are apolitical: his place at home has been usurped by his siblings, and he has protective feelings about France. Although his boyhood friend Jonno has become a courier for Sligo's nationalist rebels, 'the Mercury to all the dark men in the town', Eneas has no interest in their 'ideals and plots' (*WEM*, p.30). Throughout the novel, Jonno's Virgilian role as Mercury the messenger, always nagging Aeneas to move on, is complemented by Miltonic allusions to his role as Lucifer, the light-bearer. Early in the novel Eneas sees Jonno tumble from the wall of the blind rector's orchard where he has been plucking forbidden fruit (blind Milton's walled Paradise), and the image remains in his mind: 'forever he is falling there,

Jonno, boy of lightning, falling' (*WEM*, p.16). When he becomes friendly with the 'boy of lightning', Eneas enjoys his access to 'the nether world, the interesting hell of Jonno Lynch's heart' (*WEM*, p.18). Jonno the nationalist is the devil, or at least the Bad Angel to Eneas's Irish Everyman.

The metaphor of the journey common both to medieval Christian allegory and classical epic also structures this novel, in which Barry maps a picaresque narrative trajectory that takes his protagonist from the British Merchant Navy through the Royal Irish Constabulary, the British Army and the East African Engineering Enterprise Company. Every institutional allegiance that Eneas professes is anti-nationalist or colonialist. Despite his apolitical protestations, he knows what his actions imply:

> It was better, and more discreet with the politics going about those days, to cross from wily Connaught into the indifferent and more English-minded counties, for to take the King's shilling in Belfast. Or for to become an honest Jack Tar anyhow (*WEM*, p.34).

The dissonance between the idea of 'taking the King's shilling' and becoming 'an honest Jack Tar', between betrayal of Ireland and loyalty to the Crown, informs all Eneas's commitments.

As a tribute to an under-represented but historically significant class, the Catholic Irish Unionists, Barry's portrait of Eneas would be unproblematic were it not so sanitized. Despite his involvement in numerous wars, Eneas never kills either an Irish rebel or a German soldier. All the violence of a century of Irish history is committed by someone else: either by the Black and Tans, or by the followers of Michael Collins like his boyhood friend Jonno Lynch. Eneas is constructed as a victim, not as a political agent. His service in the British Merchant Navy is innocuous:

> They are fetching machine parts in Galveston and he understands in his heart that he may still serve the King and save France from this vantage point (WEM, p.35).

But it is enough to ensure that he gets no job when he returns to Sligo for the first time, because he has been 'busying himself during an English war' (WEM, p.53). The employment blacklist and the loss of Jonno's friendship prompt the most significant decision of his life:

> Eneas looks at it all with simple eyes and having no desire to loiter the rest of his days, joins at the hint of his Pappy the Royal Irish Constabulary. He's not the complete eejit as Jonno may believe, he's not the last innocent on earth. He knows why there are places in the peelers when there are places nowhere else. The RIC is composed no doubt of lost men, ordinary fellas from the back farms of Ireland, fools and flotsam and youngsters without an ounce of sense or understanding. And the legends of the RIC are all evictions, murders and the like, though many an Irish family was reared on those wages, and many a peeler was a straightforward decent man. Still, the word Royal is there before all, and they carry arms, and the top men are all out-and-out Castle men. But no matter. He can't live a life to please Jonno Lynch, much as his heart is grateful for the adventures of his youth. Or he would lead a life to please Jonno Lynch if Jonno still had a grá for him, a friendly love for him. But he does not, clearly. And a fella must work, must toil in the dry vale of the world (*WEM*, pp.55-6).

Barry frequently uses the word 'simple' as an explanation for loyalty to the Crown: the phrases 'ordinary fellas' and 'straightforward decent man' belong to the same exculpatory linguistic register. He also implies that if Jonno still loved Eneas, he would not have joined the peelers: his disastrous decision is caused as much by lack of affection as by his poor employment prospects.

Service in the Merchant Navy might have been forgiven by the Sligo nationalists, but not service in the RIC: when the Anglo-Irish War began in January 1919 with the killing of two Irish policemen, the constabulary's position as the local face of the enemy was highlighted. In the earliest drafts of his novel Barry cast Eneas in an even more provocative role: 'He has worn the clothes of the Black and Tans, and he must go' (*Papers*), but this idea was abandoned. Until later drafts, Barry also avoided a direct presentation of Eneas's time in the constabulary, jumping from his discharge from the Navy to the Treaty, and describing the intervening three years only in a brief retrospect:

> It had been a good bet the Royal Irish Constabulary in a land without work and even worse prospects for those who had gone out to fight the war. With decent enough pay and a pension and a sense of putting order on a disastrous situation. Well, no, the pay stank. The pension was a pauper's pittance. But he had always admired the police and was careful to join up in the full manner as a Sligoman and not an ex-merchant seaman as such and he kept away as much as he could from the auxiliaries who were dangerous men even to befriend such was their sense of their own power and such was their brief from London (*Papers*).

Instead of wearing the clothes of the Black and Tans (or the Auxiliaries, a second force made up of English ex-officers), Eneas is now distinguished from them: he signs up as 'a Sligoman' and not as a veteran of the British merchant navy. In the published text, which does describe his time in the RIC, Eneas still keeps his distance from the Tans and the Auxiliaries, but expresses admiration for their courage, and sympathy for the appalling experiences that have shaped them:

> Many of the Auxiliaries are decorated boys, boys that ran out into no-man's-land and took positions that only bodiless gods could have, and rescued men from the teeth of slaughter and saw sights worse than the drearest nightmares. And they have come back altered forever and in a way more marked by atrocity than honoured by medals (*WEM*, pp.57-8).

Like the phrases 'ordinary fellas' and 'straightforward decent men', the intimate word 'boys' contributes to a rhetoric designed to deflect blame. Barry's pervasive linguistic mannerisms reveal his political agenda: describing a police comrade who will shortly be murdered by the IRA, he writes:

> Doyle is a policeman of the old school, loyal as a child to the kings and queens of England, Scotland and Ireland and the princes of Wales also. His father was a simple cabinkeeper in Leitrim (*WEM*, p.59).

'Loyal as a child', son of a 'simple' father, Doyle is established as a boy for whom the complex questions of national identity do not arise; not as a man responsible for his own political choices, who has profited from his investment in the kings and queens of England.

Eneas is similarly distanced from the bloody business of reprisals. His job is picking up the remains of victims, not doing the shooting himself, and even this distresses him: 'Eneas in his heart cannot say that he enjoys the policing he is set to do. He had had in mind the more usual duties of the RIC, in days more peaceful, when he joined, and never had the ambition to be a carter of corpses' (*WEM*, p.59). When Jonno approaches him after the Treaty and suggests that he should redeem himself in the eyes of the nationalists by assassinating the Black and Tan Reprisal Man, he refuses on principle: 'Maybe the freedom of Ireland and all that is right and proper. But, killing a man is a very particular thing, a particular thing, it is, Jonno, and I couldn't do it' (*WEM*, p.83). There cannot have been many members of the RIC who got through the War of Independence without using their guns, and Barry shows himself aware of this credibility problem when Jonno asks, 'Aren't you after shooting men yourself, Eneas McNulty?' But Eneas denies the charge: 'Oh, as you opine, Jonno, I have fired off a few bullets in my time. I didn't hit anyone but I surely tried' (*WEM*, p.114). Simple, innocent Eneas is unable to kill even when he gives it a shot.

Barry's only concession to the patriots was, by the time his novel was published in 1998, already something of a cliché. As in *The Steward of Christendom*, the nationalist figure exempted from the general excoriation is Michael Collins, who luckily for his reputation died before he had to begin the messy business of running the country he had liberated. Collins is an all-purpose hero, guerrilla turned statesman, Republican turned Free Stater, a man with something for everyone. It is easy to like Collins, especially if you dislike de Valera. In fact, hatred of de Valera, and by implication the Ireland over which he presided for so many years, may be a major impetus behind the recent Collins love-fest. It provides a way of attacking Republicanism, both the historical and the contemporary varieties, without foregoing the advantages of patriotism:

> Bit by bit Eneas understands that a fella by the name of Mick Collins is the big man behind the wild lads willing to kill for the lovely trout of freedom. No decent description of him exists in police files, but a field of stories growing fast with brambles and tares attaches to the name. And yet the name rises immaculate and bright as a sovereign from the mire of events that muddy all normal men. It's a mystery. Eneas could call Collins the enemy except in his private mind he does not … it seems to Eneas that that same Reprisal Man is more his enemy than the invisible Mick Collins. But both are men of blood no doubt. (*WEM*, p.60)

Eneas is aware of the Big Fella's responsibility for violence: 'It was not Jesus Christ that Collins was by any means, a man with thousands of murders to his account' (*WEM*, p.99). Yet in quasi-religious diction he acquiesces in the 'mystery' of Collins's 'immaculate' name.

Nevertheless, as Collins signs the Treaty in London, Eneas weeps on the beach at Strandhill, while nationalists celebrate in his father's dancehall. (Barry ignores the fact that the Treaty was signed on December 6th, no time of year for hanging about on an Irish beach in your dancing clothes). His tears are prescient, for his lover Viv is soon warned by the local patriots 'to keep away from traitors or she would have her hair cut very short for herself' (*WEM*, p.108). As 'this murderous freedom' (*WEM*, p.109) degenerates into Civil War, Eneas, admonished once more by Jonno/Mercury, prepares to leave Ireland under sentence of death:

> He feels like a fabled wanderer of old and he hasn't left the spot yet. He has not endured shipwreck maybe but maybe he has – the shipwreck of freedom so general and welcomed in the land' (*WEM*, p.110).

Eneas travels to England and takes a job on a Grimsby trawler, 'For an Irishman might affect to hate England and love America, but they are both and were ever equal refuges to him' (*WEM*, p.125).

The Grimsby section of the book, added only in the later drafts, is a bridge designed to carry Eneas over the seventeen years between the Irish Civil War and his enlistment in the

British Army during the Second World War, and reveals by its relative abbreviation the schematic political allegory of the plot. Eneas is a loyalist Everyman who represents those Irish people who at significant historical moments chose Crown over Country. The first drafts of the novel, therefore, took Eneas off the beach at Strandhill in December 1921 and abruptly dumped him on another beach at Dunkirk in June 1940. Although the parallel settings were felicitous, the large time-lapse was clumsy: the insertion of the Grimsby episode therefore serves formal as well as political purposes. Most importantly, however, it facilitates an attack on de Valera's policy of neutrality and his refusal to grant asylum to Jewish refugees during the Emergency. As Eneas is returning from the Northern fishing grounds, he sees a large liner headed towards Europe, whose passengers 'seem to him dark-clothed and infinitely sober, like prisoners beyond reprieve, like children being ferried far from hearth and happiness' (*WEM*, p.131). Barry alludes to the voyage of the *St. Louis*, a ship that in May 1939 carried 937 Jews away from Germany, but was refused entry into Cuba, the United States, and Canada, and forced to return to Europe. The asylum-seekers were eventually accepted by Britain, France, Belgium and the Netherlands, but except for Britain these countries were occupied by the Nazis, and 250 of the original 937 passengers died in the Holocaust.[76] In his local paper Eneas learns that:

> … the ship he has seen holds a strange cargo of Jews being returned to Germany, certain there to be imprisoned as enemies of Christ and country. That no port on God's earth would take them, and that they had lain outside Dublin port and been refused and Southampton, and what affects him strongly, not only had crossed the Atlantic to be refused by the President of America himself, but had anchored not far from Galveston in the Gulf of Mexico, the very heartland of emigrants and lonesomeness. For it is a cargo of hated people, all folk like those Finans of Sligo, with their perfect shop and their weather all about of foul remarks. As a hated man Eneas feels the force of their useless journey. And he thinks of that fella De Valera, now king of Ireland, piously refusing the ship entry, and it makes a racket in his noggin (*WEM*, p.132).

De Valera's asylum policy, under which fewer than seventy Jews were admitted to Ireland during the Emergency, was not generous,[77] and in the novel his refusal to rescue these homeless souls weighs heavily against him: 'For what is the world without rescue, but a wasteland and a worthless peril?'(*WEM*, p.132).

Nevertheless, there is no evidence that the captain of the *St. Louis* sought asylum for his human cargo in Dublin. Neither Thomas and Witts's investigation of the incident, *Voyage of the Damned*,[78] nor Keogh's study, *Jews in Twentieth-Century Ireland*, mentions such a request. The US Holocaust Memorial Museum maps the ship's direct return to Antwerp: there was no detour to Dublin. Barry distorts the historical record in order to blacken de Valera, and the Jews provide a convenient stick with which to beat the Irish nationalists. Even Eneas's own mother is represented as anti-Semitic; she is 'always severe about Finan's because they are a Jewish family and in her open opinion, call her a Christian if you liked, the Jews had crucified Christ Himself in the old days of the Romans, they were all in on it' (*WEM*, p.100). In contrast with her bigotry, Eneas's vision of the ship and his desire to rescue its passengers provides an unimpeachable ethical motive for his enlistment in the British Army:

> And out he goes indeed, ever mindful of those old fields of France, but also now of that strange ship he saw strangely gliding over the cold waters to Germany as if in the sunken morning of a terrible dream (*WEM*, p.134).

When Eneas encounters displaced French people fleeing from the German invaders he finds confirmation that de Valera 'is a poor man not to help Europe' (*WEM*, p.134). In these homeless French he sees 'an echo and a remembering icon of those perished souls along the Irish seaboards a hundred years before, when the hag of Famine showed her dark face and dripping bones' (*WEM*, p.135). Apparently the memory of the Famine ought to have persuaded de Valera to join in the defence of Europe against Hitler. The analogy with the Famine, however, which is not mentioned elsewhere in the book except to suggest that those who behaved most cruelly to the starving poor were often the Irish themselves, is in the French context somewhat forced. Nor is the complex issue of Ireland's wartime neutrality debated in the book: it is simply assumed to be craven and wrong.

Eneas's exploits in the British Army are as peaceful as his behaviour in the RIC. Fleeing from the beach at Dunkirk, he is bizarrely kidnapped by an old French peasant who needs help with his grapes. Abandoning violence for viniculture, he spends months tending the 'fields of France', and after the harvest he is returned to England by French fishermen, nursing a mild case of shellshock, but satisfied by his avoidance of combat:

> As health returns he begins to feel a certain pride for all he has done as a soldier. What better thing than to spruce a French farm, better than maiming and killing he hopes (*WEM*, p.157).

Better, certainly, but also somewhat unlikely: no-one in authority asks where he has been all summer.

Honourably discharged from the Army, Eneas returns again to Sligo hoping that his sentence of death has been forgotten. But the spirit of Hitler awaits him there too, for his nemesis Jonno has become a Blueshirt:

> I think he fancies them Germans in the days to come. The United Republic of Germany and Ireland or some such, with Jonno for gauleiter maybe' (*WEM*, p.180).

To imply that Jonno's form of nationalism leads inevitably to fascism, Barry extends the Blueshirt period, which was definitively over by 1936,[79] into the early forties. Although neither the anonymous letter that reaffirms the sentence of death against Eneas, nor the group of black-coated men who chase him through the park, are identified with Jonno, his position as Eneas's devilish opposite is sustained by his association with Hitler.

The last stage of Eneas's wanderings, during which he digs canals for the East African Engineering Enterprise Company in a Nigeria on the brink of decolonization, is ideologically complex. Popular identifications between the Catholic Irish and Africans or African-Americans, pejorative in the nineteenth century, were positively reaffirmed at the end of the twentieth.

Michael Farrell's assertion that the Catholics were the 'white negroes' of Northern Ireland,[80] and Roddy Doyle's tongue-in-cheek claim that 'the Irish are the niggers of Europe'[81] are only the most famous of a series of historical, fictional, poetic, and cinematic analogies between the European victims of Empire and their black brothers.[82] Barry also emphasizes the cross-racial alliance between Eneas and his Nigerian comrade Harcourt. His evocation of their friendship, the closest adult relationship Eneas has ever known, and his only consolation for the 'bare rooms of his progress through the world', is one of the most moving portions of the novel. Yet it also carries a forced and deliberate ideological charge, and depends on an historical improbability. Harcourt tells Eneas that he spent the Second World War in 'your sweet neutral country', working undercover for British Intelligence:

> I was assigned to travel between Belfast and Dublin on the trains and talk to servicemen in their civvies and the like and to talk to any foreigners, you know, that might like to be talked to and have information they might or might not be aware they had (*WEM*, p.215).

This is a wholly implausible job for a black man in the lily-white Ireland of the Emergency. Harcourt's peaceable service in the British Army echoes Eneas's non-violent sojourn in the French vineyards, and it enrages the freedom fighters of Lagos just as Eneas's service to the Crown infuriates the Sligo patriots. Barry spells it out – 'Did it ever occur to you, brother Eneas,' says Harcourt, 'that Lagos is almost the same word as Sligo, give or take an i or an a?' The year is 1958, and 'the disaster of freedom' is coming to Nigeria:

> What's afoot is freedom, that dreaded thing. He recognizes the passionate alarm of the smart police as they drive all tooth and nail through the major boulevards … the patriots are trying to tear the old Britishness out of Nigeria, erase the men and emblems of the very Queen herself … New heroes of this trouble, but old foes and contemptuous enemies of Harcourt and his imperial ways (*WEM*, pp.240-1).

The kinship between the Irishman and the African, therefore, is not the kinship of former slaves, but of former native collaborators: Barry reverses the nationalist implications of the notion that Ireland is a 'third-world country'. Freedom for Nigeria means exile for Harcourt; Irish freedom has turned Eneas into a displaced person. Both return to the metropolitan heart of the Empire that they have served, and live out their final ten years running a hotel for old sailors on the Isle of Dogs. Although Eneas will never have a wife or a child, Harcourt is his substitute 'bride', and the love between these two elderly men is touchingly realized.

But the book does not end there. The final episode, set in 1970, stretches historical plausibility even further than the idea of a black undercover agent working the railway line between Dublin and Belfast. Barry brings the septuagenarian Jonno back for a final indictment of nationalism and what it is about to cost Irish people in the North. Jonno has previously been an IRB courier, a Collins man, a Free Stater, a Blueshirt, and an adherent of Fine Gael. The Blueshirts and Fine Gael were hostile to the IRA, so the trajectory of Jonno's sequentially coherent political positions leads away from the Republicanism of his youth. In old age, however, the Blueshirt has become an IRA gunman, and Barry seems unconscious of the ideological incompatibility between his current and former political allegiances:

> All comes round, Eneas. All comes round. Nothing going on for forty, fifty years, then, bang-bang-a-doodle, we're back in business. Have to show the young the ropes. Fight's on again, boy. Oh, we'll have the great days now. Freedom for the poor lost Catholic Irish of the North. That's the new story (*WEM*, p.297).

Moreover, he has come to shoot Eneas, fifty years too late, because the eruption of the Northern Troubles necessitates a clearing of the old blacklists before new ones are created. This apparently fantastic conclusion has some basis in fact: in the nineteen sixties Barry's grandfather traced his missing great-uncle to a hotel on the Isle of Dogs, as in the novel his brother Jack traces Eneas:

> When my grandfather went there he was told that Charlie did live there, but was out that day, and to come back in the morning. Next morning my grandfather duly returned, but found the little hotel burned to the ground. He assumed that Charlie had taken flight when he heard 'a man from Sligo' was looking for him and burned the hotel to cover his traces. Or indeed my grandfather feared he might have been followed from Sligo by his brother's enemies, and that they had caught and killed him. Either way, he never could find any trace of his brother again.[83]

Barry constructs his denouement on the basis of his grandfather's fears, which were more dramatic than plausible, and which turned out to be ill-founded: his uncle Charlie died in an old folks' home, not in a burning hotel.

Indeed, political allegory rather than historical probability dictates Jonno's return: he is still Lucifer, the boy of lightening, thinly disguised as a Provo senior citizen. Eneas's convenient ignorance of current events permits Jonno to explain the complexities of the Northern situation in crude Republican shorthand:

> 'The North, Eneas. Haven't you been reading the news?' 'The North of what?' 'Hah, you're the wide-boy. Always was the wide-boy. North going to go up like a bloody ould November bonfire. Liberty. Love of country. Things you don't understand, Eneas. Things that make great men. Great notions. Powerful classes of feelings. Patriots! Belfast, Derry, Portadown. Lisburn – haven't you been decking the news, boyo?' (*WEM*, p.297)

Jonno's staccato litany is meant to demonstrate how the 'heavy weight of Nationalist history', the old narrative of oppression and revolution, has spawned a second round of the Troubles, which will destroy 'simple' and peaceable old men like Eneas. If we read the whole novel in the light of its abrupt closing scene, in which Jonno is accidentally killed by his own sidekick (Republicanism will split and self-destruct) and Eneas dies in a quixotic attempt to save the body of his former friend from the flames of the burning hotel (symbolic of hellfire), its revisionist project is unmistakable.

The message of both *The Steward of Christendom* and *The Whereabouts of Eneas McNulty* is that the history of Ireland in the twentieth century has been bedevilled by the patriotic idea of 'freedom': decolonization spells disaster. This position can certainly be argued: indeed it has been argued ad infinitum; but both texts would have been more powerful had they been less driven by their anti-Republican thesis, less concerned to refute a one-sided version of history by offering an equally one-sided and sometimes factually misleading rebuttal. Freedom was indeed a disaster for Thomas Dunne and Eneas McNulty (and for numerous others) because they chose to be loyal to the Crown at a moment when that loyalty no longer paid off. Barry's gift for characterization and skilful deployment of pathos ensure that readers engage sympathetically with these displaced and defeated policemen, while his desire to restore their stories to the national memory is understandable, given his own family history and his stated commitment to inclusion, 'balance', and 'peace'.[84] Nevertheless, his subordination of two such richly imagined individuals to a schematic political allegory lessens the impact of their personal tragedies.

Illustration 6: Alison Deegan and Lorcan Cranitch in *The Only True History of Lizzie Finn.* Abbey, 1995

Illustration 7: Birdy Doyle as Birdy Sweeney in *The Only True History of Lizzie Finn*. Abbey, 1995

9 | Redressing the Irish Theatrical Landscape: Sebastian Barry's *The Only True History of Lizzie Finn*

Anthony Roche

During the 2004 centenary of Ireland's National Theatre, the Abbey chose a series of staged readings of eleven plays to represent each of the decades since its founding. The period '1984-1994' was represented by Sebastian Barry's 1990 play *Prayers of Sherkin*. It was good to see Barry acknowledged as one of the most outstanding of contemporary Irish playwrights. But a staged reading (or, better still, a new production) of 1995's *The Only True History of Lizzie Finn* would have provided a valuable opportunity to re-evaluate a play that has never had its due share of attention or recognition. It would also have served to emphasize the play's searching exploration of the issues and tensions surrounding the self-conscious formation of an 'Irish' theatre movement at the turn of the previous century. This idea will be explored in the following pages, both in terms of a close reading of the play itself but also in sustained dialogue and counterpoint with the life and career of J.M. Synge, the greatest dramatist the Irish theatre has produced.

It is by now something of a critical truism that Sebastian Barry's plays highlight figures whose lives do not fit into the accepted grand narrative of Irish history. Further, the individuals they dramatize are members of his own family about whom little was said because they had in some significant way transgressed the taboos of Catholic Nationalist Ireland and so were consigned to oblivion. In the case of Lizzie Finn, her unspeakable offence was to have been a dancer on the music-hall stage. It becomes necessary to put some critical pressure on the term 'family' here, not biographically but in terms of the world of the theatre. The act of theatre is among other things about finding a space in which to re-imagine or re-invent oneself, marking out a space of relative freedom in which to escape one's determining biological and sociological history. J.M. Synge's biography is virtually impossible to write, not only because so many of the primary documents necessary to that story have been destroyed but because he came from a family in which self-expression was virtually prohibited.[85] Many of Synge's plays, none more so than *The Playboy of the Western World*, are concerned with finding one's tongue and improvising a role to play in life. Such dramatic self-fashioning is not carried out in isolation, but in intimate contact with all of the others involved in the collaborative act of theatre. The term 'family' is frequently invoked to account for the intensity and closeness of the relationships involved. Synge, famously, was to become engaged to an Abbey actress, Molly Allgood, for whom he specifically wrote the parts of Pegeen Mike and Deirdre of the Sorrows. That those relationships do not always endure beyond a particular production or a set number of years does not lessen their power, particularly in theatrical terms. Sebastian Barry's *The Steward of Christendom* is remembered by those who saw it not only for the luminous quality of its lines or for that rarest of things on the contemporary stage, a touching and positive account of father-son relations, but for the committed and mesmerising central performance by Donal McCann. Less than five years after the opening night, and having toured in the part for some time, Donal McCann was dead, tragically young, from cancer, and we could only reflect on the performances we would not now see and recall with gratitude those we had. Sebastian Barry has written, powerfully and movingly, of how he attended Donal McCann in those last painful months and of the grief he suffered at his parting. It speaks to an unusually high degree of the sense of theatre as 'family'.

In *Lizzie Finn* itself, there is in the published Methuen text (most unusually) no mention of the cast who performed in the play's first production, on the main stage of the Abbey Theatre in October 1995, directed by the then-Artistic Director Patrick Mason. And yet not to know the cast of that production is to miss a crucial element in the play's conscious deployment of 'theatre as family'. The title role was played by Barry's wife, the actress Alison Deegan, for whom he had earlier written the part of another ancestor, Fanny Hawke, in *Prayers of Sherkin.* And the role of Lucinda, Lady Gibson, the formidable mother-in-law with whom Lizzie Finn has to engage when she travels home to Ireland and her husband's country estate, was performed by Joan O'Hara, the playwright's mother and one of Ireland's leading actresses. This casting of his wife and his mother has a particular resonance for one of the play's key themes, the coming together of a man and a woman from different social spheres in an act of marriage and a potential procreation which will extend the family line into the future. But, as suggested earlier, Barry is interested in the idea of 'theatre as family' in a more than biological sense. This is beautifully illustrated and developed in the play by another key piece of casting. In seeking to rescue particular individuals from oblivion, Barry is on to particularly rich terrain when it comes to actors or actresses; for where the playwright leaves a script for future productions, the actor (like most of those involved in the theatrical process) leaves no direct reproduction of their original artistic contribution (as there is in film, for instance). The most we have are still photos and press reviews of their performances, but these fall far short of the lived experience and if anything serve only to mock in their remove and very stillness the animation and full presence to which they refer. Certain play texts, however, bear within them the traces of those actors for whom their parts were first written. As Synge created the roles of Pegeen Mike and Deirdre for Molly Allgood, he no less wrote the part of Christy Mahon for William G./Willie Fay. Fay's diminutive physical stature is memorably conjured in Synge's 1905 *The Well of the Saints* by Molly Byrne, when she commends the blind Martin Doul for his 'queer talk … if it's a little, old, shabby stump of a man you are itself'.[86] And the combination of a small, initially unimpressive physical presence with considerable histrionic ability is at the centre of Synge's conception of the Playboy. In *The Only True History of Lizzie Finn*, there is a secondary character called Birdy Doyle, described as '*a small pinched man in his forties*'. He is one of the music-hall acts which accompany Lizzie Finn's dancing, and is so presented at the opening of Act One, Scene Three:

> Good evening to you. My name is Birdy Doyle. I will be doing for you now the Birds of Ohio. (*Pause.*) The Crested Jackhammer. (*Whistles it.*) The Yellow Miner Bird. (*Whistles it.*) The Ohion Sparrow. (*Whistles it.*) The Ohion Spotted Dove. (*Whistles it.*) The American Wood pigeon. (*Calls it.*) The Broken Man. (*Calls it.*) The Red-Throated Thrush. (*Whistles it.*) The Lonesome Plover. (*Calls it.*) That was, the Birds of Ohio. My name is Birdy Doyle. Thank you. (*Goes solemnly.*)[87]

The actor who played the part in the Abbey production was Birdy Sweeney, and the part was self-evidently written for him, the '*little man with the sharp face*' (p.8) who himself looked rather like a bird. He acquired a new first name from decades spent in the music-halls where he perfected an act doing bird impressions. Well on in years, Birdy Sweeney turned to the 'legitimate' stage and contributed a number of memorable performances to Irish theatre in the early 1990s, from one of the bar habitués in Garry Hynes's Abbey production of Eugene O'Neill's *The Iceman Cometh* to the sorrowful but resigned sea-god Poseidon at the start of Lynne Parker's production of *The Trojan Women* in Brendan Kennelly's version at the Peacock. Sebastian Barry's play was the one occasion where Birdy Sweeney brought not only his mock-serious sense of presence and his expressive voice and body to a legitimate role but also the non-articulate animal sounds he had perfected over the years. In this collaboration between actor and playwright, the worlds of the music-hall and of 'legitimate' theatre which have so consciously been kept separate in the Irish cultural world were forced to acknowledge an intimate interdependence (something which can also be seen in the plays of Sean O'Casey and Brendan Behan). Birdy Doyle has only one more brief appearance – in the farewell party for Lizzie Finn on the eve of her marriage to Robert Gibson – where his desire to take a drink finds reiterated expression in the one line: 'We must drink a fond farewell' (pp.21-22). But though Birdy Doyle departs from the play when the locale shifts to Castlemaine in County Kerry, Birdy Sweeney does not. He is required to play two more roles, in an act not so much of theatrical 'doubling' as 'tripling'. When Lizzie and Robert attend Lord and Lady Castlemaine's party, Birdy Sweeney reappears as the Factotum who brings on the fancy foodstuffs they are to eat, all of which turn out to be birds: quail, partridge, and pheasant. When the Factotum asks Lizzie if she knows 'the noise that fella [i.e. the particular dead bird] makes' (p.49) and she replies no, he whistles each of them in turn. Lizzie is moved to remark:

> **Lizzie:** You know, you remind me of a man I knew once in the music-hall. You're the very spit of him. You don't know the Birds of Ohio, by any chance, do you?
> **Factotum:** No, ma'am, only the birds of Corcaguiney (p.50).

The final pay-off on this theatrical gag occurs with Birdy Sweeney's third appearance, as the Anglican clergyman presiding at the funeral of Lady Gibson. Confronted once again with his distinctive bird-like features and thin, grey-haired melancholy, Lizzie risks the question, 'You don't know the birds of Ohio, do you?', (p.61) to the cleric's complete bafflement. Doubling in the theatre traditionally has arisen as a matter of economics in any play with a large cast, from Shakespeare on. And frequently an effort is made to disguise not only the body but also the physical features of the actor so the resemblance is lessened and the audience can retain credibility in the discrete existences of the different characters. But twentieth-century dramatists like Bertolt Brecht and Caryl Churchill want us to recognize that we are in a theatre. They deliberately utilize the doubling of actors to enable the audience consciously to identify the different characters as just that, fictitious creations presented to us by the performers. Birdy Sweeney is meant to be recognized in all three parts, not only by Lizzie but by us. At one level, the persistence of her music-hall companion into the alienation of her new life as Lady Gibson is a sign of Lizzie's desire to connect the old life with the new. It is also part of Barry's determination not to leave the world of the theatre behind when the scene switches from England to Ireland, but rather to see the Ireland of the play as theatrically constructed. This point will be developed later. It is enough now to remark that any future production of *Lizzie Finn*, when it comes to casting Birdy Doyle, the Factotum and the Reverend, will have to trawl the popular stage anew or come up with an actor especially accomplished in the art of making bird noises. For not only is the part being recreated in each new production but so is the contribution to it by its first performer, deeply embedded as it is in the script and its requirements.

The very first scene of *Lizzie Finn* is set backstage in a '*dressing room*' (p.5) and acknowledges the extent to which this is a play about the theatre. It shows Lizzie and her friend and fellow performer Jelly Jane getting ready to go on stage. The nightly rituals they perform, changing from one set of clothes into another, helping each other to apply the appropriate makeup, checking each other's appearance as in a mirror, show the cooperative nature of the theatre. But they also extend 'theatre as family' into the less conventional, more radical and heterodox zone of gender relations. Lizzie and Jelly Jane behave to each other in ways that might be termed 'sisterly', especially as deployed in a non-biological sense by twentieth-century feminism. Foregrounding of the backstage space which they share exclusively as women allows for a freer exchange than in the more circumscribed world of late Victorian social discourse, as the pair trade bawdy verbal exchanges and complain about their physical ailments. They also enjoy a considerable degree of physical intimacy as they shed most of their garments and move about backstage. The contrast with the formal heterosexual wooing is considerable. Robert and Lizzie dress elaborately and other in the course of the play, whether married or single. The male double standard in this heterosexual regard is examined when Robert comes to the music-hall to enjoy the mild erotic spectacle of the dancing girls and is confronted by a near-naked Lizzie. His 'instinctive' reaction is to seek to cover her with his coat. The two women backstage are of course preparing to provide such voyeuristic spectacle for the men. But they are also performing for each other, in the in-between space where they have taken off their formal wear and before they have donned the erotic costume which is explicitly described by Lizzie as a 'man trap' (p.6). In the course of the play's first act, both Lizzie and Jelly Jane will acquire suitors, be proposed to and accept offers of marriage. But the play registers a sense of loss as well as gain. The text establishes more clearly than was apparent in the Abbey production that there is a strong vein of same-sex desire running through their relationship.Nowhere is this more keenly felt than in their last scene together, where the primary impression is of lovers parting: 'Oh, Jelly Jane, Jelly Jane, I'll miss all this. I was warm in our bed'(p.24). Earlier, they envisage transferring their womanly partnership from the stage to the outside world by planning 'next year [to] open the shop' (p.6), a shared dream which their marriages put an end to. When they part, Jelly Jane gives Lizzie a memento, a little stone angel, a religious icon to watch over her. It is also an androgynous figure, which suggests the fluidity of gendered relations made possible in the theatre. A more muted renewal of same-sex desire is enacted in Act Two by Lizzie's interest in the servant Teresa, whom she spends much time measuring and fitting for a dress. At the end of the play, Lizzie buries the stone angel on the beach; it is a burial of other possibilities she has entertained both with Jelly Jane and with Teresa before she goes off forever with Robert.

Emphasis is laid throughout on Lizzie as a working woman, as someone who has signed a contract for the work she performs, and who does so with 'style' (p.6). The institution of contracts at the Abbey Theatre in November 1905 may have driven many of the amateur actors out, but it enabled Molly Allgood to leave her daytime job and take up the profession of actress on a full-time basis.[88] It was a profession she pursued even after her marriage in 1910 to G.H. Mair, a critic for the *Manchester Guardian*. Yeats's experiences in the theatre brought him into contact with actresses and other working women – such as the dancer Ninette de Valois – as well as enabling him to witness at first hand the transformation of Lady Gregory from society lady into a producer and a playwright. All of this provided quite a contrast with the fin de siècle, pre-Raphaelite images of women Yeats projected in his 1890s verse. When a Senator in the 1920s, he responded to the Free State Government's efforts to force women to leave their employment upon marrying by referring to his experience in the theatre:

> The Minister said one of the objections to appointing women to certain posts is that they may get married. I wonder if that is so? My only experience of the matter has been gained in the theatre, and I have not noticed that when an actress gets married she retires from the stage.[89]

When Lizzie marries Robert, she retires from the stage. But when they decide to leave the bankrupt family estate at the close and to look for fresh theatrical pickings in Cork, there is no legal obstacle to Lizzie resuming her former trade. Robert also counters and exposes the hypocritical condemnation Lizzie suffers from his mother and the other gentry of Castlemaine by pointing out how it is his wife's accumulated earnings from her maligned dancing career on the stage that are keeping the estate going. This ironically reverses the connection made in recent biographies of the Protestant playwrights of the Irish Theatre Movement, which reveal that their artistic careers were subsidized by rents from the reduced properties still owned by their families.[90] The Abbey Theatre's high art was funded by the Horniman tea trade, before the Irish taxpayer subsidized it directly from 1925 on. Art and commerce have always kept closer acquaintance in Irish theatre than many would care to admit.

The play's second scene initiates the courtship between Lizzie Finn and Robert Gibson. It may seem at one level as if the play is a series of disparate, short scenes (there are 16 in the first act and 14 in the second) in which it may be difficult to discern continuity, especially between the England of the first half and the Ireland of the second. This is certainly something which any production of *Lizzie Finn* would have to confront. At the Abbey, Patrick Mason's direction did justice to the playing of the individual scenes; but the lavishness of the overall production muffled the symbolic and visual continuity which connects those scenes. What gives the play cohesion and unity is its self-conscious theatricality – as for instance in the doubling of roles between the first and second halves (in addition to the persistence of Birdy Sweeney, Tilly from the dancing troupe becomes Teresa the Big House servant). But more than anything else there is the play's emphasis on clothing or, more precisely, on costuming, theatrical and social. As Fintan O'Toole has noted, Sebastian Barry's 'plays place great weight on the imagery of clothing'.[91] The play's first scene has focused, to an almost fetishistic extent, on Lizzie's starry knickers, as emblem of the erotics of her stage performance. As she walks in the next scene along the strand in her formal 'civvies', braving a strong wind, Lizzie encounters an animated hat whose flight she intercepts. The headband identifies its owner as Robert Gibson, who soon arrives in hot pursuit, hatless and windswept. There is almost as much of a play with the conventions of courtship in the ensuing scene as in a Wilde comedy, with Lizzie providing a hairpin to keep Robert's hat firmly and formally in place. But beneath the formal exchanges which keep them locked into the separate worlds of man and woman, Robert and Lizzie work to establish a common ground as Irish exiles. They are both from Ireland and both from Kerry, strangers in a strange land. Robert terms his headgear 'a Kerry hat' and rapidly identifies Lizzie's 'way of talking [as] … a Kerry person also' (p.7). They no longer identify themselves as Irish but rather as displaced, deracinated figures:

> **Lizzie:** I don't know what I am now.
> **Robert:** No more than myself (p.7).

Robert is on his way home from the Boer War, deeply traumatized by the loss of his three brothers in the conflict. They are to be represented later in the play as '*three army uniforms in a rough rack*' (p.25) in the family household, ghostly presences referring to the three men who wore them. But they radiate symbolic significance, since so little is said about the individual personalities of the three Gibson brothers who perished and so much about the imperialist cause in which they served and died. The three uniforms and the death they connote are challenged by the servant Teresa producing and flourishing Lizzie's starry knickers and the life they attest to. When Robert first voyeuristically views them, it takes him a while to match their wearer in the music-hall with the polite young woman he formally encountered the day before at the sea front:

> *The music of the cancan.* **Robert** *settles in to watch it.* **Lizzie** *and* **Jelly Jane** *come on, begin the dance … It's only after a while that* **Robert** *recognises* **Lizzie***. He scans the playbill, touches the hairpin briefly that's still in his hat, gets up, … starts to peel off his greatcoat, and in a fever rushes the stage, and wraps, or tries to, his coat about* **Lizzie** (p.9).

Robert is staging a one-man riot. The scene cannot but evoke the row over the staging of *The Playboy of the Western World* and in particular the audience breaking up in disorder over the word 'shift'. A woman signing herself 'A Western Girl' wrote to *The Freeman's Journal* to protest Synge's play flaunting so provocatively

> a word indicating an essential item of female attire, which the lady herself would probably never utter in ordinary circumstances, even to herself.[92]

The women in Synge's play at least have the decency to stay physically clothed. But their author was alert to the hypocrisy involved; and Yeats recalls Synge approaching him during the riots and saying:

> A young doctor has just told me that he can hardly keep himself from jumping on to a seat, and pointing out in that howling mob those whom he is treating for venereal disease.[93]

In the face of the howling, the actors asserted their professionalism and commitment by continuing to deliver their performances and (as best they could) their lines. Lizzie too mounts her counter-protest, objecting to the way in which Robert's actions are designed not only to breach the boundaries between stage and audience but to create a sense of shame around what is being presented: 'It's my true work. Go away from me in my work!' (p.9). From Robert's point of view, he is saving and protecting her; to the disinterested spectator, he looks to be physically attacking her. The report of the scene in the English newspapers the following day makes the connections with *The Playboy* riots even more explicit. Robert's nationality is seized on to represent him, not as the respectable English gentleman his clothes would proclaim, but as representative of the 'wild Irish'. As he finds out when he asks another of the dancing troupe about Lizzie:

> She was attacked last night in the music-hall. It's all over the town. It was in the *Gazette*. An Irishman, sir, with a great head of black hair and a wild face, and eyes that would burn your heart out of your chest … They're looking for the man, to lock the demon up. But I expect he ran for it. He'll be in Dublin now (p.14).

The newspaper portrayal of the respectable Robert Gibson as the 'wild Irishman' recalls and calls into question the ready representation of the *Playboy* rioters as an unruly, savage mob. When he meets Lizzie again, he apologizes, claiming that he only recognized the full enormity of what he had done when he read the report in the papers. She in turn counters that they are preparing not only a prison for him but a strait jacket in an asylum. Again, this is language redolent of Synge's plays, right down to the reference to the 'queer looks' Robert is attracting (p.15). The scene suggests Robert and Lizzie's imbrication within certain institutional forces, forces they think they can escape by moving to Ireland. But – as the multiple references to the authorities, the prison and the asylum in the Irish setting of Synge's play make clear – 'going home' will provide no simple one way transit to a clear, open space.

Act One Scene Twelve of *Lizzie Finn* stages Robert and Lizzie's approach to Ireland and is one of the most extraordinary scenes in Irish drama, primarily for the extent to which it opens up gaps of perception in what is habitually presented as seamless and organically integrated. In the play text, the couple approach Kerry in a pony and trap. But in Mason's production, a significant shift occurred; here, they are aboard a ship. The effect of the change is to move them outside the landscape, and to present the latter as just that, a scenic representation of Ireland in one of its most picturesque and traditional guises. There is also a continuous perceptual shift: the closer they approach to shore, the more discrete iconic images they can pick out, and the more those details manifest difference. At first sight, the land they are approaching is identified as Kerry, the same Kerry that was used by Robert as the ground of mutual sympathy with Lizzie when they first met in England – his Kerry hat, her Kerry accent. Now, '*exhilirated*', he exclaims: 'Glorious, oh, glorious, my lovely Kerry' (p.28). The possessive pronoun is revealing and is amplified when he identifies the woods she cannot recall as 'my woods, Lizzie', rapidly amended and amplified to 'Your woods. Our woods'. What Robert comes to focus on is the house, not the little houses in the village, but the Big House among the trees. Lizzie and Robert, looking at the same visual image, are discerning two utterly different socio-political realities. As Luke Gibbons has pointed out, the Irish landscape offers no escape from history, but is ineradicably marked by a legacy of social and political division.[94] For it now dawns on Lizzie as they approach the home to which Robert has beckoned them, and for which she has forsaken her beloved dancing, that her husband is of the landlord class and that she is not. For in her reveries about Ireland with Jelly Jane, she has remembered her father and family legacy as landlessness, a wandering of the roads of Corcaguiney with occasional forays into the houses of the rich to sing for their supper. She now enters the Big House as its mistress; as Robert says, 'you're strong and right and legal here' (p.29); but the passage will not be an easy one.

It is noteworthy in Irish drama how rarely Ireland is represented from outside. The setting is almost invariably from within the country, thus implying a position of authenticity, of rootedness. Much ink has been spilt questioning the terms of that authenticity and representation, most notably with Synge and *The Playboy of the Western World.* Almost a century later many of the same arguments re-emerged in relation to the London-born son of Irish emigrants, Martin McDonagh, and his decision to set his plays in the West of Ireland, in locales with real place names (Leenane, Inishmaan, etc.). *The Only True History of Lizzie Finn* is set both in England and in Ireland; and again one is moved to remark how rare a phenomenon this is, and how unusual, since many Irish plays have to do with exile and emigration. In Brian Friel's *Dancing at Lughnasa* there is a shocking speech by the narrator Michael in Act Two detailing what will happen to his aunts Agnes and Rose when they leave Ballybeg for England a short time later, the utter destitution they will face. But England and its destitution are only verbally referred to; the visual scene remains Ballybeg in late summer. A rare exception is Tom Murphy's *A Whistle in the Dark*, whose story of Irish émigrés is set entirely in England; but his later *Conversations on a Homecoming* is fixed firmly in a west of Ireland pub. It is extremely rare to have the two settings represented, as in *Lizzie Finn* the effect of this bi-location is to prevent the Irish landscape from entirely dominating, to provide another perspective from which it may be approached and so examined. It also makes manifest the traffic between the two countries which so much of the visual side of Irish drama is designed to efface. But more than being set in England, the first half of *Lizzie Finn* is set in a theatre and is a reminder of how much the history of Irish theatre has been and continues to be bound up with the theatre of the adjacent island. We see the Irish landscape being constructed on the stage. In the scene before Robert and Lizzie's approach, the English music-hall is rolled away to be replaced by the garden and drawing room of the Big House, and by the three army uniforms which signify its colonial legacy.

If most Irish plays written for the Revival are set in Ireland, all classes are not equally represented. The very first play submitted by Synge to Yeats and Lady Gregory, the non-canonical work *When the Moon has Set*, was the only one of the seven he wrote to be set in his own class and background, a landlord's house in County Wicklow.[95] The son of the household is in love with a Catholic nun, Sister Eileen. The familiar Synge dialect is spoken by the servants, but only by them. *When the Moon has Set* was rejected outright by Yeats and Gregory and never printed or staged in Synge's lifetime. He then turned to 'peasant drama' in his next two plays, *Riders to the Sea* and *Shadow of the Glen*, focused exclusively as they were on a class different from his own. Yeats may have set some of his most famous poems in Lady Gregory's west of Ireland estate, Coole; but that background and her class are absent from the majority of her plays, especially her popular comedies. Yeats does not examine the Big House in his own plays until *Purgatory*, written less than a year before his death; and the house is in ruins. The Protestant playwrights of the Literary Revival did not directly represent their own social background. Their critique of the Catholic bourgeoisie, formulated as social conformity and rampant materialism, is displaced onto the romantic personae they adopted, the houseless tramps, vagabonds and people of the roads. A rare exception is Lennox Robinson, whose 1926 play is defiantly entitled *The Big House* and which provides a fascinating comparison with the representation of the Big House in Sebastian Barry's play.[96] For what Barry is attempting to do in *Lizzie Finn* is to repair the greatest omission in the Irish theatrical landscape by writing back in and restoring the Big House setting which Synge and Gregory, in particular, effaced from their dramas.

In both Barry's and Robinson's two plays, the imposing façade presented by the Big House to the outside world is deconstructed from within by the movement from room to room. Lucinda, Lady Gibson has greeted Lizzie on her arrival with stiff formality and imposing hauteur. But she presents a very different picture when she arrives among them in Act Two, Scene Three, appearing '*rather suddenly upstage, looking a little lonesome and dishevelled'* to remark: 'Oh, here you are, of course. I got rather muddled. We're not in the drawing room at this time of year' (p.41). Not all the rooms are occupied during the long Irish winters because they are too cold and costly to heat. With each of the first three scenes of Robinson's Big House play, the iciness and inanition take greater hold:

> **Alcock:** There must be a fire in the music-room tomorrow, the Steinway is getting damp.
> **Mrs. Alcock:** Very well.
> **Alcock:** This room is cold too.
> **Mrs. Alcock:** You got perished sitting all the evening in that icy library. Sit near the fire and poke it up.[97]

Both houses are a matriarchy, presided over by a formidable matron. Robert's mother and Mrs. Alcock respond to the perception of their world coming to dissolution by asserting a personal authority. They also seek to detach themselves from their immediate environment and its increasingly hostile political order by asserting their Englishness. Lucinda talks repeatedly about handing the house over to Lizzie, or 'Mrs. Gibson', as she insists on referring to her, and retiring to her people in Yorkshire. Mrs. Alcock increasingly stresses her Englishness as the reason she has never felt at home in Ireland. Their husbands, by contrast, appear much more settled, but in a fatally lethargic way. Robert's father is long dead but is compared to his discredit with other males of the family who were exemplars of Victorian technological progress. Mr. Alcock is still alive but prone to whimsy; he plans nothing more industrious in the course of the play than writing a letter to Taoiseach W.T. Cosgrave protesting the planned execution of a neighbour's Republican son (the letter is neither written nor sent). At one point, he remarks:

> Really, I feel inclined never to get up, just lie in bed till the summer and read the classics, and never, never look at a newspaper or hear any horrible 'news'.[98]

In the gender politics of the Big House, if the fathers have settled in to almost complete inanition, the sons have been bred up to serve the British Empire in foreign wars. In relation to the Big House drama, they are notable by their absence. The first act of Robinson's play is set in 1918, just after the close of the First World War. One son has died in the war, the return of the other – Ulick – is imminently expected. The fatal dramatic development occurs when we hear that he, too, has been killed. But the ghost of the young man continues to haunt the remainder of the play through the depredations of the Anglo-Irish War and the Civil War and is the fitting inhabitant at the close of a Big House purged of its terminal iciness by being burned to the ground. And this is where the other key concern of Barry's play, the male complement to Lizzie's former life as a dancer in the English music-halls, comes into focus: the Boer War. Lucinda, Lady Gibson remembers her four sons playing by the fire in the Big House. When her sons have been raised, they have all gone out to fight for the imperial cause in the Boer War; only one has returned. It is clear from Robert's condition when he first meets Lizzie that he is on the verge of a nervous breakdown. As one of the walking wounded, he may have physically survived the Boer War; but he returns to Ireland and the Kerry Big House as much a ghostly revenant as the figure in the Lennox Robinson play.

The key scene in Act Two of *Lizzie Finn* occurs at Lord and Lady Castlemaine's dance. Lizzie endures a more protracted and socially embarrassing version of the scene she has already endured with her mother-in-law about her former life and profession. Lord Castlemaine does his best to sanitize the stage and the less savoury connotations of 'actress' by referring to Shakespeare:

> You must never think we are so provincial here as not to honour the stage. We hear a great deal about the stage that is unsavoury and we know it is bunkum. After all, my dear, Shakespeare was an actor (p.48).

Allusions such as this keep the subject of theatre well to the fore in the play's second half, and contribute strongly to the sense that *Lizzie Finn* is a dramatic meditation on the social and political conditions surrounding the formation of an Irish

National Theatre. That sense is somewhat contradicted by the date given by the playwright in the apparatus – *in the 1890s*. But a more precise, and significantly later, dating may be arrived at through the references to the Boer War. Robert is on his way home from that war, which started on 11 October 1899; and as Ben Levitas has written, 'the outbreak of hostilities between Britain and the Boers polarized Irish politics … in the first months of 1900'.[99] This would move the action of the play from a vague '1890s' into a precisely historicized 1900, the very turn of the century and the middle of the three-year experiment of the Irish Literary Theatre. Nor is this conjunction of the Irish reaction to the Boer War and the experiment to create a distinctive Irish theatre fortuitous. They are brought together in *Lizzie Finn*'s most important scene in ways curiously prophetic of more recent cultural analysis of the growth of Irish political and cultural separatism at the turn of the century. P.J. Mathews has demonstrated how the pro-Boer enthusiasm which swept Dublin brought a more politically informed response to that season's dramatic offerings by the Irish Literary Theatre.[100]

The progress of the war drove a wedge between Irish unionists. Those who had nationalist sympathies broke with their more conservative kindred. Edward Martyn resigned from his positions as magistrate and Deputy Lieutenant of Galway over it; 'even Lady Gregory … found herself falling out with Lecky over the war in South Africa'.[101] This split within southern Irish Unionism is dramatically revealed by what occurs between Robert and Lord Castlemaine during their extensive discussion of the Boer War and the fate of his three brothers. Lord Castlemaine utters the approved Unionist sentiments: 'though they died, they died well, they died for these three kingdoms and in service of their great Queen' (p.51). Robert's response is as unexpected as it is heterodox. He condemns the pro-imperialist British cause as 'unjust', denounces its general as 'a fool' and reveals that he has resigned his commission 'two years ago after they [his three brothers] were so wastefully killed'. The date of the play is now pushed even further into the new century; and for most of those present at the Castlemaine ball it is later than they think. Robert has gone even further in his apostasy towards his Ascendancy background, changing sides and affirming his Irishness by accepting 'a captaincy in the Boer army. I crossed to Kruger, as it were. His Irish Brigade, to be exact' (p.52). There is, so far as I am aware, only one other reference in the Irish theatrical canon to Kruger and the Boer War. It occurs in one of the questions put to Christy Mahon by the habitués of the Mayo shebeen:

> Maybe he went fighting for the Boers, the like of the man beyond ... Were you off east, young fellow, fighting bloody wars for Kruger and the freedom of the Boers?[102]

The answer in Christy's case is 'no'; in the Barry play, this question is redressed into a 'yes' as far as Robert Gibson is concerned. The couple are bonded, branded and dismissed from the Castlemaine household with a political and a sexual slur: 'A man who is pro-Boer can eat his supper somewhere else. And take his dancing woman with him' (p.53). The Boer War had exacerbated tensions and polarized feelings within Irish Unionism and Robert's mother is made to feel the full brunt of her son's betrayal at church the following Sunday. Lucinda prefers the myth of her sons dying in their uniforms for the Empire rather than being barred from the company of the elect. That sense of her son's betrayal, of his promoting 'the death of truth and rightness in my own house' (p.56), is compounded by the spectacle, not just of Robert's having allied himself to a 'dancing woman', but of the servant Teresa cavorting around the house in Lizzie's starry knickers. The theatricalization of the Big House is at one with its dissolution. Lucinda walks into the sea, followed by the aged retainer, Bartholomew, who has consistently inveighed against the new social order. At the close of Lennox Robinson's *Big House,* the butler Atkins can only stigmatize the rising class (that class from which he has come) as 'a low, mean, murdering crew, the people in this place'.

The conclusion of *Lizzie Finn* is pitched in more egalitarian and individualistic terms. Lizzie Finn, as her husband remarked early on, did not lie down and die in Corcaguiney. Nor will he and she remain immured in the Big House as it crumbles into the sea. They will not passively share the historical obliteration which is claiming his mother and her class. As far as being defined historically by the clothes they wear (as his brothers were, to their cost), the couple view their garments theatrically, to be taken on and off at will. As Robert says in admiration of his wife – 'We are all very much equal under the clothes that history lends us. If you can sing, or dance, or go soldiering, so much the better for you' (p.35). In their union with each other, Lizzie and Robert acknowledge that they are pledged to the future and not the past, that they will have a shared life and bear children, not for the greater glory of any creed or faith, but to endure, to persist, to throw a line into the future. They will go on.

10 | Out of history: from *The Steward of Christendom* to *Annie Dunne*

Nicholas Grene

For the reader who comes to *Annie Dunne* (2002) already familiar with *The Steward of Christendom* (1995), the relationship between the two texts is something of a puzzle. The novel cannot be accounted a sequel to the play, even though it allows us to catch up on the later lives of Annie Dunne and Matthew Kirwin, both of whom figure in *The Steward. Annie Dunne* does not require knowledge of the earlier text; indeed it re-cycles key materials from the play. Annie tells to her young great-nephew at length and in detail the story of the sheep-killing sheepdog (*AD*, p.16-8) that is the dramatic concluding monologue of *The Steward* (*SC*, p.64-6).[103] The incident of the boy Thomas Dunne finding his Christmas present prematurely and the angry confrontation with his mother that follows (*SC*, p.47) is re-deployed but to very different purpose in the climactic concluding chapters of *Annie Dunne.* Annie in the novel broods repeatedly on the circumstances of her father's life, his career as an officer in the Dublin Metropolitan Police, his sad end in Baltinglass County home – the very stuff of which *The Steward* is made. Landscape, local references, glancing allusions, all cross over from one text to the other. The strange Siamese twinning of play and novel seems to involve a re-imagination of the same Dunne family situation from a different time and vantage-point.

In this, however, the style and form of the novel, and the all but explicitly autobiographical presence of the author as the unnamed four-year-old 'boy', introduce a new dimension. The two works, taken together, encourage us to re-think the nature of Barry's enterprise in writing *The Steward*, and his 'family' plays and fictions more generally.

Roy Foster voices a widespread view of Barry's plays in his Introduction to *Our Lady of Sligo*:

> Barry writes history plays in a special sense … His project is one of recovery – stitching back into the torn fabric of Irish history the anomalous figures from an extended Irish family.[104]

Scott T. Cummings speaks of Barry appending his characters' stories to the received historical record as an imaginative and subtly revisionist addendum.'[105] The figures around whom he builds his plays are members of his own family but not, for the most part, members of the family about whom there are public records. He has sought out the black sheep and dark horses of his family's legends rather than any one whose life can be charted through definite dates, facts and documentary knowledge. These ancestors had been forgotten but also in some measure suppressed from family memory. To recall them, or rather to re-imagine them, was also to re-imagine the larger history of the nation and the parts of that narrative that have tended to be forgotten or suppressed.

The Irish of the diaspora, proud of their origins, aware of the colonial circumstances that had forced them to emigrate, would probably prefer not to think that they, like Trooper O'Hara in *White Woman Street*, (Barry's great-grand-uncle on his mother's side) had taken part in another colonial project, the mass-slaughter of Native Americans on their own continent. 'Soldiers are we', we sing in our national anthem, 'whose lives are pledged to Ireland. Some have come from a land beyond the wave.' We think perhaps of Eamon de Valera, born in New York, when we intone the phrase about those coming from 'a land beyond the wave'. We do not normally think of an extreme English Protestant community living on an island off the coast of Cork, like the one Fanny Hawke leaves in *Prayers of Sherkin* to marry Barry's great-grandfather; yet these too are a part of the history of Ireland and what it is to be Irish. Are we all soldiers with lives pledged to Ireland? Some of us in the past, certainly, were soldiers in the British Army, like Jack O'Hara in *Our Lady of Sligo*, Barry's maternal grandfather, who served in World War II in the Royal Engineers, or his great-uncle, imagined in *The Whereabouts of Eneas McNulty* as a Sergeant-Major at Dunkirk. Barry, in retrieving these lost souls of his own family, is also writing back into the story of Ireland those parts of it which our nationalist master-narrative has most signally left out, the pieces of our past that do not fit with the way we want to imagine our history.

Most in need of rehabilitation was Barry's great-grandfather, Chief Superintendent Dunne of the Dublin Metropolitan Police, the man who led the baton-charge on Jim Larkin's locked-out workers in 1913 when four men were killed. This, as Barry admitted in his introductory essay to the play 'Following the Steward', was someone he himself initially wanted to keep dark: 'I was in fear of it being discovered that I had such a relative, hiding you might say in my very blood. I was eager to conceal him, indeed to keep him concealed, to seal him in, where he lay unnamed and unmentioned in official history' (*SC*, p.vii). Connected as he was with public events, Dunne's situation made *The Steward* a more explicitly historical play than Barry's others. Audiences, and subsequently readers, were encouraged to view it in this light by the programme materials published with the play's first edition: the famous image of the defiant Larkin, arms aloft, addressing the crowd from the balcony of the Imperial Hotel in 1913; a photograph of Victoria's royal visit to Ireland in 1900; notes on Michael Collins and Robert Emmet. In his erratic memories, Dunne recalls the key events of the period, the 1913 Lockout, the Easter Rising – 'that rebellion at Easter time, that they make so much of now' (*SC,* p11) – the handover of Dublin Castle to Collins in 1922, and the Civil War that followed. In her acute analysis, Claire Gleitman pairs *The Steward* with Frank McGuinness's *Observe the Sons of Ulster Marching Towards the Somme* as comparable reconstructions of history.[106] Barry's achievement in the play was to restore to our sense of Irish history the empathetic imagination of that most erased of figures, the Catholic loyalist.

Annie Dunne is set in a very specific time, the summer of 1959, but with almost no sense of the historical implications of that time. Again and again, Annie remembers back to her father's glory days in the DMP, 'as chief superintendent, the highest rank a Catholic could hold' (*AD*, p.181). She thinks back further again to the reign of White Meg, last steward of Humewood, the stern father to Thomas Dunne in *The Steward*, grown in folkloric memory into impossible majesty: 'Oh, never a word did he speak as he came up the village road, so people say, like it was a song, nor looked right nor left, nor greeted nor offended anybody, but fetched himself in the gates of the estate as if a sort of solitary God' (*AD*, p.97). But these past dignities are only there to enforce the sense for Annie of how time 'has knocked us off our perches' (*AD*, p.98). She is conscious of the loss of class status in Kiltegan consequent on the change of regime, but conscious of it along with other more personal griefs and injuries: her bowed back due to childhood polio, the resultant mockery of the other schoolgirls in her Leeson St convent, her unmarried, unwanted status that leaves her dependent on the charity of relations, grateful for the haven of her cousin's small farm in Kelsha. In *Annie Dunne* Barry leaves behind the macro-narrative of Irish history, to which the drama of *The Steward* was connected, for the micro-narratives of lives that fall outside the scope of history altogether.

1959 was the year when Eamon de Valera's long reign as Taoizeach came to an end; 1958 was the year of T.K. Whitaker's landmark report that laid the groundwork for the government's Programme for Economic Expansion. None of this is reflected in *Annie Dunne*. The book is set in a basic rural present outside the periodization of history. Annie and Sarah live according to the rhythms of the day, rising at first light to start the chores of house and farm, of the week that brings round washing day, of the seasons, as spring leads on to high summer. *Annie Dunne* is dated so specifically in 1959 not because any given public event took place in that year, or because Barry wants to convey the atmosphere of Ireland in the 1950s, a decade that continues to preoccupy, even obsess, so many Irish writers. The year of the action is chosen because that was the summer Sebastian Barry and his sister Siobhan, like the novel's unnamed 'boy' and 'girl', spent in the care of the real-life Annie Dunne and Sarah Cullen.[107]

In terms of the date of composition *The Steward* came before *Annie Dunne* and it is concerned with the experiences of an older generation, so it is natural to think of the novel as following on from the play. But the materials of *Annie Dunne* in fact provided the imaginative starting-point for the earlier work. 'All the country stuff in the play was my own country stuff you might say from childhood, when I was four or so and staying with Annie and Sara. [108] I gave it to Thomas as the only gift I had for him.' (*SC*, p.ix). In *Annie Dunne* Barry is working with the original sources back-projected into historical time in *The Steward.* We can see that in the way in which incidents from the play are used more integrally in the substance of the novel. In Act II of *The Steward*, there is a scene dramatising the paranoid delusions of Dunne in his last years of country retirement and Annie's efforts to dispel them:

> **Thomas:** ... what about that filthy mass of men that came up the yard last week and rattled our latch, and shouted in at me, while you were at the well?
> **Annie:** It was only a crowd of tinkers, Papa, that thought you were a woman alone, and wanted to frighten you (*SC*, p.62).

In the novel this is dramatized as the climactic event of Chapter Six, the terrifying onslaught of the tinkers, Sarah, and then Annie with her, trying desperately to hold down the latch being rattled from outside by the unseen assailants, the small children behind them, 'two old women and two scraplings' (*AD*, p.69). This is based closely on an actual event, as Barry remembers it, as though in a perpetually stopped present. In the book, though, it functions to enforce the sense of the special vulnerability of the ageing, unmarried women living alone. The latch just barely held down by the women against the tinkers is a telling image of potential male violation.

'There was an old woman that lived in the wood, willa, willa, wallya', sings Thomas near the opening of *The Steward* (*SC*, p.6). It is apparently just one of the random shards of memory that make up the mosaic of his ramblings, like the snatches of song in the mad scenes of *King Lear*. But it too had an identifiable origin the significance of which emerges in *Annie Dunne*. The ballad about the old woman who kills the baby was a special song of the real-life Annie, and sufficiently close to the imaginative matrix of the novel that 'Weile, weile, wáile' was one of Barry's initial, preferred titles for the book. He remembers hearing it with the literalism of the four-year-old as though it were an actual series of events, sung as it was with a whole series of verses detailing the trial and execution of the murderous old woman. In the novel it is trailed first in the voice of Jack Furlong, the strange, solitary rabbit man:

> His little song drifts down over the spent heathers,
>
> There was an ould woman and she lived in the woods,
> Weile, weile, wáile,
> There was an ould woman and she lived in the woods,
> Down by the river Sáile (*AD*, p.58).

We are thus prepared for the climax of Annie's violent anger against the boy over the ruined birthday present, culminating in a verse from the song cited without introduction or comment in a section all to itself:

> She stuck the penknife in the baby's heart,
> Weile, weile, wáile,
> She stuck the penknife in the baby's heart,
> Down by the river Sáile (*AD*, p.177).

The toy fire engine that appears in both texts – in *Annie Dunne* it is a 'fierce green,' red in *The Steward* – was in fact a birthday present purchased by Annie as in the novel, not the Christmas gift it becomes in the play. The details in both, however, are as Barry remembers them: the toy hidden away, discovered by the child before the day itself, wrecked by skating up and down on it, provoking the fierce anger of the great-aunt/mother who buries it in the dungheap. In this case, however, the text of the play is truer to the actual revenge taken by the young Barry: 'I sought out her favourite laying hen and put a yard-bucket over it, and it wasn't found for a week, by which time the Christmas was over and the poor hen's wits had gone astray from hunger and darkness and inertia' (*SC*, p.47). In the novel the boy is exculpated from this crime; it is Billy Kerr who imprisons the hen in the bucket, the falsely accused boy runs away and his ultimate reunion with Annie brings about the reconciliation that is the book's concluding note. A similar emotional resolution is achieved at the close of *The Steward*, with the unexpected forgiveness by his father of the child Thomas who has hidden away with the sheepdog under sentence of death:

> And I would call that the mercy of fathers, when the love that lies in them deeply like the glittering face of a well is betrayed by an emergency, and the child sees at last that he is loved, loved and needed and not to be lived without, and greatly (*SC*, p.66).

The tale of the dog had no identifiable source, was written for *The Steward*, and reappears in *Annie Dunne* as a secondary re-telling.[109] But in both texts the fierce intimate emotions of childhood are primary: love, hatred, fear, humiliation, the terrors of separation and the release of reunion.

Barry resisted telling the story of *Annie Dunne*, the memories of his own childhood, from the viewpoint of the child. He had used this narrative perspective in his first short story 'The Beast' drawing on the Kelsha experience, in which virtually all the materials of the later book are present: the visit to the Dunnes of Feddin – in the story referred to as the sisters of 'Aunt Anne' – the purse dropped in the mud, the runaway pony, the feared workman who wants to marry Sarah, the attack by the travellers, the misused fire-engine buried in the dungheap, the boy's revenge.[110] But for the novel he felt that this conventional child's eye view would be too limiting. In *Annie Dunne* we are never given access to the boy's thoughts and feelings; he is unnamed, rather as the boy Michael in Friel's *Dancing at Lughnasa* is invisible on stage.[111] However, Friel takes over a standard convention of autobiographical fiction by refracting the child's remembered life through the voice of the adult narrator. The mature Michael stands in relation to his seven-year-old alter ego, present but unseen, as the grown-up Pip or David Copperfield do to the suffering younger selves they recollect. This too was a road not taken by Barry. Instead we get the occasional glimpse of the boy in *Annie Dunne* as a portrait of the artist as a young child. Annie watches him watching her pluck a hen she has just killed, and he reminds her of his grandfather:

> The little boy hangs a side of his rump on the chopping block, with its thousand stripes of the axe, and never offers a word, his face unchanging, like, it occurs to me, Matt when he is painting. I have watched Matt working the odd time secretly, noting how he does not move his face except to lick his lips, his left foot forward of his right as he stands at his easel in a summer meadow as may be, capturing some instance of beauty he has found in our Wicklow (*AD*, p.111-12).

There is a complex process of representation going on here: the writer re-creating in imagined fictional form a sense of his own childhood being, as observed by his much loved great-aunt.

At one early stage in the composition of *The Steward*, Barry experimented with using Annie as a surviving narrator recollecting the past life of her father, like Pyper in *Observe the Sons of Ulster*, but he soon abandoned the attempt. It may be that there was a similar problem to that which prevented Barry writing *The Whereabouts of Eneas McNulty* as a play:

> Eneas McNulty has a sort of silence and confusion at the heart of him. As I usually write plays in long speeches, this was awkward, because Eneas did not want to speak in that way. The interior world of the novel, the descriptive and psychological world, was more suitable for the painting, you might say, of Eneas McNulty.[112]

Annie Dunne is not as silent a figure as Eneas McNulty, but certainly the endlessly active, irritable and obsessive character of Annie rendered in *The Steward* would not have been convincingly capable of the richly reflective periods given to the elderly, semi-senile Thomas. Annie needed the expansive, interiorized mode of the novel to be allowed full expression.

In both fiction and drama, a highly wrought poetic prose has been the hallmark of Sebastian Barry's writing. He takes the licence of earlier Irish dramatists to give to his dramatic characters an eloquence and articulacy beyond the ordinary. However, in his best plays, as Ger Fitzgibbon argues:

> the language itself carries the stamp of the truly accomplished dramatist: the rhythm, syntax, sound and texture of his writing resonates with the particularity of a specific character in a specific moment; it demands, provokes and rewards performance.[113]

By contrast with this the discursiveness of fiction allows a principle of compensation for speech deficit. The inner world of an Annie Dunne is rendered with a rich specificity she could never manage to voice herself. 'Perhaps', she senses about the 'girl', 'she does not have words for what she wants to say' (*AD*, p.13). The same could be said of Annie herself; the words are the imaginative gift to her of the writer.

Conventionally the post-Romantic author recalls the sights and sounds and textures of childhood as the vivid stuff of memory, the Wordsworthian first things of the world. Barry shifts this perspective in *Annie Dunne*, reconstituting what is for him memory as the immediate sensations of his great-aunt. There is a double recuperation involved here; he restores his own lost sense of things – he is only four at the time of the novel's action in 1959, 'too young to know his writing,' yet already with the aspiration to write 'every day' (*AD*, p.3). The four-year-old could not plausibly remember with the novel's fullness of detail the cottage of his relatives in Kelsha. Barry therefore imaginatively delegates those memories to Annie. But for her too this represents a restoration of a luminous and comprehensive grasp of things she can never have had. The point of view hovers between the child and the protective old woman, both endowed with the vocabulary of the mature writer.

The style of *Annie Dunne* is fully literary; Barry does not attempt to restrict himself to a vocabulary or manner credibly mimicking that of an ageing Irish country woman of limited education, even if her better-read father is occasionally credited as the source of a literary allusion – 'this side idolatry, as Ben Jonson says of William Shakespeare, according to my father' (*AD*, p.131). The subject of the book brings the novel at times close to Synge, the Synge of the Wicklow essays who depicted the oppression of the hills, the fears and horrors of madness and the workhouse. 'The county home is a fearful place. That is where the homeless and the country destitute go, the withered girls and the old bachelors finally maddened by the rain … The Wicklow rain has madness in it like an illness, an ague' (*AD*, p.26). There is a muted Lawrentianism in the treatment of sexuality, the uncontrollable force of the pony Billy only mastered by his namesake the intrusive Billy Kerr; the rhythms of natural life, its seasonal changes, are rendered with Lawrence's sort of hyper-reality. In terms of literary precursors, the writing in the book is perhaps closest to Virginia Woolf. In a famous formulation, Woolf stated the principles of modern fiction such as hers:

> Examine for a moment an ordinary mind on an ordinary day. The mind receives a myriad impressions – trivial, fantastic, evanescent, or engraved with the sharpness of steel. From all sides they come, an incessant shower of atoms.[114]

Barry's objective like Woolf's is to catch the effect of this 'shower of atoms' in a pointillist, lyric style expressive of the very texture of experience and sensation. The similarity is the more startling because in *Annie Dunne* we are far from the middle-class, aesthetic sensibilities of Bloomsbury. Yet the hard labouring and inarticulate Annie Dunne is to be denied nothing accorded to the consciousness of a Mrs Dalloway or Mrs Ramsay.

At times the metaphors and similes used by Annie are ones that might well suggest themselves to a country person; but they are turned with a literary leap of the imagination, not according to the norms of orality where even the most vivid phrases tend to be traditional, inherited, employed generically. So, for example, there is the description of the children's shyness and embarrassment on arrival: 'For a moment they are stuck, like beasts in the gap between two fields' (*AD*, p.4). The idea of social paralysis, yoked to the image of cattle floundering in the churned-up mud of a gateway, has the new-minted originality of writing, not the familiar piquancy of speech. The happiness of Annie and Sarah at having the children with them is characterized with a homely domestic image: 'A glee suffuses us, like beaten egg whites folded into sugar' (*AD* 7). The word 'suffuses' stands out from its linguistic company. Barry enacts the feelings of Annie Dunne in language that is often obviously not her language:

> Towards the end of the day these times I go slower and slower, like a bad clock. My movements lessen and I reach across gaps with parsimonious expense of energy. Even my words stretch longer. I feel a sudden fear that we are too old to guard these little ones. A hundred tasks and now, two creatures as vigorous as steam engines (*AD*, p.5).

This renders effectively the waning strength of the hard-pressed elderly woman faced by the new burden of looking after the young children with their irrepressible vitality. But the words do indeed stretch longer, beyond the scale of any an Annie Dunne might credibly have in her active vocabulary: 'My movements lessen and I reach across gaps with parsimonious expense of energy.' The sentence is crafted with an undisguised writerly control of syntax and a writer's fullness of phrasing.

Annie Dunne needs fullness of expression to compensate for a fullness of being that life has denied her. In *Steward* Barry concentrated on Thomas Dunne, a figure written out of Irish history. But someone like Annie Dunne was never in public history to be written out. She has gone from looking after her father to looking after her brother-in-law Matt and his children, a marginal, supporting character throughout. With the death of her sister Maud and Matt's second marriage, she is left dependent on the charity of relatives, and after the humiliation of one rejection, is deeply grateful to her cousin Sarah Cullen for taking her in. Always there is the fact of her childhood polio that has left her back bent, depriving her of the possibility of a husband and family of her own. It is this thwarted story that makes her so hungry for the caring, maternal role she finds unexpectedly in looking after her nephew's children for the summer. It is this same story that creates her paranoid fear of Billy Kerr and the possibility of his marrying Sarah, taking from her once again the fragile security she has found in the cottage in Kelsha and her loving relationship with her cousin.

Annie is given an inner expressiveness in the novel that makes painfully clear her inability to speak those emotions she feels. We see her, for instance, in the sweetshop of Mrs Nicodemus, convinced that the shopkeeper dislikes her, swayed by her own conflicting feelings, unable to voice any of them in the most commonplace of words, and driven back into a passion of self-execration:

> Of course this is why she dislikes me. I have no grace, no truth, no womanly understanding. I am not a mother. I am a humpbacked woman that might make a humpbacked child. I am not like her, or any other human person. Moreover, I do not really feel sympathy for her, I feel it for myself. I am a charlatan, and in my emotions maybe almost a cretin. It is a terrible thing, to be there in the shop like a cretin. Will the Lord not save me? (*AD*, p.104)

Behind this there are echoes of another hunchback, Richard of Gloucester:

> I had no father, I am like no father;
> I have no brother, I am like no brother;
> And this word 'love', which greybeards call divine,
> Be resident in men like one another
> And not in me: I am myself alone.[115]

But where Shakespeare makes of Richard a loveless monster, autistically incapable of fellow-feeling, Annie Dunne constantly belies her own self-description as a cretin of the emotions because we have access to those emotions she cannot speak.

Barry charts in *Annie Dunne* the microclimates of the inner life. By contrast with *The Whereabouts of Eneas McNulty*, the picaresque novel that immediately preceded it, *Annie Dunne* is minimalist in scope and action: one summer of one woman's life in which nothing very significant seems to have happened. In the book's own scale of significance, however, Annie lives in an alternating systole/diastole state of peace and agitation, contentment and disturbance, joy and suffering. So, for example, in Chapter Six, it is into a scene of perfect repose within the farmhouse that the sound of the approaching tinkers comes:

> It is a simple moment, all labour done, the natural anxieties of being alive all stilled and soothed. The turf fire mutters in the murky hearth. The clock seems less anxious to seek the future, its tick more content, slower. All is in the balance of a kind, the weight and the butter in the scales in sufficient harmony.
>
> Then we begin to hear them (*AD*, p.67).

At the end of Chapter Fourteen, after the visit to Matt in the hospital that had been the Baltinglass County Home, the resolution of Annie's feelings about Matt and the exorcism of the ghost of her father brings a sense of blessedness that is the exact opposite of the alienation experienced in Mrs Nicodemus's shop:

> I am buoyant, almost, I am thinking, graceful, or at least, full of a kind of grace, bestowed upon me. High clouds rage in the upper sky, they rage with sunlight pouring down through them in yellow torrents. There may be a change in the weather coming. I know what I look like to the passing cars, an old countrywoman without trap or newfangled vehicle to her name, but I do not care. I know my worth (*AD*, p.196).

Such an assurance of grace, however, cannot be sustained and the next chapter brings Annie's most anguished ordeal with the disappearance of the boy.

The fact of love between Annie and the children is the central *donné* of the book; the novel is written, as it were, as a tribute of love by its author to the great-aunt who nurtured him. But that feeling itself is not unproblematic. A moment of closeness to the boy provokes in Annie a reflection of its uncommonness:

> I stroke the black hair of his head, thinking of all past times, and present times, the river of time upon which we are merely carried, small boys and girls, loves expressed but rarely, loves confounded in the main (*AD*, p.120).

This is borne out not only by the set-piece scenes of anger and antagonism between child and woman, the incident where he deliberately drops her purse into the drain, her revenge upon him for the destruction of his birthday present. Love has to reach out over a basic gap of mutual incomprehension. The novel itself may be a retrospective effort of the imagination to understand the elderly relative whom a four-year-old can only have dimly apprehended as a separate person. What it dramatizes is the reverse process, the efforts of Annie Dunne to grasp the mysterious being of the children. And in this nothing is more shocking than her glimpse of their sex-play and the suggestion it raises of incest and child abuse, little as Annie may know of such things. Suddenly she, supposedly the adult protector of the young, is more innocent than they, at a complete loss as to what to do. She can only pray:

> What sloughs of despond, what pits of darkness have they seen? God enfold them, embrace them, retrieve them, perfect them, restore them. I cannot. All I have is the made-up love of a woman with a hump on her back like half the moon (*AD*, p.93).

That love, we are made to feel, does much for the children in the novel, but she can only guess at what it does.

> Fair seed-time had my soul, and I grew up
> Foster'd alike by beauty and by fear.[116]

For Barry, as for Wordsworth, the experience of the child is primary, formative, fundamental. Barry, though, raises the possibility that the world of the child may be a dark place of knowledge as well as of wholesome beauty and fear. Annie senses in the boy at one point a 'stain of desperation':

> It makes me wonder about him, if he hasn't something unusual within, some quaint understanding beyond his years, or despite

> them. He is what they used to call *sean-aimseartha*, an old-fashioned child (*AD*, p.119).

It is as though encoded into the being of the young boy is not only all that he will be – 'the child is father to the man' – but also all the lives that have gone before. Barry has said that his experiences of Kelsha 'seeped into me as a child, and showed themselves in all their aspects to me in what would amount now to visions, the ancient cinema of childhood'.[117] Equally, however, it is as if, like Saleem Sinai in *Midnight's Children*, the stories of all his family have 'leaked into' him as well. The memory of the child is not just his personal memory; it is the inheritance of sorrow and loss, pain and destruction that comes down to him from all the others who have gone before. The imagination of the writer goes out to the otherness of those others, but it is an otherness that he intuits within himself. In that sense, *Annie Dunne* is the geno-text for the family plays and fiction that preceded it.

One sentence is close to the thematic heart of the novel, as Annie reflects, sleepless and silent, outdoors in the dark night: 'Under the starlight I stand, ruminating, like a creature myself, an extra thing in the plenitude of the world. I know I am nothing' (*AD*, p.43). To conjure up the life of an Annie Dunne is to give her back a share in that 'plenitude of the world', a share she may never have had in life. This, as much as the rehabilitation of figures from history, seems the underlying project of Barry's work as it appears in *Annie Dunne*. Imagining the lost lives of the past, lives that led down to his own, leaked into him, is a kind of benediction or making whole. The lost lives are irrecoverably lost, not just because they are dead, forgotten, not known. They probably had no words to render what they were even when they lived. And their lives were things of pain, of deprivation and deformation anyway, of the ordinary cruelties of lovelessness, hatred and oppression, manifest in them as the mere detritus of history. Making them over in play or novel is conceived as a kind of grace for lost souls. '*Tout comprendre, c'est tout pardonner*': there may be nothing much to forgive in the life of Annie Dunne, as there certainly is with other characters of Barry. Still, the effort to understand her wholly is felt as both a memorial and an absolution. *Annie Dunne* gives us visions from Barry's own 'ancient cinema of childhood'; at the same time it fulfils that aspiration expressed by Jack at the end of *Our Lady of Sligo* that

> our children's children might look at our photographs and have some pride in us simply as people that had lived a life on this earth and were to be honoured at least for that.[118]

11 | 'Something of us will remain': Sebastian Barry and Irish History

Roy Foster

Within the wide arc thrown by his plays and novels Sebastian Barry has gathered a gallery of characters whose lost lives reflect the fractures and losses of Irish experience: to borrow a great phrase from Ezra Pound, they appear on the stage as 'ghosts patched with histories'.[119] The old sheep farmers Mick and Josey in *Boss Grady's Boys*, the island Protestant sect of *Prayers of Sherkin*, the ex-DMP Superintendent Thomas Dunne in *The Steward of Christendom*, his soldier son Willie *in A Long Long Way*, the dying alcoholic Mai O'Hara in *Our Lady of Sligo*, the disgraced politician in *Hinterland*, the wandering pariah Eneas MacNulty, Lizzie Finn and her displaced Ascendancy husband Robert Gibson, the cross-dressing imperial doctor James Miranda Barry in *Whistling Psyche*: the secretive personal histories of these people are invested with dramatic tension, while their integration into the wide canvas of Irish history lends a peculiar resonance and pathos to their stories.

As Barry's oeuvre comes more clearly into focus, it seems that certain historical themes predominate: people left over in the margins and interstices, through religious exclusion, or a change of regime, or a redefinition of loyalty. The connection between allegiance and identity is a recurring theme, as well as the necessity of reconciliation. Both these themes are also wound into the thread of family relationships which unites much of his work, particularly the tension between fathers and sons: it is significant that so much of the inspiration comes from Barry's own family, stories handed down, resentments preserved, evasions sustained. But these personal preoccupations are transcended by his historical sense, and Barry's evident commitment to understanding rather than judgement – never better expressed than in the heart-breaking soliloquy that closes *The Steward of Christendom.* The last memory of Thomas Dunne, wandering in his wits in the County Home, recurs to a childhood trauma and the memory of dereliction of duty – concerning a dog that worried sheep, his own concealment of the malefactor, and his father's astonishing forgiveness of the act.[120] But for the audience, this personal recollection is inextricably connected with the memory of later traumas which have earlier beset the old policeman – the 1913 Lock-out, 1916, the Tan War, and finally handing over authority at Dublin Castle to Michael Collins – an act which carried its own hint of absolution, swiftly negated by Collins's death. Another layer of historical meaning lies in the fact that this soliloquy is delivered to the friendly ghost of Thomas's son Willie – who, before his death on the Western Front in 1918, had come to question the imperial values by which his father lived.

Many of the lives investigated by Barry are inextricably tangled into what James Miranda Barry calls 'the great muddled wool-basket of Empire'.[121] In *Whistling Psyche*, Dr Barry's own confusion of gender and destiny brilliantly mirrors the uncertainty of Ireland's position in the Victorian empire- part colonized, part colonising, neither the one thing nor the other, like James Miranda Barry himself – 'that other sort of creature, neither white nor black, nor brown nor even green, but the strange original that is an Irish person' (*WP*, p.11). Rearranging Sebastian Barry's works by chronology of topic, rather than in the order he wrote them, presents a suggestive development of this theme. The freakish Dr Barry comes out of late-Georgian Ireland:

> a jangling of destructed metres, the cries and worse silences of those that hunkered in weeping cabins, and the laughter and polite, useless talk that passed the strange time for the grandees of Cork (*WP*, p.24).

First performed in 2004, the play's action takes place as Barry meets Florence Nightingale in the anteroom of Hades, at the end of the nineteenth century – visualized as a grand Victorian railway station – but the play's subject-matter is firmly located in the mid-nineteenth century. (James Miranda Barry himself died in 1865.) *Prayers of Sherkin* (1990) is set around 1890, and also casts back to the establishment of the visionary Purdyite sect a hundred years before. *The Only True History of Lizzie Finn* (1995) opens around 1900, in an English music-hall, but shifts to an isolated Big House in Kerry, haunted by deaths in the Boer War. *White Woman Street* (1992) brings to the American West of 1916 a wandering Sligoman, Trooper O'Hara, who cannot get Ireland out of his mind. *A Long Long Way* (2005) is set in Dublin and the trenches of Flanders, from 1914 to 1918. The same era and the same events are revisited in *The Steward of Christendom* (1995), though the play itself takes place in 1932. In *The Whereabouts of Eneas McNulty* (1998) the eponymous hero is born around 1900, and the novel tells the story of his life till his death about 1970. *Our Lady of Sligo* (1998) happens 'circa 1953', but Mai O'Hara (also born with the century) recurs to the palmy days of her youth in the twenties, and the decline and disillusionment that follow. *Annie Dunne* (2002) deals with rural Wicklow in 1959, where the modern world is nervously kept at bay, but a sense of impending change is all around. Only *Hinterland* (2002) was set, audaciously, at the time of writing, and seemed to recount the political scandals of the current Irish moment; but its treatment of Irish politics since the 1960s, and the themes of authority, corruption, allegiance and historical memory, will ensure it further (and fairer) hearings. They also place it closer to the heart of Barry's musings on Irish history than was realized at the time of its first run.

What are the continuities that link these anomalous outsiders and their individual histories? It is clear that Barry's tragic imagination is determined upon linkages. When Fanny Hawke in *Prayers of Sherkin* is vouchsafed her vision of Matt Purdy, founder of the sect, he prophesies, like a seer in a Greek tragedy, the fate of a dynasty: the lives of her future children:

> All about them lies a cruel century of disasters and wars that I did not foresee. I steer you back into the mess of life because I was blinder than I knew. I saw a vision in time, that will not serve me outside time. I give you back to the coming century, Fanny, and your children are calling you. There are lives that are waiting to be made in a black century, and though they will see suffering, yet they will value their lives. Oh, in darkest heart they will cherish them (*LF*, p.105).

This might be the playwright's voice, not only prophesying his own existence but laying out his agenda for plays dealing with Irish history, circling around family stories, severances, exilings and returns. Even his early experimental novel, *The Engine of Owl-Light* (1987), which might seem at odds with much of his oeuvre, deals with someone who 'having been a largely extra citizen of Ireland, Africa, Europe and America, went back to Sligo with fifty pounds and an unshakeable wish to be alone'[122]: shades of Eneas, or Jack O'Hara. Over and over again, his characters export Ireland to elsewhere. An Indian 'tent town' puts Trooper O'Hara 'in mind of certain Sligo hills, and certain men in certain Sligo hills; the English had done for us, I was thinking, and now we're doing for the Indians' (*WWS*, p.144). James Miranda Barry, organizing hospitals and revolutionizing medical treatments in Cape Colony, Jamaica, St Helena, Canada and the Crimea, seeks 'in the machineries of Empire … compassion hidden like a gem in mud', always remembering the poverty of Ireland in the famines of 1810-1812 during his youth:

> For necessary then to all Irish persons was subterfuge and subtle guiles, things not unknown to me now and long since, things ever carried before the spectacle of my private story like obliterating lights. But wherever in the world I have found a version of Ireland, a palimpsest of that once-easy kingdom, I have striven again to create that old balance and medium among destroyed and enmired peoples, as if by my qualities and

> doctoring abilities I might restore to the earth a true translation of the text of Ireland's happiness, however forlorn in the attempt, even however foolish and by civilized people reviled for my instinct and dreams. For nothing is more discommoding to the general stability and luxuries of accommodated folk than the spectre of change and the sword of reform that cuts through not only the noisome horrors of what happens in the dank margins of things, but also inevitably the sweet-scented calicoes and poetries and philosophical affectations and religious contentments of the officers and high servants of a long-established and increasingly encushioned Empire (*WP*, p.15).

This reflection indicates that Sebastian Barry's view of Ireland's part in the Empire is very far from a simple effort at rehabilitating a forgotten tradition, much less a coded attempt at 'Raj revisionism'. This has not prevented at least one critic from attacking him for providing 'in-service reading for a fairly standardized brand of revisionism'.[123] While unwillingly declaring admiration for *A Long Long Way*, Barry's most recent work, the same reviewer felt it necessary to rap Barry over the knuckles for supposed past sins against nationalist verities. Even one of the most subtle and probing critiques of Barry's work to date is constrained by similar contortions, claiming that he is recognized as 'an ideological ally by the Conservative British paper the *Daily Telegraph*' on the strength of a book-review praising *The Whereabouts of Eneas McNulty*. ('Political naivety', a failing attributed to Barry in the same piece, might be better applied to the belief that freelance contributors to the literary pages of a daily newspaper inevitably subscribe to its editorial line.)[124] The real insights of this essay, based on a close reading of Barry's manuscript drafts, sit oddly with a dismissal of *Eneas McNulty* as 'an anti-nationalist allegory' about 'a native collaborator', who operates in an 'exculpatory linguistic register' by a writer with suspect political views.[125] Under such scrutiny, even the recurrent treatment in Barry's work of Michael Collins as a charismatic lost leader is read as 'a way of attacking Republicanism, both the historical and the contemporary varieties'.[126] It is hard to believe that such a *parti pris* political judgement would be levelled at – for instance – Neil Jordan.

The complex layers of Barry's versions of Irish history, as seen through free adaptations of his family's stories, come more clearly into focus in *A Long Long Way*. This novel returns to the lives of Thomas and Willie Dunne, father and son, a world carried away in 1916 – both by the Rising in Dublin, where Thomas tries to maintain civic order, and by the horrors of the Somme. Barry is at one with recent historians in seeing World War I as the hinge of the decade-long Irish revolution from 1912 to 1922. From the beginning, despite the large number of Irishmen who enlisted, the focus of loyalty was uncertain, and in Ireland the ostensible unity behind the war effort in 1914 was, as an important recent study has put it, 'suspicious and conditional'.[127] The same might be said of the larger issue of loyalty to a British government which had apparently failed to face down the Ulster Unionists' refusal to countenance Home Rule, though the measure had passed through Parliament. As the war's horrors continued, British policy towards Ireland's contribution continued obtuse, especially in threatening conscription. The Home Rule leader John Redmond's gamble of throwing the National Volunteers behind the war effort rebounded upon him; the dissidents in the Volunteering movement, who formed the breakaway Irish Volunteers, would mount the apparently hopeless but psychologically transformative Rising in 1916, precipitating families like the Dunnes into an agonizing conflict. In *A Long Long Way*, Willie, home on leave from Flanders, is swept up in the merciless repression of the rebellion. He finds himself 'facing a shivering man, a very young shivering man in a Sunday suit and a sort of military hat, and an ancient-looking revolver held in both his hands, raised towards Willie's chest' (*LLW*, p.92). The insurgent calls him a 'Tommy' and thinks he is Scottish; Willie assumes that his antagonist is German. The rebel is shot down in front of him and dies horribly, a flood of blood 'covering the pavement of Wicklow granite' and drenching Willie's uniform – where traces of it remain as he embarks again for France. In the face of all these confused assumptions and allegiances Willie's incomprehension is almost childlike, even after a history-lesson from the more politically-minded Jesse Kirwan:

> 'These Volunteers you mentioned, your crowd,' said Willie, 'were they the crowd was firing at us?'
>
> 'What? No, you gammy fool, that's the other Volunteers. You got to keep up, William. We were one and the same up to the war breaking out, and then some of us said we could do what Redmond said and fight as Irish soldiers, you know, to save Europe, but a few of them – well, they didn't want that. You know. A handful, really. But the names, you know, I know them well. Some of the best of us.'
>
> 'I don't understand this volunteer thing' said Willie. 'You're volunteers, you say – but you know I'm a volunteer too – I volunteered for the army.'
>
> 'Ah Jesus, Willie. That is different altogether. You're a volunteer for fucking Kitchener. You can't be this thick. Look it, boy. The Ulster Volunteers were set up to resist Home Rule. So then the Irish Volunteers were set up to resist them, if necessary. Then the war came, as you may have noticed, and most of the Irish Volunteers did as Redmond said and came into the war, because Home Rule was as good as got. But a few broke away and that is who you just saw on the lovely streets of Dublin! Of course, Willie, the Ulster Volunteers came in too, but not for Home Rule, for God's sake. But for king and country and everything kept as it is. You see it now?'
>
> Well it was a veritable tornado of volunteers, that was the truth. If he never heard the word volunteer again it would be too soon.
>
> 'So where does it leave you, Jesse?'
> 'I don't know, do I, Willie? Where does it leave you?' (*LLW*, p.95)

Willie's exposure to what has happened in his native city haunts him, and causes the terrible breach with his father; but the echoes of the Dunnes' conflicted allegiance carry on down the years, conditioning the responses to Thomas in the Baltinglass County Home during the 1930s (where one of the attendants more or less blames him for Robert Emmet's execution in 1803), and still preoccupying his daughter Annie's agonized memories in 1959.

Barry is interested in what he has called elsewhere (in relation to Jennifer Johnston's fiction) the 'minor officers and denizens' of ascendancy Ireland, now 'a dwindled and diminished species'.[128] The exactness with which he presents the Pasley family in *A Long, Long Way* should be noted: Wicklow Protestants, not 'grand', somewhere between strong farmers and minor gentry, working their own land. Visiting their house to tell them how their son died in Flanders, Willie is at first unsure whether Mrs Pasley is the cook or the lady of the house; meanwhile her husband is out liming the lower field. But this is a world well known to his father Thomas in his youth – son of a hereditary steward of Humewood, who had married the daughter of a master coppicer in the woods of another great Wicklow estate, Coolattin. The Pasleys are not 'Ascendancy' in the sense of those vanished worlds:

> It was like the kitchen of any farmhouse, with a big fire of turf and logs, and a scrubbed deal table, and the flagstones a little wet from the mop, and the old clock going at its work. But there was a door open into the rest of the house and Willie could see the genteel transformation there, with flatter plaster walls and pictures, and an old red carpet, and by another much bigger entrance a brass box of sticks and umbrellas. It gave him a strange pleasure suddenly to think of Captain Pasley walking there, and sitting, not as a captain but as the son of the house, a farmer and a living man (*LLW*, p.257).

They and their kind are not grandees of Georgian mansions and Church of Ireland bishoprics, Protestant though they are; the same might be said of the Hawkes of Sherkin, or the ex-Presbyterian music-hall artist, Lizzie Finn. They live their lives separately from the Catholic majority, but are not presented as threatening dispossessors: when Sarah Purdy thinks of offering Patrick Kirwin soup in *Prayers of Sherkin*, the reference to proselytism is merely an oblique and ironic echo.[129] What Barry is trying to describe is a far more complex and nuanced *couche sociale* than the simple dichotomy of planter-and-native.

Willie Dunne's visit to commiserate with the Pasleys is the only comforting outcome of his disastrous last leave home, when he loses his lover and is rejected by his father. At the same time, he realizes the old differences of Irish life have been driven deeper by the war:

> When they got to the graveyard at Kilcomman, Mr Pasley brought Willie quietly in. He brought him over to a bright new stone, with its carving excellently done.
>
> 'There you are,' said Mr Pasley. 'Of course, his body doesn't lie here, more's the pity. But you know all about that.'
>
> It said the captain's name and that he had died 'in the empire's service in the cause of righteousness and freedom'. Willie nodded his head. He didn't think that Mr Pasley would be too sorry that Home Rule would not be coming after all, as people said. He didn't think he would be, no. In the cause of righteousness and freedom- and farming, they might have put, he thought. And liming (*LLW*, pp.260-61).

It is also the end of 'imperial nationalism', buried in the Flanders mud like the medal for 'gallantry', on Willie's body when he dies. 'Maybe the helpful acidic earth has eaten into the blackness and the quiet medal is clean and brown, showing, if only to the worms, its delicate design of a small crown, and a small harp' (*LLW*, p.292).

The Pasleys, like the grander Gibsons in *Lizzie Finn*, send their sons to fight in imperial wars; often all that comes back is the empty uniform, a powerful establishing symbol in that play. But Protestants are not the only Irish who serve the Empire. This is one of several points where Barry's work chimes with recent preoccupations in Irish historiography: the many ways in which Irish Catholics, often middle-class nationalists, made their careers through imperial channels (especially in India).[130] This is one of the identities and allegiances that Willie Dunne realizes have gone for ever, just before his death:

> He knew he had no country now. He knew it well. Finally the words of Jesse Kirwan had penetrated deep into the sap of his brain and he understood them. All sorts of Irelands were no more, and he didn't know what Ireland there was behind him now. But he feared he was not a citizen, they would not let him be a citizen. He would have no pride to be walking through Stephen's Green, he would not have the mercy of youth or the hastening thoughts of age. They may stone him too when he

> returned, or burn the house of himself; to the ground, or shoot him, or make him lie down under the bridges of Dublin and be a lowly dosser for all the rest of his days … No, he did not understand Jesse Kirwan entirely, but he would seek to in the coming years, he told himself. At least in the upshot he would try to know that philosophy. But how would he live and breathe? How would he love and live? How would any of them? Those that went out for a dozen reasons, both foolish and wise and all between, from a world they loved or feared, but that equally vanished behind them. How could a fella go out and fight for his country when his country would dissolve behind him like sugar in the rain? How could a fella love his uniform when the same uniform killed the new heroes, as Jesse Kirwan said? How could a fella like Willie hold England and Ireland equally in his heart, like his father before him, like his father's father, and his father's father's father, when both now would call him a traitor, though his heart was clear and pure, as pure as a heart can be after three years of slaughter? What would his sisters do for succour and admiration in their own country, when their own country had gone? (*LLW*, p.286-87)

These are the very questions addressed in The Steward of Christendom, The Whereabouts of Eneas McNulty, and Annie Dunne; while the final 'descendancy' of this tradition is central to Our Lady of Sligo. When Mai O'Hara's daughter Joanie, who bitterly resents her decayed father in his rotting Dunseverick bungalow, attacks him in a vitriolic tirade by her mother's hospital bedside, she is conjuring up a displacement that is both personal and historical:

> **Jack:** All I ever wanted was a fire in the evening and to put my feet up and read my book by the fire.
> **Sister:** I think if we could all just …
> **Joanie:** There was never a fire lit in the house, what are you talking about? And all your old poetry books, Tennyson, *Around the Boree Log*, Kipling, strewn about in boxes. And when an electrician is called because finally a fitting has fallen out of the wall, you always say, don't mind the state of the place, we've just moved in. And we'll have been there a year, two years, and even if it was twenty years you'd still; be saying it. And your gun cases and pouffes from Africa and ivories and fancy Nigerian tables and what not, and your uniforms and everything, all put in the garage and robbed, robbed out of it, because you were

> too taken up with other things to unpack them. Things that might have looked well and I could have looked at them and been proud, my bloody father the major.
> **Jack:** (*to* ***Sister***) … Royal Engineers … (*Desperate*) Bomb disposal.
> **Joanie:** Oh, shut up.
> *Silence for a bit.*[131]

In fact, as the history of Jack's relation Eneas McNulty demonstrates elsewhere, the evidence of imperial service is not something to be proudly displayed in independent Ireland. While Jack dimly recognizes this, he clings doggedly to the fact that he did 'rise in the world' by that route; gentrification came by way of being an old Nigeria hand, British Army major, engineer, Fellow of the Royal Geological Society. But it was all a half century or so too late. As Mai cruelly but accurately details it, he had chosen obsolete models:

> At least Jack turned himself into the thing he had admired in Sligo as a child, those Middletons and Jacksons and Pollexfens, big-house Protestants who would never have spoken to the likes of him. And by the time he did that, those people were gone, or sunken back into a different life, and all their sons or many of them killed in the Great War. Jack tried to turn himself into a sort of British gentleman but by the time he achieved it, death and independence had erased his template. There were no posh Protestants left in Sligo to notice the Catholic butterfly painfully emerged from the dank caterpillar he had been. It probably broke his heart just as much as marrying me did (*OLS*, pp.49-50).

Mai's own history reflects the social history of a class (more secure than Jack's) which has recently drawn the attention of historians: the Home Ruler bourgeoisie of the era immediately before the Irish revolution, who expected to inherit the earth.[132] In the year of Mai's birth, 1900, the Home Rule Party reunited under John Redmond, and apparently sustained its hegemony over Irish politics; the Liberal government of 1906 came to depend on Irish votes in the House of Commons, just as Gladstone had done twenty years before, and the prospect of Irish autonomy achieved by constitutional means seemed inevitable from about 1910. For Mai Kirwin at twenty, the first woman to wear trousers in Sligo, Junior Tennis Champion of Connaught, Commerce student at the new National University, the world was at her feet. All this reflects contemporary reality; women had been graduating from the old Royal University since the 1890s, and their educational opportunities had been greatly boosted by university reform in 1908. In other ways too, the Catholic middle class were solidly entrenched in worlds previously dominated by the protestant elite – the legal profession, medicine, the civil service.

But from the turn of the century the bourgeois Redmondites were being traduced as 'shoneens' and 'Castle Catholics' by the new ideologues of Sinn Fein; the idea of nationalism within the empire, adhered to by an intellectual like Tom Kettle as well as a policeman like Thomas Dunne, was already outmoded, and after the revolution it looked at best self-delusive and at worst, treasonous collaboration. The revolution was just as much directed against the class of Mai and Jack as against the British oppressors (in fact, many if not most of the Dublin Castle officials had long accepted the coming of Home Rule as inevitable and even desirable). From 1922 the new Free State wrote the *ci-devant* Catholic bourgeoisie out of history, along with the ascendancy elite which they had been poised to replace. W.B. Yeats's notional 'dream of the noble and the beggar-man' stood for an Ireland without intermediate classes or confused allegiances, and this suited the purposes of nationalist state-builders as well as romantic reactionaries. Yeats himself was descended on his mother's side from those very 'Middletons, Jacksons and Pollexfens' held up to Jack O'Hara – though in reality they too were mercantile rather than 'Big House' Protestants. But Barry is in search of exactly those confusions of identity, those intermediate spaces where people are caught looking over their shoulder, afraid to face the future. Long before we meet Annie Dunne, worrying her life away in her Wicklow farmhouse in 1959, we have heard her bitter prophecy of the new Ireland in 1922:

> It will be whins and waste everywhere, with bits of stones sticking up that were once Parliament, Castle and Cathedral.

> And people going around like scarecrows and worse. And Cuckoo Lane and Red Cow lane and all those places just gaps with rubbish in them … The like of Collins and his murdering men won't hold this place together. They haven't the grace and style for it. So you needn't mourn your shops and hats and haircuts, Dolly Dunne – they won't be there' (*SC*, p.278).

Though her father intuits that Collins has his own grace and style, the future is with de Valera, who to Jack and Mai (devotees of shops, hats and haircuts) seems 'deadening, deficient', threatening to 'isolate us, as if we weren't enough of an island already' (*OLS*, p.24).

By the time of *Hinterland*, de Valera has become a moral arbiter of the past – whom the corrupt phrasemaker Johnny Silvester tries to recruit to his own advantage:

> **Cornelius:** Well, I think by tradition the Irish journalist has played an important role in history. Nationalism. The Irish Press. The opposing view. De Valera and so on.
> **Johnny:** Would de Valera be proud of his country now? Every damn thing going to a tribunal. This account, that account – drink? – no? – the fucking Cayman Islands, who gives a fuck about all that, it was just money, not blood. *(Makes a drink for himself)*
> **Cornelius:** Blood money. Judas in the Potter's Field.
> **Johnny:** Were we forever to live like slugs under the rock of the British economy? If we were careless in our financial dealings, weren't the fucking banks on our side? They are trying to hang us now – they are trying to hang me. It's ancient history![133]

That 'ancient history' belongs to a country very far from the desiderata of Thomas Dunne, Eneas MacNulty, the O'Haras, or even Boss Grady's Boys, Josey and Mick – for whom Michael Collins also looms as a half-mythic figure, emblematic of a future that never happened. But there are, in fact, no alternative futures. Despite odd transforming rays of light, Barry's vision is a dark one. History is presented as a juggernaut, like fate in classical tragedy. The characters observe it, comment upon it, even comprehend it, but for all their knowingness they remain impotent. Those great floods of speech which gloss and articulate their trapped lives present the audience with a dramatic imperative: understanding and thus expiation. Over and over again, the image recurs of redemption laying a suffering soul to rest. But this is located in a universe ruled by history rather than religion.

'It's only history chooses a person's circumstance', Robert Gibson tells his new wife Lizzie Finn (*LF*, 203): heroine of a story so complex and referential that it might be more successful as one of Barry's history-novels than a two-act drama. The commitment which Barry brings to his exploration of the Irish past is founded on his belief in crossing barriers and taking risks, in terms of style as well as subject. The terseness of his novels is set against the great floods of speech in his plays, but both modes articulate and demand historical empathy as a condition of entering their enclosed worlds. In both genres, using an extraordinary ability to ventriloquize voices, speech-patterns, idioms over two centuries of Irish history, Barry has linked intricately-knotted patterns of long-gone Irish individuals and communities to his own extended family, held in a resolutely historical perspective. This has been a preoccupation for longer than is, perhaps, realized. The epigraph to that youthful novel, *The Engine of Owl-Light*, chosen from the seventeenth-century polymath Sir Thomas Browne, has in a sense guided him throughout:

> To palliate the shortness of our Lives, and somewhat to compensate for our brief term in this World, it's good to know as much as we can of it, and also so far as possibly in us lieth to hold a Theory of times past as though we had seen the same.[134]

Above all, he has determined to rescue figures adrift in history's flood, and salvage a sense of belonging. 'Like the spider, although we will decay, something of us will ever after remain.'[135] The final cry of Annie, the most defiant of Thomas Dunne's children, may stand as the credo of an author as bent upon redeeming the forgotten, marginalized and awkward minor actors of Irish history as Joyce or O'Casey – writers who echo, in their different ways, through his work. In that epigraph to *The Engine of Owl-Light* Thomas Browne also reflects that people who realize 'how things long past have been answered by things present, how matters in one age have been acted over in another' may feel themselves 'to be as old as the World' (*EOL*, p.6). Sebastian Barry is just fifty, and there must be much yet to come. But his range and power of imagination already promise to outreach most of his contemporaries.

12 | *Hinterland*: The Public Becomes Private

Colm Tóibín

In the first years of the new century the young Irish playwrights wrote about bad fathers. In May 2000, for example, Marina Carr's play *On Raftery's Hill*, in a joint production by Druid in Galway and the Royal Court in London, was performed at the Kennedy Center in Washington DC as part of a festival of Irish culture. Some in the audience at the opening night were old Kennedy stalwarts; others were loyal devotees of Irish culture. It was clear from the silences and the gasps and the shocked comments at the interval that this Irish father on the stage was not familiar to them. '*The kitchen of the Raftery household*', where the play was enacted, lacked charm, to say the least. There was no dancing at Lughnasa; there were no wild or comic Irish characters; there was even no bitter melancholy; the language was colourful in ways which did not seem to appeal to the audience. The dark cruelty of the father was relentless. Incest, rape, violence, vicious attacks on animals were all central to the drama and its impact. It was an Ireland which anyone who attended to page four of *The Irish Times*, which by the mid 1990s was daily covering cases of family horror, knew and recognized. But for those whose image of Ireland came from their memory or from the glories of *The Quiet Man* or *Riverdance*, this dark Ireland was new and strange.

In 2004 three first plays by Irish writers dramatized a world dominated by bad or mad fathers. In these plays, fatherhood was to be mocked, subverted, shown in all its madness and perversion. Stuart Carolan's *Defender of the Faith*, for example, was, once again, set in a rural kitchen. The setting was South Armagh in 1986. As in Marina Carr's play, Foucault rather than Freud was the dominant spirit, where power over others was the goal, where mindless control and cruelty lay in a fierce embrace on the hearthrug. Foul statement made a constant raid on the inarticulate.

In Mark Doherty's *Trad*, first performed at the Galway Arts Festival in 2004, the word 'Da' became almost a chant in the play, as a mad father, well past his sell-by date, led his dim-witted son into the temptation offered by hideous prejudices, many non-sequiturs, hilarious wild goose chases and bizarre urges and desires. In *Take Me Away* by Gerald Murphy, produced by Rough Magic, the father was a manic figure, unprotected, asking absurd questions, lacking all forms of authority, a joke on the stage. Like *On Raftery's Hill*, *Defender of the Faith* and *Trad*, the mother in *Take Me Away* was entirely absent. Thus the father was left exposed in his foolishness, his exaggerated needs, his mad requests, his ultimate humiliation.

In his play *Hinterland* Sebastian Barry sought to move the drama about fathers and their failures from a purely domestic space into the public realm, or into what seemed at first like the public realm. For an Irish audience the character of Johnny Silvester was clearly, and also deceptively, a closely researched version of Charles J. Haughey, who became Taoiseach in 1979 and remained in that position through some of the 1980s until he was ousted in 1992. Later, in his retirement, Haughey was plagued by allegations, which he himself subsequently confirmed under oath, that he had taken large sums of money from prominent businessmen for his own private use, and had held an enormous overdraft at Allied Irish Banks. If Ireland needed a public figure to become its disgraced father, then Charles Haughey offered himself freely for the role and played it with a distant tragic dignity in his lonely exile in his Georgian mansion in North County Dublin.

This was the house of Hinterland. The stage directions set the play in 'the private study of a Georgian mansion, outside Dublin. All the paraphernalia of a successful political life – citations, presentations, election posters framed'. [136] The opening speech, however, offered a clue to the great ambiguity which would surround the text and its dramatic intentions. In what was, ostensibly, a stilted letter to his aunts in Derry about the effects of partition, Silvester mentioned his father who was 'hardly the same man after partition, and his physical breakdown may well have been hastened by the same imposition' (*H*, p.7). Partition, he wrote, separated 'father from fatherland' (*H*, p.7); the play dealt over and over with the matter of fathers – Silvester was haunted by his own father's failure, his wife by her own father's reputation, and their son by Silvester's own disastrous fathering.

What distinguished these fathers in Irish plays of the first years of the twenty-first century was that none of them was a tragic hero; they were not caught between two worlds as one collapsed and the other took its place. In these plays, there was only one world, the one which had collapsed and had brought down a reign of terror, or a reign of madness, with no other world come to replace it. These men were static villains, caught in dramatic headlights, willing to destroy, living in a dream of the past. They would always do their worst, and there would be no moments of redemption or recognition or reconciliation. These fathers did not change; they acted and they remembered and they justified their actions. They and those around them were frozen in a ritual in which there was no exit. They were like figures in a Trojan horse, which does not move, which has no Troy in sight.

The act of not killing the father became the dramatic core of both *On Raftery's Hill* and *Hinterland.* Letting the father live, against all dramatic expectation, became a powerful and intriguing way of offering no resolution, no easy hope, and an increased dramatic tension. It is important to note that both of these plays were written in a time of great and obvious social change in Ireland, a time of new money, new social and sexual freedom and many bright expectations. These plays became a message from the strange, dark, hidden soul of the society; their power was all the more true for being controlled, almost manipulated, in a mysterious way, by the magnetic force which suggested that the world they dramatized was not as it seemed.

The unrepentant exile of Charles Haughey was a godsend to a playwright concerned with the dramatic possibilities of intractability; he is a hero who is unready for change, on whom everything is lost. Johnny Silvester's kingdom in *Hinterland* has already been taken from him; his house, where his wife weeps, is his prison. As his servant leaves him for the night, Silvester uses the precisely the same line from *Othello* as Charles Haughey used in the Dail on the day of his resignation. 'I have done the state some service.'[137] Just as he begins then to quote Yeats's lines about 'an aged man' he is visited by Cornelius, a dead colleague, whom an Irish audience will instantly recognize as Brian Lenihan, who held many ministerial portfolios in Fianna Fail governments, and was defeated for the Presidency by Mary Robinson in 1990. One of Silvester's earliest comments to his old friend mentions his heart transplant; Brian Lenihan, as an Irish audience would know, had a liver transplant. [138]

Hinterland thus contains large numbers of references to details from the career of Charles Haughey which are given to Johnny Silvester as part of his past. Both Silvester and Haughey, for example, were praised by pensioners for giving them free travel.[139] Both men gave a silver teapot to a female British Prime Minister.[140] As Silvester had betrayed Cornelius during his bid for the Presidency, so too Haughey betrayed Brian Lenihan in the 1990 Presidential campaign.[141] Both Haughey and Silvester have to face tribunals to investigate their financial affairs.[142]

These clues to the emotional or political core of the play are, however, deeply misleading; they represent a sort of decoy to distract the audience from what is really happening. Almost any imaginative writer who sets to work creating a set of motives and signature tones for a character from history ends by writing a sort of autobiography. Sometimes this can happen unconsciously; the character begins as a set of facts, and slows melts into a set of fictions. The process is gradual and tentative;

it may have its origins in speculative drafting, seeing how some new ingredient might work, realizing that, while the main character need not be changed, some of the surrounding circumstances will not fit the drama. Slowly, the play, or the novel or the story, becomes a dramatization of an aspect of the secret self.

In considering the relationship between the play *Hinterland* and Sebastian Barry's secret self, it might be useful to quote in full the second stanza from a poem from his collection *The Pinkening Boy*, which was published in 2004, and written in the same few years as the play *Hinterland.* The poem is called 'The Trousers'. The first stanza deals with the poet's interest in joining the Royal Marine Yacht Club, his inability to join because his father was not a member, his plans with his father to buy a yacht

> and sail
> wherever the spirit took us, to Dalkey island,
> to the inland mysteries of the French canals
> though neither of us knew a sail from a bedspread,
> and still don't.

The second stanza reads:

> So what a surprise to meet him in Dawson Street
> last Friday, after years of separation,
> family troubles keeping us apart. He passed
> like a retired sea-captain with a long white beard,
> the trim of his coat quite sailorlike,
> the hint of the South Seas in the sun creases
> about his eyes, his tentative and nautical hello -
> not sure of his ground, the tilt of the hard earth.
> As if in the intervening years he had indeed
> gone off to the Caribbean or rounded the Horn
> nonchalantly enough, and the Royal Marine Yacht-club
> owed me an apology. And as he hurried on,
> quite shipshape at sixty-seven,
> his sea-legs not yet attuned to land,
> it was his neat trousers particularly I noticed –
> the cut of his jib, the breeze athwart the main. [143]

Hinterland is as concerned with the failures of fatherhood and the surrounding grief and estrangement as the poem 'The Trousers'. As has already been stated, Johnny Silvester summons up his father in his opening speech, as his wife Daisy does hers almost as soon as she arrives on stage. Daisy's father, like Charles Haughey's actual father-in-law, was a politician, 'the soul of probity' (*H*, p.19). Both Johnny and Daisy will continue throughout the play to make reference to their respective fathers, as though they are desperately trying to eek out an identity for themselves, even one that depends on myths and shadows. So too Aisling who comes to interview Johnny, refers over and over to her own father. ('My father is a good decent person, I have to say. As fathers go.' [*H*, p57]) As Daisy bemoans her husband's infidelities, she mentions the needs of their son Jack:

> A little boy waiting for his father to come home. Do you know what a little boy is, Johnny? I'll tell you. He's a tiny contraption of bones and skin, tuned like a radio to give out and receive certain signals. When a little boy is sick, his whole body strains to broadcast a special signal, he wants a very simple thing, to be cuddled in the arms of his father (*H,* p.24).

Daisy carries on discussing the power of the absent father to do damage in a set of speeches which are the most emotionally forceful in the play:

> I pity all the little boys of this world. Because, when the signal is not answered, the pain is so great, so oddly great …A true father would feel that call from three thousand miles and travel all day and night to reach his child. Nothing can put that little scenario back together again and time goes on swiftly and then there is nothing but a tangle of broken wires, good for nothing because it can finally neither receive nor send a signal (*H*, p.25).

When Jack, their son, arrives on stage, it is clear that he is a tangle of broken wires, still half a child demanding and offering love. Daisy, by this time, has mentioned a particular mistress of her husband's who had written a book. For an Irish audience, this would have been instantly accepted as a reference to the journalist Terry Keane, who published a series of articles in *The*

Sunday Times about her long affair with Charles Haughey and who made no secret of the affair in her column in *The Sunday Independent.*[144] Once more, a precise reference to an actual event in the life of Charles Haughey had been inserted into the play.

The problem, however, was not this reference to Haughey's personal life, but the presence of Silvester's son Jack on the stage. Charles and Maureen Haughey, as is well known, have three sons, all of whom benefit from exceptionally strong mental health; there has not been a sign of a breakdown or a hint of a twitch among them. But healthy children, in general, are no use to a playwright. Suddenly, with the son Jack, the play had moved into areas dictated by its own necessities, the proper realm of fiction. In one sense, the play had always been there, since its emotional life arose not from a set of public events but from a series of meditations about fathers and fatherhood. But in scene after scene, the connections between the Silvesters and the Haugheys had been made abundantly clear. Now the script had departed from the story of the Haugheys to tell another story, one of grief and estrangement and the damage fathers cause to their sons, which belonged more to the emotional life of the poem 'The Trousers', in which a son inspects his father as he passes him silently on the street, than to the many volumes by journalists which told the story of Haughey's reign and his downfall.

The controversy surrounding the play thus centred on the use of Haughey as a central character and the distortion of the facts for dramatic purposes. It simmered in the newspapers and on radio and came to a head at a post-show discussion in the Abbey Theatre two weeks after the opening of the show, on 20 February 2002. The actors, the director and the theatre's literary manager took part, the author watching from the wings.

Jocelyn Clarke, the literary manager, remembers 'an unusually full post show discussion house' in which the first speaker from the audience disagreed with the director's statement that the play had 'grace'. 'The characters', she said, according to Clarke, 'were small minded and petty, especially the politician, and his relationship with his wife and son were not credible.' Clarke remembers that a young man then stood up 'and wondered how Barry could use the life and figure of a still living politician for his play – what right had he to do that to Charles Haughey's family, and to a lesser extent Brian Lenihan's family'. Clarke set about defending the play:

> I replied that *Hinterland* was not a biographical drama about Charles Haughey's life and times but about an imaginary politician whose life and times were based on figures and events in Ireland's recent political history, and which were very much in the public domain. That a playwright chooses to write a play about a political figure whose life story has similarities to the story of a living or dead politician does not make it a play about that politician's life or career.

'The audience', Clarke remembers, 'grew more restive. "That's not true", cried somebody. "It's about Charles Haughey", shouted somebody else. "It's been all in the newspapers". I replied:

> that it had not been Barry's intention to write a play about Charles Haughey. Indeed, *Hinterland* should be seen in the broader context of his work, and his ongoing theatre project to explore a nation's history through the prism of Barry's own family and its history. It could be argued that *Hinterland* is a biographical play in the sense that Barry primarily uses elements from his own biography rather than Haughey's or any other politician's and that as far as I was aware Haughey was still happily married, and he has several sons, none of whom suffer from a mental illness.'[145]

Thus the ambiguities surrounding the play and its intentions were spelt out. Its emotional shape came from the author's private life and that of his family; some of its detail came from the public domain, from aspects of the life of the former Taoiseach. Some of the audience believed that the author had no right to confuse the two, and the play had been damaged by the confusion. The theatre's literary manager suggested that to see the play as solely about Haughey or as a distortion was a fundamental misreading of the play.

Act Two of *Hinterland* centres on Jack's father-fed neurosis and Johnny's affair with Connie, the woman whom the audience recognized as the journalist Terry Keane. The act opens with Jack trying to hang himself. When Daisy comes in on this scene, she says to her husband: 'Listen, you can be the king that ruined his country but I won't let you be the father that ruined his son' (*H*, p.44). And it is in this sense that the personal is all that matters which impels *Hinterland*, with Daisy as a sort of chorus, musing always on the career of her husband as a father rather than as a party leader. His neglect of his son is offered as an event that supersedes politics, but stands for the rot at the heart of them as well:

> You were running for office, or running the country. Ah, yes. But it denies something at the heart of life. At the heart of families, of countries, of political parties even. If that slight signal [which the child in need gives out] is not attended to, there is really no family, party or country. Because the oldest law on earth has been violated (*H*, p.25).

Thus Barry subtly works the connection between a man who calls himself 'the father of the nation' (p.59) and the domestic father, insisting on the failure of the latter as a sort of poison which infects the public realm. But he is also using elements in the career and personality of Charles Haughey as a metaphor for what is essentially a private ache. This might seem, as it did to some of the Abbey audience at the discussion, a sort of confusing battle between private and public, an invasion of Haughey's privacy and the privacy of his wife and children, a distortion of the facts for mere artistic purposes, a dishonest and misleading play on public affairs while all the time masking a personal, private pain. Many of these accusations which were made about the play missed the point, which is that all fiction comes from a direct source and makes its way indirectly to the page or the stage. It does so by finding metaphors, by building screens, by working on half truths, moulding them towards a form which is both pure and impure fabrication. There is simply no other way of doing it. Most plays, novels and stories use the same stealthy process. Barry, by stealing Haughey, simply exposed an age-old system. Fiction, by its very nature, is a form of deceit. *Hinterland* inhabits beautifully and controversially the interstices between the world as we know it, raw and shapeless, and the world as imagined, tested richly and suggestively by private and hidden experience.

Illustration 8: Kathryn Hunter in *Whistling Psyche*. Almeida, London, 2004

Illustration 9: Kathryn Hunter and Claire Bloom in *Whistling Psyche*. Almeida, London, 2004

13 | 'In the dank margins of things': *Whistling Psyche* and the Illness of Empire

Claire Gleitman

Sebastian Barry's most recent play, *Whistling Psyche*, takes place in the Beckettian waiting room of a Victorian railway station, where two aged people pass the time (which does not pass) by reciting their life stories as they await the arrival of something that might release them from this purgatorial spot into what appears to be the 'strange eternity of death'. Although the absurdist echoes are resonant, Barry's two characters are rooted in history in a manner that distinguishes them from their Beckettian predecessors: one, we learn, is Florence Nightingale and the other is James Miranda Barry, a scandalous footnote in the annals of British history and a probable ancestor of the author himself. At first glance, the famously prim 'lady of the lamp' and the cross-dressed military doctor seem to have little in common other than the medical profession to which both were committed. However, in this elegant poetic drama comprised of alternating monologues, their stories gradually intertwine as we come to see their rich similarities despite their mutual antipathy. To borrow Dr. Barry's phrasing, both were pilgrims who did their work in the grim hospitals and asylums at the neglected edges of the British Empire. These houses of the dying and the mad come to be emblematic of the madness of Empire itself, to which Barry and Nightingale were tied both ambiguously and ambivalently. Both chose to work from within the empire in order to reform it; both 'penetrate[d] into districts of desolation' (*WP*, p.43)[146] in the course of doing their work; and each despises the other for what s/he perceives as the other's artificiality and pretensions. Florence Nightingale castigates Barry for his low-born putting on of airs, while Barry equally castigates Nightingale for using her pretty face to get her way with drains and bandages (*WP*, p.48). Yet, as Nightingale slowly comes to see, she and Barry both endured a kind of 'confusion almost unto madness' thanks to the compromises forced on them by their time, place and gender. Indeed, what each character reviles in the other are precisely the transgressions of empire that made them extraordinarily effective reformers – while also consigning them to a lifelong state of poignant lonesomeness, with pets as their closest companions.

The play begins by situating us in time and space and simultaneously unsettling our confidence in that situation. On the waiting room's paneled walls are framed prints depicting territories into which British imperial tentacles once reached, as well as a portrait of Queen Victoria herself. Yet the stage directions suggest that this seemingly concrete representation of an historical moment should melt into something less tangible: '*the edges of the room*', Barry writes, are '*fraying into the evocative decrepitude of a graveyard monument*' (*WP*, p.9). There is a clock on the wall indicating the time, but over the course of the play its hands never move. Dr. Barry's uniform suggests mid-19th century, but the author tells us: '*if this place has a time, it is around 1910*'. 1910 is the year Florence Nightingale died, which accounts for her arrival at this way-station at this moment. Perhaps not coincidentally, 1910 is also the year when, according to Virginia Woolf, 'human character changed'. More specifically, if whimsically, Woolf assigned the change to 'on or about December 1910'.

All human relations have shifted – those between masters and servants, husbands and wives, parents and children. And when human relations change there is at the same time a change in religion, conduct, politics, and literature.[147]

This change, Woolf argued, was best represented with attention to character of a particular kind ('I believe that all novels begin with an old lady in the corner opposite' [*CB*, p.102]); further, it necessitated new methods for representing such characters' inner lives, methods that were likely to be fragmentary and 'spasmodic' (*CB*, p.119). The characters in *Whistling Psyche* are intermittently conscious of having lived at a moment perched just prior to monumental changes – changes, as we shall see, from which Barry especially recoiled, even though they might have liberated him to live and work without a permanent, suffocating disguise. Both figures were essentially creatures of their historical moment while also being, somewhat despite themselves emphatically ahead of their time. Sebastian Barry reveals his characters by making use of monologues – or soliloquies, rather, as the two rarely address one another directly. While some critics of the 2004 Almeida Theatre production complained that this lack of interaction rendered the play un-dramatic, Barry's reliance on monologues is a perfect device for allowing his characters to expose their inner selves in a manner that such buttoned-up people would never do in conversation (least of all with each other). Indeed, monologues abound in the contemporary Irish drama, most notably in Brian Friel's *Faith Healer*, as well as in the work of Marina Carr (in *The Mai*, for example) and in most of Conor McPherson's plays. Among other things, monologues function in these dramas to enable an unrestrained revelation of self that might seem jarringly unrealistic in ordinary, naturalistic dialogue. For all their ornate lyricism, in *Whistling Psyche* the monologues proceed in stream-of-consciousness fashion, as the old ladies (one cross-dressed convincingly as a man) sit in their opposite corners and fill the uncertain time by speaking, sometimes 'spasmodically', about a past to which they can never be fully reconciled but which they persist in relating, partly to keep threatening silence at bay.

Whether or not the playwright intended for us to hear echoes of Virginia Woolf, her remarks provide a resonant backdrop for *Whistling Psyche*. 1910 was also the year that Edward VII died, and the Edwardian Age died with him, the last gasp of the 19th century. Edward's mother, Victoria, had died in 1901, but her son carried the empire into the 20th century, along with the imperial assumptions around which the English organized their lives and their world. In 1910, Europe was a mere four years from the final catastrophe of August 1914 and the beginning of the slaughter that ultimately unraveled that empire. *Whistling Psyche*, then, is set in the twilight of a certain kind of world (is the 'graveyard monument' evoked in Barry's stage directions the tombstone for the decaying Victorian age?), the only world that Dr. Barry and Nightingale ever knew and within which they struggled with the uncomfortable positions that they assumed against the harsh choices offered to them as a result of their gender, their respective classes, and their nationalities. They were women in a time and place that severely restricted the sway of women outside the home. One was poor and the other was wealthy in times and places that assigned to those categories nearly immutable roles. Their behavior was circumscribed drastically by the political, social and national contexts within which they resided. The play's intricate web of words provides poetic objective correlatives for the various systems within which these characters struggled, as well as correlatives for the structural and systemic ways they overcame the constrictions or at least endured them.

Dr. Barry's first lines refer to a beloved series of poodles that he owned in his life and for which the play is named. His devotion to this rather fussy breed offers suggestive hints regarding his own complex nature. 'You will not need to be told', he tells us, ' … of the beauties and exactitude of the poodle' (*WP*, p.9). Beauty and exactitude are among the adjectives one might choose as antonyms to the operations of empire that Barry spent his life trying to mitigate. As he acknowledges later in the play: 'the work of an empire is deadly, and done to a short song' (*WP*, p.23). Yet soon after speaking about the poodle breed, Barry applies one of these same adjectives to the waiting room, which he decides is 'undoubtedly in England'; you can tell, he maintains, 'by the sheen and exactitude of it' (*WP*, p.9). Like Thomas Dunne in Sebastian Barry's earlier masterpiece, *The Steward of Christendom*, *Whistling Psyche's* main character is an Irishman who admires 'exactitude', or neatness and order; hence his conflicted admiration for the empire he dutifully if ambivalently serves. His poodles, Dr. Barry tells us, all hailed from 'old England', each of these vestiges of Old England he names Psyche and identifies as 'an image of my own human soul' (*WP*, p.10). The arrival of the ships transporting each new poodle from England to Cape Town, where he was stationed for many years, brought 'to me again Psyche, renewed and familiar' (*WP*, p.11). Thus it seems that each Psyche is a small patch of Old England sent out into the fetid edges of the empire where Barry labors, to restore his soul and renew him. He is sustained, in other words, by these little furry fragments that derive from the imperial center.

At the same time, Barry tells us that his time in Africa was joyful, and he attributes this to his own liminal status within the colonized territory. Both the natives and the colonizers he describes as bewildered', 'sick and mad'; yet he stood apart from that confusion, because:

> I am that other sort of creature, neither white nor black, nor brown nor even green, but the strange original that is an Irish person ... my heart, my white heart blackening secretly with age, was with the soiled lunatics that cried out like large owls in the bright asylums (*WP*, p.11).

By virtue of being an 'other' sort of creature, of being no identifiable color, of *lacking* exactitude himself, he is able to elude the absolute categorizations that would identify him as colonist or colonizer, since as an Irishman working for the British he could be considered to be either or both. His ambiguous status in terms of gender goes a long way toward explaining his life-long identification with 'the outcast and the forsaken' to whom he dedicated his life, despite his failure to say so here.

Though we cannot anticipate the connection, Barry's simile regarding the lunatics who 'cried out like large owls' is an early evocation of the pet to which Nightingale was devoted: 'a little owl, Athena ..., as neat and square as a soap-stone statue' (*WP*, p.16). Yet this moment that might unite the characters at least in terms of their admiration for neatly compact pets also introduces us to the ferocious enmity that Barry felt for Nightingale. After noting that he served 'the despised and lonesome of the world' (adjectives, of course, that describe him also), Barry laments his own erasure from the historical record and contrasts it angrily with Nightingale's fame. As he does so, he lights a cheroot. The gesture is intriguing; can there be any prop more masculine than a cigar (even if sometimes a cigar is just a cigar)? Precisely as he arrives at what is so profoundly galling to him – that Nightingale did not need to dissemble her gender and was lionized for the work that she did as a woman – he engages in the most overtly male behavior that his non-gender status will permit. This action, coupled with his failure to speak to her, offends Nightingale: ' ... he will not speak. He would rather pollute his surroundings' (*WP*, p.13). Thus in this moment of their first near confrontation, he clings to a masculinity that is in fact not natural to him, as she clings to a prim conventional femininity from which, to some extent, she struggled to escape throughout her life.

While we were told that Dr. Barry's face was 'anxious' when he first arrived on stage, Nightingale is said to be 'as confident as a child in its own room' (*WP*, p.13). Unlike the doctor, she seems fully comfortable in her strange surroundings and eager to engage in conversation with the man who shares the stage with her, though she does not recognize him. Yet Barry admits to hearing only 'something low and mean' when she speaks (*WP*, p.14). Assiduously ignoring her, he resumes his own story, and describes his childhood in a manner that again recalls Thomas Dunne. The Ireland of Dr. Barry's birth is full of 'musical cows' and 'bucolic choral singing', like the 'clover honey-smelling' fantasy of childhood that Dunne evokes in the opening lines of *The Steward of Christendom*.[148] But Dr. Barry tells us that the prelapsarian Ireland of his younger years, where even destitute country people could throw themselves 'on the pleasant and easily given mercy' of their wealthier relations, gradually gave way to something new and horrific as a result of the potato famine that 'changed all things' (*WP*, p.14). There is the smallest hint of the gathering darkness in Barry's description of Cork cows that are 'crazy in the afternoon' (later, Barry will commit himself to the task of caring for lunatics in the empire's asylums, and Empire itself is referred to by Nightingale as ' terrible illness that smote the mind' [*WP*, p.20]). In almost every respect, though, he depicts early 19th century Ireland as pure pastoral plenty. Further, what destroys this idyll is said to be entirely natural: 'hunger and pestilence leaped forth upon the same green fields with fang of wolf and embrace of bear' (*WP*, p.14). As he proceeds to lament what was lost, he credits the colonists with creating the idyll in the first instance, though he neglects to mention their role in failing to contain the famine:

> The landed people turned their gaze inward because outward, upon the white roads of Ireland and in the mudded huts so like unto those later that I found in the rural plethoras of Africa, limbs withered to sticks and stenches of misery and terminality amassed themselves so that any possible scales of landlord and labourer were quite broken, and a bleak nightmare beyond words took the place in the book of life where once those old colonists and native rich had tried … to make a rural idyll in their inherited fields (*WP*, p.14).

Barry's benign representation of the world that famine washed away is striking, especially coming as it does from an Irishman: those fields, one might argue, were *stolen* rather than 'inherited' from their rightful Irish owners in the early years of colonization and plantation. But the edenic Ireland Barry conjures is characterized by a perfect balance between landlord and laborer, colonist and colonized. Its demise is due, in his judgment, not to colonial theft but to a natural disaster that overwhelms the Irish physically and the colonizers spiritually; the latter are so appalled by the suffering of the native Irish that they turn 'their gaze inward'. Moreover, it is a desire to recreate 'that old balance and medium' that Barry believes to have existed in old Ireland that motivates him to do his life's work. This reformer's impulse, it seems, is in some respects retrograde; he longs for a return to 'the ancient text of Ireland's happiness', which he locates in the early 19th century, a time when Ireland was an English colony, but (in Barry's view) a well-run one.

It is noteworthy that what propels him into action is the fact of 'misery and *terminality*' and 'the *noisome* horrors of what happens in the dank *margins* of things' (*WP*, p.5, emphasis added). Almost immediately afterwards, Nightingale describes the wretched condition of nurses as they existed a generation before:

> A nurse in my good mamma's day was a poor fallen type, heavy with fat and evil intent, consuming jars of *noisome* beer … , women who themselves were abandoned to the sanitary horrors and *terminal*, dark corridors of the hospital itself, a place where … the hopelessness of *a sort of end of earth* took hold of everyone (*WP*, p.17, emphasis added).

As 'the daughter of wealthy people', Nightingale found herself with two options. She could opt for a nurse's life, which attracts her, although her description of it recalls both the horrors of the Irish famine and of life in Africa as Barry describes them. (Thus she suggests unwittingly that the misery at the end of the Empire exists also within its center, in English hospitals.) Or she could opt instead for what she describes as another kind of horror within the center of Empire: that is, the conventional, pampered life of an upper-class English woman. But in her 'cushioned domains', as she calls them, Nightingale felt imprisoned 'in the same dailysome rictus that held' her sister and mother. Her neologism ('dailysome') faintly recalls Barry's use of the word 'noisome' as well as Nightingale's own, just as the image of the imprisoning rictus is picked up again later when Nightingale describes her mother's 'philosophy … on the sofa':

> Plato based his philosophy on the soul, my mother on the sofa. Indeed, she based herself on it … She wished to be allowed to

> lie, and to be inserted at length into the maw of death, horizontally, like a letter into a letterbox (*WP*, p.27).

Thus Nightingale's position in the devouring jaws of aristocratic leisure, or what she elsewhere calls 'that smothering, mothering place where I mouldered, all loved and admired and understood and as good as dead' (*WP*, p.18), prompts her feverish rebellion. Like Barry, who leaves squalid Ireland for equally squalid Africa and determines to find remedies in the new locale for what seemed incurable in the old one, Nightingale flees one form of noxious horror (passive, leisured femininity) for another (the ghastly conditions prevailing within the English military hospital system), determined to attack the latter head-on. In both cases, the characters remain deeply entwined both psychologically and practically with the imperial system that is, in some ways, at the heart of the noxiousness they are determined to root out.

Indeed, after some years of working in British military hospitals in Scutari and Balaclava – where wounded soldiers lay covered in filth, food was left to decompose, and drainage systems failed to function – Nightingale issued a direct appeal to Queen Victoria, whom she visited in Scotland in 1856. While describing that encounter in the play, Nightingale delivers an impassioned paean to the queen that again recalls Thomas Dunne. Like Dunne, who extols Victoria for having 'built everything up and made it …shipshape' (*WP*, p.15), Nightingale sees the queen as the maternal 'ordering' principle in a world that otherwise would spiral out of control; her 'true offspring', says Nightingale, 'were liberties and progress'. Interestingly, Nightingale portrays Victoria as strained by the task of breeding order so that at times 'she became silent, and had the look of a panicked animal. As though the effort of Empire were like a terrible illness that smote the mind' (*WP*, p.20). Just as Barry earlier linked the 'craziness' and 'panic' of Ireland's fat cows with their life-giving potential (their craziness is brought on by the pain of their full udders [14]), Victoria suffers as she labors into birth 'her true offspring', which is a world containing subjects who stretch from 'across the Irish Sea, down to Africa and Asia and the Arab worlds'. Although Nightingale longs to escape the soul-destroying comfort to which Victoria's orderly empire would consign her, she nevertheless reveres Victoria and attributes to her 'essential grace' (and not to her own persuasiveness) the queen's adoption of Nightingale's proposals for reform (*WP*, p.20). Yet the effect of Sebastian Barry's recurring images is to expose, insistently if subtly, the conflicts with which Nightingale and Dr. Barry's relationship to their historical situation are rife. As we have seen, images of madness, panic, and pained maternity seem inextricably linked to their portraits of an 'orderly' imperial world, like barely conscious admissions of the disorder, disease and corruption that they themselves found lurking everywhere beneath the glory of Empire.

Of course, both Barry and Nightingale had the opportunity to see firsthand that the British Empire had deep structural as well as ontological problems, and they dedicated their lives to attempting to remedy some of them. Barry frequently critiques the stratified nature of military life, which allowed officers to remain at a comfortable remove from any real labor or danger, while 'other lowly beings' were obliged to do the life-threatening work of maintaining the empire – while meanwhile being treated no better than the colonized. Further, when he and his mother found themselves rescued from destitution by a figure with the androgynous name of General Miranda, who proceeded to dress the female Barry in male clothing and sent her/him to learn to be an army doctor, Barry describes Miranda as having 'liberate[d] me like the serf of a terrible empire, or a slave of received understanding' (*WP*, p.31). By suggesting that femininity and its attendant expectations constitute a form of enslavement, Barry unwittingly aligns himself with Nightingale, who also recognized that the only freedom available to her was outside the confines of conventional femininity (though she did not have to venture so far outside). Having allowed the General to rewrite his identity, Barry asserts that he no longer can remember his 'original name'. His new self completely overtook his former one, compelling him to accept a life of permanent solitude.

What he fails to see is that the same was true for Nightingale, though she was not obliged to give up wearing skirts. Nightingale might have noted the parallel, except that she chooses this moment in the play to fall asleep, thus missing Barry's stunning revelation about his sexual identity. Still, when she awakens she launches into a pertinent consideration of what conventional femininity and especially maternity might have offered her:

> Confinement after confinement like a sentenced criminal, and perchance at some bleak break of day, among the weakening light of the candles, to die in a shrieking moment, trying to bring forth just such another as yourself into these ruined realms. A private soldier had a better chance of surviving his battles! (*WP*, p.32)

Yet again a woman's lot is portrayed as a form of captivity leading to panic, and in this case death. Nightingale goes still further, explicitly comparing the perils that laboring women endure with what men face on the battlefield and pronouncing the former the greater risk. In doing so, she echoes the famous assertion of Euripides' Medea, surely one of the most transgressive female characters in literature: 'I would very much rather stand/Three times in the front of battle than bear one child'.[149]

Yet Nightingale is rueful as she muses about what it was that she sought in lieu of a conventional female life. Though Barry is envious of her fame, it is her less celebrated days of youth and vigor that she remembers most fondly, when 'I had the gallop and reach of a giraffe' (*WP*, p.33). The metaphor neatly encapsulates her duality as a woman who managed to be transgressive and traditional at once. That 'wonderful creature' the giraffe, she points out:

> … can do no other than reach higher than her fellow creatures, she is strangely comely and slender, maidenlike, but large as a dream, an animal stretched out and altered in the most fantastical manner (*WP*, p.33).

Unlike Barry, Nightingale succeeded in remaining feminine in form; yet like him, she was an 'other' sort of creature, compelled in part by her own nature (as Barry felt compelled by his strange Irish otherness) to carve out an astonishing if also desperately lonely life for herself. To accomplish this, she too had to find a way to elude exactitude, to become fluid – both 'maidenlike' and 'fantastical', both 'slender' and uncommonly large – so as to escape the rigid categories in which human beings (and especially females) were encased in her day.

Nightingale's tale of her past reaches an anguished crescendo as she describes the aftermath of the 'historied charge' of the Light Brigade during the Crimean War. For her, this event crystallized the nearly criminal callousness and bureaucratic stupidity that characterized the treatment of the wounded in her day. With heart-wrenching detail, she evokes 'the wild broken music' of the stench that emanated from the hospital barracks' airless rooms, and 'the extraordinary music of human pain' that mingled discordantly with the other, riotous tune (*WP*, p.35). But it is the fate of the horses left to starve on the battlefield that haunts Nightingale's imagination most piercingly: 'Often and often I think of those horses, I know not why, thinning and famishing in the dark aftermath of the most famous and revered action in the annals of that war' (*WP*, p.36).

This memory stalks her, it seems, because it captures the dark underside of the workings of Empire. What Tennyson's neatly repetitive, glorifying cadences veil is the gruesome, disorderly reality of imperial warfare. The disasters that befell the Light Brigade and the subsequent disregard for its horses she attributes to 'the bleak dullness of official minds' (*WP*, p.35) and, more specifically, to a petty dispute that erupted between two commanders, one Irish and one English (no strangers to disputation, by national tradition at any rate), who could not agree upon a rational approach to conducting the battle. Those men lucky enough to survive their ineptitude with only wounds were almost certain to die later in hospitals with drainage systems so completely blocked up that 'every noisome and poisonous seeping' was redirected into the vents of the hospital to infect the wounded men. Nightingale concludes: 'we were bringing [our own men] to death by the blithe ignorances and dither of those official men' (*WP*, p.37). Thus the horses discarded like rubbish become an image for imperial warfare and its bungling waste of life; 'in those times', notes Nightingale, 'a soldier was nigh equal a mere beast' (*WP*, p.36).

Nightingale's descriptions of the ghastly conditions at Scutari and Balaclava are juxtaposed with Barry's descriptions of similar blundering in the asylums that he encountered in Cape Town. He tells the story of a Major Barnes who suffered from severe alcoholism and was placed in the local asylum, where he lived in filth and isolation and quickly degenerated into a state of raving bestiality. Barry recognized that an improvement in his external circumstances was likely to result in an improvement in his mental health. But, although he temporarily succeeded in creating more humane conditions that were demonstrably beneficial not only for Barnes but for the other inmates, the asylum quickly declined to its former state of decrepitude after Barry left it: 'The officers of that asylum were allowed to return to their murderous idleness, and all was right with the world of Empire, in all its hopelessness and eternity' (*WP*, p.40).

Barry ruefully concludes that such conditions persist because people get used to them: they 'become enshrined as tradition'. As Vladimir observes in *Waiting for Godot*, 'habit is a great deadener'.[150] It was Barry and Nightingale's particular genius, as Sebastian Barry portrays them, to be able to see (and live) past habit and outside of tradition; they recognized that what others perceived as natural was in fact often irrational and perverse. Yet, as we have noted, these iconoclasts also kept one foot firmly planted in the reassuringly conventional world in which they were born. Late in the play, Barry remarks that he was viewed as an exotic and even erotically fascinating figure not only because of his sexually ambiguous demeanor, but because of his willingness to venture into 'districts of desolation like a pilgrim' with no companion 'except a poodle and a fine heart like Nathaniel at [his] side' (*WP*, p.43). This boast is rather self-deceiving and not only because the poodle, as we have seen, is a remnant of comforting old England; it accompanies Barry to his colonial outposts to assure him of his connection to Empire even as he leaves and in part disavows it.

Even more revealingly, Nathaniel is the African servant whom Barry repeatedly portrays as content in his servitude, even naturally suited to it. Often, he mentions Nathaniel in the same breath as Psyche, as if there is scant difference between the two. At the start of the play, while surveying the railway waiting station, he imagines that Nathaniel is present with him, or near him, '[s]itting patiently in the third-class waiting room' (*WP*, p.10). This unreflective acknowledgment of Nathaniel's third-class status is characteristic of Barry's reflections upon him. Elsewhere, he describes Nathaniel as polishing Barry's Cape Town house to a shine 'with his domestical genius' and tending devotedly to Barry's boots (*WP*, pp.11; 44). Most remarkably, we learn that when Barry found himself pregnant with the Cape Town governor's child, he stole away to deliver the baby 'with only Nathaniel and Psyche'. The former, Barry tells us, was 'tender and strong as a midwife', as he helped what he believed to be his male master through the agonies of a stillborn birth (*WP*, p.51). Barry does appreciate how astounding this experience must have been for Nathaniel, whom he imagines must have viewed him as some sort of demon. Yet he presumes: 'because he loved me as a servant, he did what was asked of him, without question or reproach' (*WP*, p.52).

In short, Nathaniel is portrayed as the essence of docile slavishness, unquestioning and even loving in his servitude. Moreover, Barry projects some traditionally female qualities upon his servant when it serves him to do so: Nathaniel is domestic and he is a tender midwife. Thus he becomes at once a fluid, transgendered creature like his master *and* a reassuringly happy slave. He becomes, that is, precisely what Barry needs him to be in order to secure Barry's own, wavering sense of self. It is left to Nightingale to describe Nathaniel – on the one occasion in her life when she crossed paths with Barry, during a hospital inspection at the height of the Crimean War – in a manner that we sense is closer to the truth. She describes him as 'a dejected African serving man trotting after [Barry] like a shadow' (*WP*, p.46). The dejection that she perceives in Nathaniel Barry never glimpses for a minute, perhaps because doing so would force him to acknowledge his own conflicted relationship to an empire that enslaved both women and colonized people, that required Barry himself to play an artificial role in order to prosper for a time within it, and that banished him back to the margins once his (or her) true identity was revealed. Still, Barry adopted many imperial assumptions about colonized people and, as we will see in a moment, about women, even as he dedicated his life to improving the lot of 'the despised and lonesome' with whom he did not completely wish to identify himself.

Barry recognizes that his disguise was not so effective as to completely conceal his ambiguous nature. On the contrary, in an intriguing meditation, he speaks about the effect that his elusive sexual identity has upon others. He imagines that the mystery of his nature prompted a 'hidden lust' in women in particular, who longed to unveil him in both a literal and a figurative sense. The result, he imagines, would be transformative for them as well as for him:

> … they would with due worship undo my buttons … and find beneath … a body as crisp as an angel, the skin as white as last fires, the sex as fierce and gentle as a philosophy that would undo and explain the meaning of the world in one moment. The sex as rare as some tight metal from the deepest earth, that would somehow impale them and be impaled in one moment. And in that queer moment of ravishment I would destroy their social natures so that they issued forth into the imperial streets at dusk redeemed and at last elevated beyond the strictures of sin (*WP*, p.44).

In this astonishing passage, Barry seems to imagine a confrontation for the women with something that would shatter their assumptions about the world and clarify their vision at the same time, and a sexual act that would defy exactitude as well as traditional gender distinctions: it would be both fierce and gentle, and it would allow the women to be both female (impaled by him) and male (doing the impaling) at once. The result of this 'queer' act, he suggests, is that his own fluid nature would render theirs fluid also, dissolving 'their social natures' so as to free them from imprisoning social categories, as General Miranda freed him.

But just after Barry describes an attainment of social liberation for drawn and withering women attained through an act of 'queer' sex, both he and Nightingale recall the day when their paths crossed in the Crimea. In this fateful moment when these strikingly alike figures confronted one another, they (predictably) failed to perceive any kinship at all. Instead, Nightingale viewed Barry as 'so odd and unexpected an apparition' that she could not believe they 'share[d] the same sphere on earth' (*WP*, p.45). Oblivious to the fact that he was dedicated to the same kind of good works as she, she decided that the miseries of the English army stemmed directly from his 'evilly ignorant … customs and practices'. In her harsh description of his appearance there is a flicker of an awareness of the artificiality of his disguise: he was dressed up, she says, like a bad actor. Yet this recognition evoked only revulsion in her. Even his dog (his Psyche) disgusted her.

Although Barry *did* recognize a kinship between them, this recognition merely sent him into a rage: 'She did no more than I had been doing for thirty years, and that without changing out of her skirts … She had not had to change out of her skirts to be the personage she was' (*WP*, p.48). His pained resentment prompted him to scold Nightingale for daring to do what he himself longed to do (and did do, although in disguise) – to venture into 'a male place' as if it were her right. Barry deems Nightingale's actions a violation of 'things as they were'. His rage, one senses, is in part self-directed. Lacking Nightingale's courage, he rages against these 'things as they were' while also fervently clinging to them. When he describes himself berating her, he says that he 'fix[ed] her there before all those rough hearts and souls', and the image is arresting, since both Barry and Nightingale struggled not to be fixed, to free themselves from rigid categories. Yet at this moment Barry strove to fix her. Correspondingly, he fixed himself in the role of authoritarian male, a role that denied him any real human companionship throughout his unhappy, if also adventurous and productive, life.

Nightingale's first response is ire when she finally recognizes Barry, in the present tense action of the play; yet she is moved to sympathy by his reaction when she recalls his miserable end. Barry's actual sexual identity was only discovered after his death, by what he calls (with characteristic self-loathing) a 'dirty Irish nurse' who came to lay him out for burial. It was she who spied out 'that little lonesome cleft' that betrayed his real gender (*WP*, p.56). Once it was exposed, Barry's considerable accomplishments dissolved from historical memory and his name became 'mired', as Nightingale puts it, 'in a filthy story' (*WP*, p.49). Barry concedes that this is so and pronounces himself: 'nothing … A filth, a darkness' (*WP*, p.49). Recalling his earlier, slightly dissimilar use of that phrase at the start of the play, one can see that many of his actions were impelled by a yearning to restore cleanliness to menacing filth, both in poorly maintained institutions and in his own fragile sense of self. Speaking about his habit of giving each new poodle the same name as the last one, he says: 'So that I might go out into the walled garden at night in the clean filth of the dark and call that same important name, *Psyche*' (*WP*, p.10). Just as the dog grants him a sense of renewal and a connection to old England with its "sheen" rather than to 'dirty' Ireland, it may well have granted him temporary relief to pronounce Nightingale 'a disgrace and a defamation', thus projecting onto her what he feared existed in himself (*WP*, p.45).

The play moves toward its close with a recounting by both characters of tales of disappointed love; Barry's ended in scandal and Nightingale's ended with her rejection of a potential lover who proclaimed that she 'should have been born a man, because I was like a man and worse than a man' (*WP*, p.52). While Barry declares himself 'the mourner of himself' because of his ruined history, Nightingale maintains that she is incapable of 'mourn[ing] myself', and proceeds to accept and even welcome the inevitable passing of all things (*WP*, p.57). Barry picks up and extends the same theme in his last monologue, in which he reflects upon the ephemeral nature of sparrows and empires alike: 'The clocks disprove us all', he notes (*WP*, p.60). In this place where time is frozen and clocks' hands do not move, Barry points to the transitory nature of human existence and the inexorable passage of time, which washes away all vestiges of 'the little eddy we made across the pond of daily life'. In his final lines, he looks forward to that moment of redemption when God 'takes each and every one and makes him new, returns him to the crisp clear lines of the original mould' and relieves him of his sins (*WP*, p.60). Characteristically, he imagines release taking the form of a return to exactitude, which is also a return to some kind of original purity. Nightingale also stays true to form, as she imagines herself devotedly ministering to Barry in heaven in order to help provide the forgiveness for which he longs. As the play ends in its published version, the characters are brought together physically for the first time: their hands just touch, '*perhaps*' (says the playwright) '*by accident*' (*WP*, p.61). It is worth noting that, in the Almeida production, the characters were granted a far more intimate closing tableau: Nightingale removed Barry's jacket, his shirt, and his bindings to reveal, just for an instant, his breasts, and the two characters embraced. While this gesture allowed for a powerful moment of connection between them that was surely cathartic for the audience, I am unconvinced that we have seen Dr. Barry achieve the degree of self-acceptance necessary to allow for such extraordinary self-exposure. Hence my own preference is for the original ending, with its mere hint of a touch. This is a far more subtle and tentative suggestion of achieved intimacy, but perhaps one which is all the more moving for that reason.

Whatever the final gesture, the play concludes with a pair of *ubi sunt* monologues, in which Sebastian Barry's characters bid elegiac farewells not only to their lives but to the imperial age, which seemed impregnable to change (Dr. Barry, we will recall, referred to 'Empire, in all its … eternity', [*WP*, p.40]), but proved to be as evanescent and flawed as all other human constructs. Indeed, what *Whistling Psyche* indicates with its intricate network of images is the hopelessness of reforming something that is diseased at the core. Despite their most fervent efforts, Barry and Nightingale cannot root out the illness that is Empire, though they did far more than many of their contemporaries to mitigate its horrors. Although they repeatedly attempt to distinguish between the center of Empire (which is old England and Victoria and thus good) and the margins (Ireland, Africa, Scutari), the inside (which has exactitude) and the outside (which is disorder), the play's recurring images work to blur these distinctions and to reveal that the noxiousness on the fringes of Empire results from the noxiousness at its heart, and perhaps vice versa. Nightingale's description of the blocked drains in the Scutari hospitals, which redirected 'noisome' fluids and vapors back into the hospitals to re-infect wounded men, is an apt image for imperialism itself and its attempt to remake foreign cultures in its own image while itself remaining absolutely eternal and unchanged. As *Whistling Psyche* makes evident, the consequence is a kind of mass dissemination of pestilence and madness that infects cultures and individuals alike. Both Barry and Nightingale attempted to escape to the margins of Empire not just to enact reforms but to free themselves from the empire's stultifying social categories. But to different degrees they carried those categories within them and even to some extent imposed them on others. The full dissolution of those categories, and the liberation that Barry imagines might result from an act of queer sex, in fact occurs for Sebastian Barry's lonely creations only in the moment of their deaths – and, perhaps, in the moment when their hands just touch and they become 'an unexpected couple', united by their remarkably similar histories and finally willing to accept their kinship, as their lives and the world that shaped them vanishes into darkness and the curtain falls.

14 | Bibliography of Works of Sebastian Barry

Fiction

Macker's Garden, (Dublin: Co-Op Books, 1982).

Time Out of Mind [&] *Strappado Square,* (Dublin: Wolfhound, 1984).

Elsewhere: The Adventures of Belemus, (Portlaoise, Ireland: Dolmen, 1985; Gerrard's Cross: Colin Smythe, 1997).

The Engine of Owl-Light, (Manchester: Carcanet, 1987; Kent: Paladin, 1988).

The Whereabouts of Eneas McNulty, (London: Picador, 1998).

Annie Dunne, (London: Faber, 2002; 2003).

A Long Long Way, (London: Faber, 2005).

Poetry

The Water-Colourist, (Portlaoise, Ireland: Dolmen, 1983).

The Rhetorical Town, (Portlaoise, Ireland: Dolmen, 1985).

Fanny Hawke Goes to the Mainland Forever, (Dublin: Raven Arts, 1987; 1989).

Poems

in:

The New Younger Irish Poets, ed. Gerald Dawe (Belfast: Blackstaff, 1991): 'Hermaphroditus', 44; 'Summer desk', 44; 'At a gate of St. Stephen's Green', 45; 'Fanny Hawke goes to the mainland forever', 46; 'Lines discovered under the foundations of Dublin in a language neither Irish nor English', 47; 'Trooper O'Hara at the Indian Wars', 48.

Poems from *The Rhetorical Town* in *The Field Day Anthology of Irish Writing,* Vol. 3, ed. Seamus Deane, (Derry: Field Day; Cork: Cork University

Press, 1991): 'The Tree Alphabet', 1426-1427; 'The Real Snow', 1427; 'The February Town', 1427. Also biographical info. 1316 and 1436.
The Pinkening Boy, (Dublin: New Island, 2004).

Plays

Pentagonal Dream, (Performed only. First produced by Operating Theatre at The Damer Hall, St. Stephen's Green, 1986).
Boss Grady's Boys, (Dublin: Raven Arts, 1989).
Prayers of Sherkin and Boss Grady's Boys: Two Plays by Sebastian Barry, (London: Methuen Drama, 1991).
The Steward of Christendom, (London: Methuen Drama in association with the Royal Court Theatre, 1995).
The Only True History of Lizzie Finn; *The Steward of Christendom*; *White Woman Street: three plays by Sebastian Barry,* (London: Methuen Drama, 1995).
Plays 1: Boss Grady's Boys; Prayers of Sherkin; White Woman Street; The Only True History of Lizzie Finn; The Steward of Christendom, (London: Methuen, 1997).
Our Lady of Sligo, (London: Methuen, 1998).
Hinterland, (London: Faber, 2002.)
The House of Bernarda Alba, translation and adaptation of the play by Federico García Lorca, (Performed only. First produced by the Abbey Theatre, 2003).
Whistling Psyche [&] *Fred and Jane,* (London: Faber, 2004).

Miscellaneous.

'The Beast', [Short Story] *Irish Press,* 3 March 1979, p.9.
Ed. & Intro.,*The Inherited Boundaries, Younger Poets of the Republic of Ireland,* (Portlaoise, Ireland: Dolmen, 1986).
'Fanny Hawke Goes to the Mainland Forever', *Stand Magazine,* 29:4, (1988), p.46.
'The Only True History of Lizzie Finn, by Herself', *Stand Magazine,* 29:4, (1988), p.45.
'The man in the back row has a question: IV', *Paris Review,* 142, (1997), pp.226-244.
Foreword in *Far from the Land: Contemporary Irish Plays,* ed. by John Fairleigh, (London: Methuen, 1998).
'Holding History to the Light', [reflections on *The Steward of Christendom* and *Our Lady of Sligo*] *Irish Theatre Magazine,* ed. Karen Fricker, 1:2, (Spring 1999), pp.13-17.
Preface to *The Essential Jennifer Johnston,* (London: Review, 1999; London: Headline, 2000).

'Dying to Mourn: Sebastian Barry on Donal McCann', [a response to the actor's death] *The Irish Times Magazine*, 17 November 2001.

Extract from *Annie Dunne*, *Dublin Review*, 5, (Winter 2001-02), pp.90-96.

Selected Critical Bibliography on Barry

Reviews

Gerald Dawe, 'A New Generation of Poets', [review of *The Rhetorical Town*] *Irish Literary Supplement*, Fall 1985.

Maurice Harmon, review of *The Inherited Boundaries*, *Irish University Review*, 16:2, (Autumn-Winter 1986), pp.234-237.

Fintan O' Toole, review of *Boss Grady's Boys*, *Sunday Tribune*, 28 August 1988. repr. *Critical Moments: Fintan O'Toole on Modern Irish Theatre*, eds. Julia Furay and Redmond O'Hanlon, (Dublin: Carysfort Press, 2003), pp.66-67.

Maurice Harmon, review of *Fanny Hawke Goes to the Mainland Forever*, *Irish University Review*, 20:1, (Spring-Summer 1990), pp.202-203.

Armita Wallace, 'The Prodigious Sebastian Barry', *The Irish Times*, 17 November 1990.

Fintan O' Toole, review of *Prayers of Sherkin*, *The Irish Times*, 24 November 1990. repr. *Critical Moments*, pp.109-112.

-----, 'Sebastian Barry', [short commentary on Barry's work] *The Irish Times*, 13 June 1992. repr. *Critical Moments*, pp.313-318.

Michael Billington, 'Family Tree Surgery: Donal McCann astonishes in *The Steward of Christendom*', *The Guardian* [Features], 5 April 1995.

Fintan O' Toole, review of *The Steward of Christendom*, *The Irish Times*, 9 May 1995. repr. *Critical Moments*, pp.150-152.

Benedict Nightingale, 'A Great Actor Meets an Emotional Challenge', [article on Donal McCann with reference to *The Steward of Christendom*] *The New York Times*, 19 January 1997.

Ben Brantley, 'A Life and a Country Stripped of Illusions', [review of *The Steward of Christendom*] *The New York Times*, 22 January 1997.

Helena Mulkearns, 'High Drama in New York', [review of *The Steward of Christendom*] *The Irish Times*, 25 January, 1997.

Vincent Canby, 'Out of the Din of Madness, the Music of Words', [review of *The Steward of Christendom*] *The New York Times*, 2 February 1997.

Maggie Gee, review of *Prayers of Sherkin*, *Times Literary Supplement*, 6 June 1997.

Kevin Myers, *'Irishman's Diary'*, [on the publication of *Plays 1*] *The Irish Times*, 28 June 1997.

Mary Morrissey, *'The Song of Wandering Eneas'*, [review of *The Whereabouts of Eneas McNulty*] *The Irish Times*, 28 February 1998.

Lloyd Rose, 'The Studio's Irish Times', [review of *The Steward of Christendom*] *The Washington Post*, 7 April 1998.

Bob Mondello, 'Second Chances', [review of *The Steward of Christendom*] *Washington City Paper*, 10 April 1998.

Sarah Kaufman, 'Memorable Celtic Themes', [review of *The Steward of Christendom*] *The Washington Post*, 24 April 1998.

Lindsay Duguid, 'Ireland, Where is that Country?', [review of *Our Lady of Sligo*] *Times Literary Supplement*, 1 May 1998.

Benedict Nightingale, review of *Our Lady of Sligo*, *The New York Times*, 10 May 1998.

Aoibeann Sweeney, 'The Wanderer', [review of *The Whereabouts of Eneas McNulty*] *The New York Times*, 18 October 1998.

Susan Dooley, 'Wandering Towards Redemption', [review of *The Whereabouts of Eneas McNulty*] *The Washington Post*, 29 October 1998.

Mel Gussow, 'An Irish Writer Redeems Black Sheep', [review of *The Whereabouts of Eneas McNulty* in reference to other works including an interview with Sebastian Barry] *The New York Times*, 28 December 1998.

Eileen Battersby, book notice on *The Whereabouts of Aeneas McNulty*, *The Irish Times*, 3 April 1999.

Ben Brantley, 'One Life's Restless End', [review of *Our Lady of Sligo*] *The New York Times*, 21 April 2000.

Matt Wolf, 'A Showpiece for Sinead Cusack', [article on Sinead Cusack in *Our Lady of Sligo*] *The New York Times*, 23 April 2000.

John Lahr, review of *Our Lady of Sligo*, *New Yorker*, 8 May 2000.

John Steel, review of *Our Lady of Sligo*, *Irish Theatre Magazine*, ed. Karen Fricker, 2:6, (Summer 2000), pp, 77-79.

D.J.R. Bruckner, 'Saving Scenes Too Vibrant to be Dreams', [review of *Boss Grady's Boys*] *The New York Times*, 7 April 2001.

Helen Meany, 'Political *Hinterland*: trials and tribunals', [review of *Hinterland*] *The Irish Times*, 19 January 2002.

Eileen Battersby, 'Poor Drama and Bad Manners', [review of *Hinterland*] *The Irish Times* [Weekend], 9 February 2002.

Emer O' Kelly, review of *Hinterland*, *Sunday Independent*, 10 February 2002.

-----, 'Barry's Chilling Study of CJ is Uneven', [review of *Hinterland*] *Sunday Independent*, 10 February 2002.

John Waters, 'Half-baked Ideas about Haughey', [review of *Hinterland*] *The Irish Times*, 25 February 2002.

C. L. Dallat, 'Hiding Behind the Outskirts', [review of *Hinterland*] *Times Literary Supplement*, 22 March 2002.

Patrick Lonergan, 'Tackling a Live Subject: the Hinterland Controversy', *Irish Theatre Magazine*, ed. Karen Fricker, 3:11, (Spring 2002), pp.8-11 .

Gerry Dukes, review of *Hinterland*, *Irish Theatre Magazine*, 3:11, (Spring 2002), pp.101-102.

Declan Kiberd, review of *Annie Dunne*, *The Irish Times* [Weekend], 18 May 2002.

Brendan Glacken, 'Happy Playwrights – enough to make you very nervous', [in reference to reactions to *Hinterland*] *The Irish Times*, 17 June 2002.

Eamonn Sweeney, 'Busted Flush?', [review of *Annie Dunne*] *The Guardian*, 29 June 2002.

Paul Murphy, review of *White Woman Street*, *Irish Theatre Magazine*, 3:12, (Summer 2002), pp.125-127.

Emily Gordon, 'Dances With Hens,' [review of *Annie Dunne*] *The New York Times*, 15 September 2002.

Max Winter, 'Tales With Protagonists Who Are Down But Not Out', [review of *Annie Dunne*] *The Washington Post*, 22 September 2002.

Derek West, review of *Fred and Jane* and *Our Lady of* Sligo, *Irish Theatre Magazine*, 3:13, (Winter 2002), pp.93-96.

Helen Meaney, review of *The House of Bernarda Alba*, *Irish Theatre Magazine*, 3:15, (Summer 2003), pp.63-65.

Michael Billington, review of *Whistling Psyche*, *The Guardian*, 13 May 2004.

Nicholas de Jongh, 'Purgatorial Pathos in Full Bloom', [review of *Whistling Psyche*] *Evening Standard*, 13 May 2004.

Susannah Clapp, 'Ten out of Tena', [review of *Whistling Psyche*] *The Observer*, 16 May 2004.

John Peter, review of *Whistling Psyche*, *Sunday Times*, 17 May 2004.

Mary Russell, 'No Wonder Sebastian Barry Was Intrigued By His Namesake', *The Irish Times* [Weekend], 28 June 2004.

John Kenny, 'His Heart is There: Sebastian Barry's challenging novel succeeds on almost all fronts', [review of *A Long Long Way*] *The Irish Times* [Weekend], 26 March 2005.

Laura Barber, 'Hear the Bleak Ballads of Willie Dunne', [review of *A Long Long Way*] *The Observer* [Review], 3 April 2005.

Mick Heaney, 'Fresh Dispatches from the family war front', [review of *A Long Long Way*] *The Sunday Times* [Culture], 10 April 2005.

Interviews

'It's Ancestor Worship, But of a Dramatic Sort', interview with Sebastian Barry by Matt Wolf, *The New York Times*, 19 January 1997.

'Singing Across the Gaps', interview with Sebastian Barry by Helen Meany, *The Irish Times* [Arts], 19 February 1998.

'My Family, the Outcasts', interview with Sebastian Barry by John Cunningham, *The Guardian* [Features], 25 March 1998.

'Terrible Tales at Bedtime', interview with Sebastian Barry by John Whitley, *Daily Telegraph*, 18 April 1998.

'An Interview with Sebastian Barry', interview by Shannon Hopkins and Virginia Mack, *Irish Literary Supplement*, 18(1), (1999), pp.24-26.

'Sebastian Barry in Conversation with Ger FitzGibbon', interview in eds. Eamonn Jordan, Ger FitzGibbon and Lilian Chambers, *Theatre Talk: Conversations with Irish Theatre Practitioners* (Dublin: Carysfort Press, 2001), pp.16-28.

'Political *Hinterland*', feature interview with Max Stafford-Clarke, director of *Hinterland*, *The Irish Times* [Weekend], 19 January 2002.

'Backlash Left Irish Writer in Fear: Dramatist tells of extraordinary reaction to satirical work about political corruption in Ireland', interview with Sebastian Barry by Angelique Chrisafis, *The Guardian*, 8 June 2002.

'The Anguish that Led to *Hinterland*', interview with Sebastian Barry by Michael Ross, *The Sunday Times* [Culture], 9 June 2002.

'Barry Recalls Upset at Criticism of his Play [*Hinterland*]', *The Irish Times*, 10 June 2002.

'Really All Danger', interview with Sebastian Barry by Maria Kurdi, *New Hibernia Review: A Quarterly Record of Irish Studies*, Spring 8:1, (2004), pp.41-53.

Criticism

Achilles, Jochen, '"Homesick for Abroad": the transition from national to cultural identity in contemporary Irish drama', *Modern Drama*, 38:4, (1995), pp.435-449.

Bertha, Csilla, '"A Haunted Group of Plays": The Drama of Sebastian Barry', *Twentieth-Century Theatre and Drama in English: Festschrift for Heinz Kosok on the Occasion of his 65th Birthday*, ed. Jürgen Kamm, (Trier: Wissenschaftlicher Verlag Trier, 1999), pp.527-544.

Cullingford, Elizabeth, 'Colonial Policing: *The Steward of Christendom* and *The Whereabouts of Eneas Mc Nulty*' in *Éire-Ireland*, 39:3&4, (Fall-Winter 2004), pp.11-37.

Cumings, Scott T., 'The End of History', *A Century of Irish Drama*, eds. Stephen Watt, Eileen Morgan, Shakir Mustafa, (Bloomington: Indiana University Press, 2000), pp.291-301.

Deane, Paul, 'Rebels without a Cause: Sebastian Barry's *The Whereabouts of Eneas McNulty*', *Notes on Modern Irish Literature*, 13, (2001), pp.28-32.

Dumay, Emile Jean, 'Passe et passage dans le theatre de Sebastian Barry', *Publication des Groupes de Recherches Anglo-Americaines de l'Université Francois Rabelais de Tours* (GRAAT), 19, (1998), pp.63-74.

Duncan, Dawn, 'Barry Rows forward with Prayers of Sherkin', *Barcelona English Language and Literature Studies* (BELLS), 11, (2000), pp.33-40.

Fitzgibbon, Ger, 'The Poetic Theatre of Sebastian Barry', *Theatre Stuff: Critical Essays on Contemporary Irish Theatre*, ed. Eamonn Jordan, (Dublin: Carysfort Press, 2000), pp.224-235.

Foster, Roy, 'Introduction' to *Our Lady of Sligo*, (London: Methuen, 1998).

-----, 'Lost Futures', *The Irish Review*, No. 22, eds. Kevin Barry, Tom Dunne and Enda Longley; guest ed. Frank McGuinness, (Summer 1998), pp.23-27.

-----, programme note to *Whistling* Psyche, directed by Robert Delamere, Almeida Theatre, London, May 2004.

Gleitman, Claire, 'Reconstructing History in the Irish History Play', *The Cambridge Companion to Twentieth Century Irish Drama*, ed. Shaun Richards, (Cambridge: Cambridge University Press, 2004), pp.224-229.

Grene, Nicolas, *The Politics of Irish Drama, Plays in Context from Boucicault to Friel*, (Cambridge: Cambridge University Press, 2000), pp.242-243.

Haughey, Jim, 'Standing in the Gap: Sebastian Barry's Revisionist Theater', *Colby Library Quarterly*, 34:4, (1998), pp.290-302.

Lynch, Vivian Valvano, '"Who is the father of any son?": Sebastian Barry's *The Steward of Christendom*'. *Beyond Borders: IASIL Essays on Modern Irish Writing*, ed. Neil Sammells, (Bath: Sulis Press, 2004), pp.239-248.

Mahony, Christina Hunt, 'Barry, McPherson and McDonagh in the States: cops, critics and cripples', *Irish Literary Supplement*, 17:2, (1998), pp.6-8.

-----, *Contemporary Irish Literature: Transforming Tradition*, (London: Macmillan, 1999), pp.182-190.

Murray, Christopher, '"Such a Sense of Home": The Poetic Drama of Sebastian Barry', *Colby Quarterly*, 22:4, (1991), pp.242-248.

-----, *Twentieth Century Irish Drama, Mirror up to a Nation*, (Manchester: Manchester University Press, 1997), pp.243-244.

O' Toole, Fintan, 'Introduction' to *Plays 1: Boss Grady's boys; Prayers of Sherkin; White Woman Street; The Only True History of Lizzie Finn; The Steward of Christendom* (London: Methuen, 1997).

-----, *Critical Moments: Fintan O'Toole on Modern Irish Theatre*, eds. Julia Furay and Redmond O'Hanlon, (Dublin: Carysfort, 2003).

Pelletier, Martine, 'D'ombre et de lumière : *Prayers of Sherkin* de Sebastian Barry', *Études-Anglaises*, 56:2, (Apr-June 2003), pp.194-205.

Wehrmann, Jürgen, 'Revising the Nation: Globalization and Fragmentation of Irish History in Sebastian Barry's Plays', *Contemporary Drama in English 10: Global Challenges and Regional Responses in Contemporary Drama in English*, eds. Jochen Achilles, Ina

Production Details of the Premieres of Sebastian Barry's Plays.

The Pentagonal Dream, produced by Operating Theatre. First presented at The Dame Hall, St. Stephen's Green, Dublin, March 1986.

Performer	Olwen Fouéré
Director	David Heap
Set Designer	John Comiskey
Lighting Designer	John Comiskey
Costumes	Clodagh McCormick
Music Composition	Roger Doyle

Boss Grady's Boys, produced by The Abbey Theatre. First presented at The Abbey Theatre, Dublin, on 24 August 1988.

Mrs Swift	Marie Kean
Josey	Eamon Kelly
Father	Oliver Maguire
Mr Reagan	Gerard McSorley
Girl	Gina Moxley
Mother	Bríd Ní Neachtain
Mick	Jim Norton
Mrs Molloy	Maureen Toal

Director	Caroline FitzGerald
Set Designer	Carol Betera
Lighting Designer	Tony Wakefield
Costume Designer	Carol Betera and Rachel Pigot
Sound	Nuala Golden
Music	Thomas McLaughlin

Prayers of Sherkin, produced by The Abbey Theatre. First presented on the Peacock stage at The Abbey Theatre, Dublin, on 22 November 1990.

John	Alan Barry
Fanny	Alison Deegan
Jesse	Phelim Drew
Patrick	Brendan Gleeson
Hannah	Doreen Hepburn
Mr Moore	Eamon Kelly
Meg	Ruth McCabe
Singer	Gina Moxley
Stephen	Wesley Murphy
Sarah	Joan O'Hara
Matt Purdy	Donal O'Kelly
Eoghan	Owen Roe

Director	Caroline FitzGerald
Designer	Bronwen Casson
Lighting	Tony Wakefield
Sound	Dave Nolan
Music	Shaun Davey

White Woman Street, produced by The Bush Theatre. First presented at The Bush Theatre, London, on 23 April 1992.

Mo	Roy Hanlon
Blakely	George Irving
Clarke	Kevork Malikyan
James	Patrick Miller
Trooper	Jim Norton
Nathaniel	David Yip
Director	Caroline FitzGerald
Designer	Kendra Ullyart
Lighting Designer	Tina MacHugh
Music	Shaun Davey

The Steward of Christendom, co-produced by The Royal Court Theatre and Out of Joint. First presented at the Royal Court Theatre, London, on 30 March 1995.

Smith	Kieran Ahern
Annie	Tina Kellegher
Maud	Cara Kelly
Thomas Dunne	Donal McCann
Mrs O'Dea	Maggie McCarthy
Dolly	Aisling McGuckin
Matt	Rory Murray
Recruit	Rory Murray
Willie	Jonathan Newman
Director	Max Stafford-Clark
Designer	Julian McGowan
Lighting Designer	Johanna Town
Sound Designer	Paul Arditti
Music	Shaun Davey

The Only True History of Lizzie Finn, produced by The Abbey Theatre. First presented at The Abbey Theatre, Dublin, on 4 October 1995.

Musician	Greg Boland
Robert Gibson	Lorcan Cranitch
Lizzie Finn	Alison Deegan
Musician	Anthony Drennan
Britannia	Lynda Gough
Annie Oakley	Lynda Gough
Colonel Cody	Roy Hanlon
Lord Castlemaine	Roy Hanlon
Zulu Warrior	James Hosty
Indian	James Hosty
Bartholomew Grady	Eamon Kelly
Cavalry Man	Darren Lawless
Pierrot	Darren Lawless
Ballerina	Shereen Lawlor
Miss America	Shereen Lawlor
Indian	Glen Mulhern
Ventriloquist	Glen Mulhern
Theresa	Fionnuala Murphy
Tilly	Fionnuala Murphy
Jelly Jane	Marion O'Dwyer
Lady Castlemaine	Marion O'Dwyer
Lucinda Gibson	Joan O'Hara
Pearley Queen	Liz Roche
Squaw	Liz Roche
Pearley King	Pepe Roche
Sitting Bull	Pepe Roche
Birdy Doyle	Birdy Sweeney
Factotum	Birdy Sweeney
Rector	Birdy Sweeney

Director	Patrick Mason
Set Designer	Joe Vanek
Lighting Designer	Mick Hughes
Costume Designer	Joan O'Clery

Sound	Dave Nolan
Choreographer	David Bolger
Music	Shaun Davey

Our Lady of Sligo, co-produced by Out of Joint and Royal National Theatre, First presented on tour at the Oxford Playhouse, England, on 26 March 1998.

Joanie	Catherine Cusack
Mai O'Hara	Sinead Cusack
Sister	Andrea Irvine
Jack	Nigel Terry
Dada	Harry Towb
Maria	June Watson
Director	Max Stafford-Clark
Designer	Julian McGowan
Lighting Designer	Johanna Town
Sound Designer	Paul Arditti
Music	Conn Buckeridge

Hinterland, co-produced by The Abbey Theatre and Royal National Theatre and Out of Joint. First presented at the Octagon Theatre, Bolton, England, on 17 January 2002.

Cornelius	Kieran Ahern
Jack	Phelim Drew
Stephen	James Hayes
Connie	Anna Healy
Johnny Silvester	Patrick Malahide
Aisling	Lucianne McEvoy
Daisy	Dearbhla Molloy
Director	Max Stafford-Clark
Designer	Es Devlin

Lighting	Johanna Town
Sound	Paul Arditti
Fight Director	Terry King
Music	Paddy Cunneen

Fred and Jane, produced by Bewley's Café Theatre. First presented at Bewley's Café Theatre, Dublin, on 21 August 2002.

Anna Nagle	Mary McEvoy
Beatrice Dunne	Colette Proctor

Director	Caroline FitzGerald
Designer	Emma Cullen
Lighting	Moyra Darcy

The House of Bernarda Alba, produced by the Abbey Theatre. First presented at The Abbey Theatre, Dublin, on 14 April 2003.

Village Woman	Glynis Casson
Adela	Isabel Claffey
Maid	Emma Colohan
Village Woman	Eileen Fennell
Angustias	Olwen Fouéré
Village Woman	Lynda Gough
Martirio	Andrea Irvine
Village Woman	Lisa Lambe
Bernarda Alba	Rosaleen Linehan
Poncia	Ruth McCabe
Village Woman	Eithne McGuinness
Prudencia	Bernadette McKenna
Village Woman	Marie McNamara
Magdalena	Justine Mitchell
Amelia	Gertrude Montgomery
Village Woman	Franchine Mulrooney

Village Woman	Deirdre Ní Chinneide
Beggar	Sile Nugent
Maria Josefa	Joan O'Hara
Village Woman	Billie Traynor
Director	Martin Drury
Set Designer	Francis O'Connor
Lighting Designer	Davy Cunningham
Costume Designer	Joan O'Clery
Sound Designer	Cormac Carroll
Movement Director	Liz Roche
Fight Director	Donal O'Farrell
Composer	Nico Brown

Whistling Psyche, produced at the Almeida Theatre, London, on 12 May 2004.

Dr Barry	Kathryn Hunter
Florence Nightingale	Claire Bloom
Direction	Robert Delamere
Design	Simon Higlett
Lighting	Tim Mitchell
Projection Design	Jon Driscoll
Music	Ross Lorraine

Contributors

- **Peter Denman** is Dean of Arts and Senior Lecturer in English at the National University of Ireland Maynooth. A former editor of *Poetry Ireland Review* he has broadcast and written articles on Irish poetry, and a monograph on Samuel Ferguson.
- **Éilís Ní Dhuibhne** is the author of fiction, drama and children's books, including *The Bray House*, *The Dancers Dancing* and *The Inland Ice*. She is a member of Aosdána, and is the recipient of two Bisto awards for children's fiction and the Stewart Parker Prize for Drama. She took her PhD in Irish Folklore at UCD, and is a curator at The National Library of Ireland.
- **Bruce Stewart** lectures in Irish literary history at the University of Ulster, where he is also Director of the EIRData Internet Project. He is Literary Advisor to the Princess Grace Irish Library in Monaco, and has edited a series of volumes of symposia which have taken place there. A frequent contributor to Irish Studies journals, he has published on a wide range of authors and periods. He is the assistant editor of *The Oxford Companion to Irish Literature*.
- **David Cregan, OSA,** is Assistant Professor in the Theatre Department at Villanova University in Pennsylvania. He recently received his PhD from the Samuel

Beckett School of Drama at Trinity College, Dublin, and has published articles on Frank McGuinness in *Modern Drama*, *Australasian Drama Studies*, and the forthcoming volume of *New Voices in Irish Criticism 5*.

- **Christina Hunt Mahony** is the Director of the Center for Irish Studies at The Catholic University of America in Washington, DC, the author of *Contemporary Irish Literature: Transforming Tradition*, and has written on Yeats, Louis MacNeice and contemporary Irish poets and dramatists. She is editing the proceedings of The Forum on the Future of Irish Studies, which convened in Florence in 2005.
- **Anthony Roche** is Senior Lecturer in Anglo-Irish Literature and Drama at University College, Dublin. He is the author of *Contemporary Irish Drama: from Beckett to McGuinness*. A former editor of *Irish University Review* he is now the director of The Synge Summer School, and currently preparing *The Cambridge Companion to Brian Friel*.
- **John Wilson Foster** is Professor Emeritus of the University of British Columbia in Vancouver. He is the author of *Forces and Themes in Ulster Fiction*, *Fictions of the Irish Literary Revival: A Changeling Art* and *Colonial Consequences: Essays on Irish Literature and Culture*. He non-literary writing includes *Nature in Ireland: A Scientific and Cultural History* and *The Titanic Complex*.
- **Elizabeth Butler Cullingford** is the Jane and Rowland Blumberg Centennial Professor in English Literature at the University of Texas at Austin. Her publications include *Ireland's Others: Ethnicity and Gender in Irish Literature and Popular Culture*; *Gender and History in Yeats' Love Poetry*; and *Yeats, Ireland and Fascism*.
- **Nicholas Grene** is Professsor of English Literature at Trinity College, Dublin. His most recent books include *The Politics of Irish Drama* and *Shakespeare's Serial History*

Plays. He is the editor of *Interpreting Synge: Essays from the Synge Summer School*, and co-editor, with Chris Morash, of *Irish Theatre on Tour*.

- **Roy Foster** is Carroll Professor of Irish History at Hertford College, Oxford. His work includes *Modern Ireland 1600-1972*, *The Oxford Illustrated History of Ireland. Paddy and Mr. Punch*, *The Irish Story: Telling Tales and Making it up in Ireland*, and the authoritative two-volume biography *W. B. Yeats: A Life*.
- **Colm Tóibín**'s recent novel *The Master* was nominated for The Booker Prize. His other novels include *The South*, *The Heather Blazing*, and *The Story of the Night*. He is also the author of nonfiction volumes including *The Sign of the Cross: Travels in Catholic Europe* and *Lady Gregory's Toothbrush*. His play *Beauty in a Broken Place* appeared on the Peacock stage during the centenary of the National Theatre in 2004.
- **Claire Gleitman** is Associate Professor of English at Ithaca College in New York. She has published in *Eire/Ireland*, *Modern Drama*, *Comparative Drama*, and the *Canadian Journal of Irish Studies*. Her work on Sebastian Barry and contemporary Irish dramatists is included in *The Cambridge Companion to Twentieth-Century Irish Drama* and *The Concise Companion to Contemporary British and Irish Drama*.
- **Fintan Walsh** holds an MPhil in Irish theatre and film from the School of Drama Trinity College, Dublin, where he is completing his PhD on issues of masculinity in contemporary drama, live art and film, and also teaching Irish theatre.

Endnotes

---

1 *The Water-Colourist* (Dublin: Dolmen Press, 1983); *The Rhetorical Town: Poems* (Dublin: Dolmen Press, 1985); *Fanny Hawke Goes to the Mainland Forever* (Dublin: Raven Arts Press, 1989).

2 *The Inherited Boundaries: Younger Poets of the Republic of Ireland*, (Dublin: Dolmen Press, 1986).

3 *The Pinkening Boy* (Dublin: New Island, 2004).

4 Christopher Murray, '"Such a Sense of Home": The Poetic Drama of Sebastian Barry', *Colby Quarterly* 27 (Dec. 1991) pp.242-47; Ger Fitzgibbon, 'The Poetic Theatre of Sebastian Barry', in Eamonn Jordan, ed., *Theatre Stuff: Critical Essays on Contemporary Irish Theatre* (Dublin: Carysfort Press, 2000) pp.224-35.

5 Terry Eagleton, 'From the Irish' *Poetry Review* 75, 2 (August 1985) pp.64-5.

6 Terence Brown 'Poetry and Partition: A Personal View', *Krino* 2 (Autumn, 1986) pp.17-23.

7 Angela Bourke, *The Burning of Bridget Cleary: A True Story*, (Pimlico: London, 1999)

8 Anne Ferry, *The Title to the Poem* (Stanford CA: Stanford U.P., 1996) p.211

9 James Berry, *Tales of the West of Ireland*, ed. Gertrude M. Horgan, (Dublin: Dolmen Press, 1966), pp.42-4.

10 Sebastian Barry, *Macker's Garden.* Dublin: Irish Writer's Co-Op, 1982.

11 Conversation with Sebastian Barry, Franco-Irish Literary Festival, 16 April 2005.

12 P.29. Not mentioning the ages of the characters is in itself an indication, if any were needed, that Barry did not target solely or primarily a juvenile audience for this book. A golden rule of children's literature is that the characters' ages be clearly specified.

The editor of my first book for children told me, 'Put their ages on the first page.'

[13] The names Nessie and Annesley appear in Barry's work, and in a probable autobiographical context, as early as 1979 in a story, 'The Beast', published in the *Irish Press*. See Nicholas Grene's essay in this volume.

[14] Although some very recent novels for young people deal with issues of homosexuality as well as heterosexuality, this was not the case in 1982, when Sebastian Barry published *Macker's Garden.*

[15] *Elsewhere: The Adventures of Belemus*. (Dublin: Dolmen Press, Brogeen Books), 1985.

[16] Francie Brady, in Patrick McCabe's *The Butcher Boy*, makes similar use of vivid free association, contributing much to the stylistic richness of that novel.

[17] *Belemus* appeared just a few years too early to benefit from that movement, and the concomitant emergence of media attention, critical research, and prizes for children's fiction.

[18] 'The Divided Mind', *Poetry and Ireland since 1800: A Source Book* (London: Routledge, 1988), p.215.

[19] *The Engine of Owl-Light* (London: Paladin, 1988), p.193.

[20] *At Swim-Two-Birds*, (Harmondsworth: Penguin, 1967), p.9.

[21] The passage is from *Christian Morals* (1716), Part III, Sect. 29, and is cited in the novel without a bibliographical reference other than the author's name.

[22] See Dermot Bolger, *Invisible Dublin: A Journey through the Dublin Suburbs* (Dublin: Raven Arts, 1991).

[23] Barry, *Boss Grady's Boys* in *Plays: 1* (London: Methuen Drama, 1997), p.5.

[24] Barry, *Prayers of Sherkin* in *Plays: 1* (London: Methuen Drama, 1997), p.53.

[25] Bert O. States, *Great Reckonings in Little Rooms: On the Phenomenology of Theater* (Berkley: University of California Press, 1987), p.103.

[26] ibid., p.104.

[27] Barry, *Whistling Psyche* (London: Faber & Faber, 2004), p.9.

[28] Barry, *Fred and Jane* (London: Faber & Faber, 2004), p.69.

[29] Frank McGuinness, *Observe the Sons of Ulster Marching Towards the Somme* in *Plays 1* (London: Faber & Faber, 1996), p.145.

[30] Marina Carr, *On Raftery's Hill* (Loughcrew, Ireland: Gallery, 2000), p.35.

[31] Jean-Paul Sartre, *Existentialism and Human Emotions* (New York: Philosophical Library, 1957), pp.15-16.

[32] Richard Schechner and Mady Shuman, eds., *Ritual, Play, and*

Performance: Readings in *Social Sciences/Theatre*, (New York: Seabury, 1976), p.195.

33 Victor Turner, *From Ritual to Theatre: The Human Seriousness of Play* (New York: Performing Arts Journal Publications, 1982), p.12.

34 Robert Welch, ed., *Irish Writers and Religion*, (Savage, Maryland: Barnes and Noble, 1992), pp.ix-xiii.

35 Turner (1982), p.41.

36 Edith Turner and Victor Turner, *Image and Pilgrimage in Christian Culture: Anthropological Perspectives* (New York: Columbia University Press, 1978), p.3.

37 Sebastian Barry. Email from the author. 18 January 2005.

38 Barry, *Prayers of Sherkin* [&] *Boss Grady's Boys* (London: Methuen Drama, 1991), p.62.

39 Barry, *Annie Dunne* (London: Faber & Faber, 2002), p.43.

40 Barry, *A Long Long Way* (London: Faber & Faber, 2005), p.121.

41 Barry, *The Whereabouts of Eneas McNulty* (London: Picador, 1998), p.53-55.

42 Because of the Abbey Theatre's rejection, Sean O'Casey's Great War play, *The Silver* Tassie(1928), was not seen in Ireland until 1935 and only fitfully thereafter. Frank McGuinness' Great War play, *Observe the Sons of Ulster Marching Towards the Somme* (1985), has tended to be discussed in the context of Northern Ireland rather than the Great War.

43 Fintan O'Toole, 'Introduction: A True History of Lies', Sebastian Barry, *Plays 1* (London: Methuen, 1997), p.vii.

44 Though they are Catholic and not upper class, the Dunne family share some features of fate and attitude with the descending or superannuated Anglo-Irish gentry familiarly depicted in literature: they are passive, graceful, distracted, have declined into eccentricity or even a degree of madness, and are, finally, oblivious to the modernizing world around them. (These features are continued in the novel *Annie Dunne*, 2002: see below.)

45 Gerald Griffin, *The Dead March Past: An Autobiographical Saga* (London: Macmillan, 1937).

46 Ella MacMahon, *Irish Vignettes*, (London: John Lane, 1928).

47 'An Irishwoman', 'The Terror by Night', *Blackwood's Edinburgh Magazine* 208 (1920), 38.

48 Sebastian Barry, *The Steward of Christendom* (London: Royal Court Theatre & Methuen, 1995), p.50. The playwright's 'Notes on the Play' precede the text (n.p.).

49 James H. Murphy, *Abject Loyalty: Nationalism and Monarchy in Ireland* (Washington DC: Catholic University of America Press, 2001), p.xii.

[50] Annie, like her father, remembers with fondness an old Ireland under British rule, an Ireland that 'was another Ireland altogether', *Annie Dunne* (London: Faber, 2002), p.95.

[51] Michael Neill, '"Servile Ministers": *Othello, King Lear* and the Sacralization of Service', The 2003 Garnett Sedgewick Memorial Lecture (Vancouver: Ronsdale Press, 2004), p.21.

[52] Gonne had a different queen in mind. The mirror opposite of Annie Dunne, she was the daughter of an Irish colonel in the British Army, and acted as hostess for him in Dublin Castle. After his death she became an Irish republican and an anglophobe and during the Great War campaigned against conscription in Ireland.

[53] Hindsight allows Barry to assign to an unnamed character whom Thomas Dunne meets in 1922 the prediction that his grandsons 'will be feral in this garden' (p.50): an allusion perhaps to the Troubles that broke out in the 1970s and kept alive by the activities of those who saw themselves as heirs to Collins and De Valera.

[54] Michael Neill, pp.11, 15, 14.

[55] *Annie Dunne*, p.95.

[56] Kazuo Ishiguro, *The Remains of the Day* (1989; Toronto: Penguin, 1990), p.115.

[57] *Annie Dunne*, p.95.

[58] Sebastian Barry, *Plays I* (London: Methuen, 1997). Subsequently referred to in the text as *SC*.

[59] Barry, *The Whereabouts of Eneas McNulty* (London: Picador, 1998). Subsequent reference *WEM*'.

[60] See Nicholas Grene, *The Politics of Irish Drama: Plays in Context from Boucicault to Friel* (Cambridge: Cambridge University Press, 1999), pp.242-60, for an excellent extended comparison of Barry and McGuinness.

[61] Sebastian Barry Papers. Drafts of *The Steward of Christendom* and *The Whereabouts of Eneas McNulty*, miscellaneous notes, introductions, and correspondence, contained in a series of boxes numbered R 14839, Harry Ransom Humanities Research Center, University of Texas at Austin. Subsequently referred to in the text as *Papers*.

[62] Helen Meany, 'Singing Across the Gaps' (Interview with Barry), *Irish Times* 19 February 1998, 16.

[63] *King Lear*, III.iv.

[64] ibid.

[65] Kevin Kenny, 'Ireland and the British Empire: An Introduction', *Ireland and the British Empire*, ed. Kevin Kenny (Oxford: Oxford University Press, 2004), p.16.

[66] Meany, p.16.

[67] John Cunningham, 'My family, the Outcasts' (Interview with Barry), *The Guardian*, 25 March 1998, p.14.

[68] Jim Haughey, 'Standing in the Gap: Sebastian Barry's Revisionist Theater', *Colby Quarterly* 34.4 (1998), pp.290-302.

[69] Padraig Yeates, *Lockout: Dublin 1913* (New York: St. Martin's, 2000), p.66.

[70] ibid., pp.58-75.

[71] ibid., p.66.

[72] Jim Herlihy, *The Dublin Metropolitan Police: a Short History and Genealogical Guide* (Dublin: Four Courts, 2001), p.62

[73] Jim Herlihy, 'An Arresting Development', *The Stage* 5 October 2000, 11.

[74] Elizabeth Cullingford, *Ireland's Others: Ethnicity and Gender in Irish Literature and Popular Culture* (Notre Dame, Ind.: University of Notre Dame Press in association with Field Day, 2001), pp.213-33.

[75] Cullingford, pp.99-131.

[76] Voyage of the St. Louis, United States Holocaust Memorial Museum, www.ushmm.org/stlouis

[77] Dermot Keogh, *Jews in Twentieth-Century Ireland: Refugees, Anti-Semitism and the Holocaust* (Cork: Cork University Press, 1998), p.92.

[78] Gordon Thomas and Max Morgan Witts, *Voyage of the Damned* (New York: Stein and Day, 1974).

[79] Maurice Manning, *The Blueshirts* (Toronto: University of Toronto Press, 1971), pp.195-6.

[80] Michael Farrell, 'Long March to Freedom', *Twenty Years On*, ed. Michael Farrell (Dingle: Brandon, 1988), p.57.

[81] Roddy Doyle, *The Commitments* (London: Minerva, 1991), p.9.

[82] Cullingford, pp.144-50.

[83] Sebastian Barry, Interview, *Penguin Reading Guides*, ww.dk.com/static/rguides/us/whereabouts_of_eneas.html

[84] ibid.

[85] W.J. McCormack addresses these problems in 'The Former Lives of J.M. Synge', the first chapter of *Fool of the Family: A Life of J.M. Synge* (London: Weidenfeld and Nicolson, 2000), pp.3-13.

[86] J.M. Synge, *The Well of the Saints*, in *Collected Works: Plays 1*, ed. Ann Saddlemyer (London: Oxford University Press, 1968), p.115.

[87] Barry, *Three Plays: The Only True History of Lizzie Finn; The Steward of Christendom; White Woman Street* (London: Methuen, 1995), pp.8-9.

[88] See McCormack, *Fool of the Family*, p.288.

[89] See *The Senate Speeches of W.B. Yeats*, ed. Donald R. Pearce (London: Prendeville, 2001), p.94.

[90] See Richard Ellmann on Wilde's 'Bray houses' in *Oscar Wilde* (London:

Hamish Hamilton, 1987), p.99, and McCormack in *Fool of the Family* on the 'two houses in Mount Street belong[ing] to J.M. Synge through the years of his Abbey Street fame' (p.60).

91 Fintan O'Toole, Introduction, *Three Plays*, p.ix.

92 Cited by Nicholas Grene in *The Politics of Irish Drama: Plays in Context from Boucicault to Friel* (Cambridge: Cambridge University Press, 1999), p.81. The word itself is valuably discussed in his chapter 'Shifts in Perspective', pp.77-109.

93 W.B. Yeats, 'J.M. Synge and the Ireland of His Time', in *Essays and Introductions* (London: Macmillan, 1961), p.312.

94 See Luke Gibbons, *Transformations in Irish Culture* (Cork: Cork University Press in association with Field Day, 1996).

95 J. M. Synge, 'When the Moon Has Set', *Collected Works: Plays I* (London: Oxford University Press, 1968), pp.153-77.

96 For a sensitive interpretation of the play, see Christopher Murray, 'Lennox Robinson, *The Big House, Killycreggs in Twilight* and "the Vestigia of Generations"', in Otto Rauchbauer, ed., *Ancestral Voices: The Big House in Anglo-Irish Literature* (Hildesheim: Verlag, 1992), pp.109-119.

97 Lennox Robinson, *The Big House*, in *Selected Plays of Lennox Robinson*, pp.178-9.

98 ibid., p.179.

99 Ben Levitas, *The Theatre of Nation: Irish Drama and Cultural Nationalism 1890-1916* (Oxford: Clarendon Press, 2002), p.51.

100 P.J. Matthews, *Revival: The Abbey Theatre, Sinn Fein, the Gaelic League and the Co-operative Movement* (Cork: Cork University Press in association with Field Day, 2003), pp.66-75.

101 Levitas, pp.51-2.

102 J.M. Synge, *The Playboy of the Western World*, in *Collected Works: Plays 2* (London: Oxford University Press, 1968), p.71.

103 The texts used throughout are *The Steward of Christendom* (London: Methuen, 1997) and *Annie Dunne* (London: Faber & Faber, 2002) with references given parenthetically throughout.

104 Sebastian Barry, *Our Lady of Sligo* (London: Methuen, 1998).

105 Scott T. Cummings, 'The End of History: the Millennial Urge in the Plays of Sebastian Barry', in *A Century of Irish Drama: Widening the Stage*, ed. Stephen Watt, Eileen Morgan and Shakir Mustafa (Bloomington & Indianapolis: Indiana University Press, 2000), p.295.

106 Claire Gleitman, 'Reconstructing History in the Irish History Play', in *The Cambridge Companion to Irish Drama* (Cambridge: Cambridge University Press, 2004), p.218-30.

107 Although Barry was to make some later visits to Kelsha, he drew

primarily on the memories of this one summer in writing *Annie Dunne*, and in much of his other work, including *Boss Grady's Boys*; even though the primary setting of the play and the main characters are derived from a time living in Cork, the rural ambience was based on his recollections of Kelsha. Personal interview with Sebastian Barry, 3 August, 2004. This interview is the source for all information not otherwise referenced in this essay. I am very grateful to Sebastian Barry for so generously answering my questions.

108 The imprecision is interesting here. Barry was born on 5 July 1955 and the birthday celebrated at Kelsha would actually have been his fourth; in the novel, 5 July is the boy's fifth birthday. Barry conjectures that he so miscounted because he found it hard to believe that the impressions he remembers so vividly date from such a young age as just four. In his short story 'The Beast', using the same materials, he makes the narrator a boy of seven.

109 Personal information from the author, 3 August, 2004.

110 Sebastian Barry, 'The Beast', *Irish Press*, 31 March, 1979: 9.

111 In 'The Beast', he is called by alternative petnames as 'Nessie' and 'Annesley'.

112 'A Penguin Reader's Guide', appended to Sebastian Barry, *The Whereabouts of Eneas McNulty* (New York: Penguin, 1998), p.5.

113 Ger Fitzgibbon, 'The Poetic Theatre of Sebastian Barry', in *Theatre Stuff: Critical Essays on Contemporary Irish Theatre*, ed. Eamonn Jordan (Dublin: Carysfort Press, 2000), p.234.

114 Virginia Woolf, 'Modern Fiction', *Collected Essays*, II (London: Hogarth Press, 1966), p.106.

115 *The Third Part of King Henry VI*, New Cambridge Shakespeare, ed. Michael Hattaway (Cambridge: Cambridge University Press, 1993), 5.6.80-84.

116 William Wordsworth, *The Prelude (1805)*, ed. Ernest de Selincourt (London: Oxford University Press, 1964), Book I, ll, pp.305-6.

117 Maria Kurdi, '"Really All Danger": an Interview with Sebastian Barry', *New Hibernia Review*, 8.1 (Spring 2004), p.45.

118 Barry, *Our Lady of Sligo*, p.63.

119 *Three Cantos*, I (first published 1917): 'Ghosts move about me/Patched with histories'.

120 Sebastian Barry, *Plays 1: Boss Grady's Boys, Prayers of Sherkin, White Woman Street, The Only True History of Lizzie Finn, The Steward of Christendom* (Methuen, London, 1997), pp.299-301.

121 Barry, *Whistling Psyche; Fred and Jane* (London: Faber and Faber, 2004), p.12.

122 Barry, *The Engine of Owl-Light* (London: Paladin edition, 1988), p.387.

[123] John Kenny, 'His Heart Is There', *The Irish Times*, 26 March, 2005, p.10.

[124] Elizabeth Cullingford, 'Colonial Policing: *The Steward of Christendom* and *The Whereabouts of Eneas* McNulty', *Éire-Ireland* (Fall/Winter, 2004) pp.11-37.

[125] ibid., pp.23 & 26.

[126] ibid., p.29.

[127] Adrian Gregory and Senia Paseta (eds.), *Ireland and the Great War: 'A War to Unite us All?'* (Manchester: University Press, 2002), p.2.

[128] Sebastian Barry, Introduction to *The Essential Jennifer Johnston* (Review, London, 1999), p.x.

[129] *Plays 1*, p.111.

[130] See for instance C.A. Bayly, 'Ireland, India and the Empire, 1780-1914' in *Transactions of the Royal Historical Society*, Sixth Series, X (Cambridge University Press, 2000), pp.377-98; S.B. Cook, *Imperial Affinities: nineteenth-century analogies and exchanges between India and Ireland* (Delhi: Oxford University Press, 1993); Barry Crosbie, 'The Irish Expatriate Community in British India, c.1750-1900' (PhD Cambridge, 2004).

[131] Sebastian Barry, *Our Lady of Sligo* (Methuen, London, 1998) p.59

[132] See especially Senia Paseta, *Before the Revolution: nationalism, social change and Ireland's Catholic elite 1879-1922* (Cork: University Press, 1999) and Patrick Maume. *The Long Gestation: Irish nationalist life 1891-1918* (Dublin: Gill and Macmillan, 1999).

[133] Sebastian Barry, *Hinterland* (London: Faber & Faber, 2002), pp.15-16.

[134] *The Engine of Owl-light*, p.6. 'He who hath thus considered the World, as also how therein things long past have been answered by things present, how matters in one age have been acted over in another, and how there is nothing new under the sun, may conceive himself in some manner to have lived from the beginning, and to be as old as the World; and if he should still live on, twould be but the same thing.'

[135] Barry, *Annie Dunne* (London: Faber & Faber, 2002), p.228.

[136] Barry, *Hinterland* (London: Faber, 2002), p.7.

[137] Bruce Arnold, *Haughey: His Life and Unlucky Deeds* (London: Harper Collins, 1993), p.282.

[138] James Downey, *Lenihan: His Life and Loyalties* (Dublin: New Island, 1998) pp.154-57.

[139] Arnold, p.61.

[140] Arnold, p.168.

[141] Downey, Chapter 13; Arnold, pp.253-355.

[142] Kevin O'Connor, *Sweetie: How Haughey Spent the Money* (Minneapolis:

Irish Books & Media, 1999), pp.36-76.

143 Barry, *The Pinkening Boy* (Dublin: New Island, 2004) p.6.

144 O'Connor, pp.85-98.

145 This account of the event is taken from an unpublished manuscript by Jocelyn Clarke, the literary manager of the Abbey Theatre.

146 In order to avoid the cumbersome s/he, for the purposes of this essay I will refer to James Miranda Barry with the male pronoun, as Sebastian Barry does in the play.

147 Virginia Woolf, 'Mr. Bennett and Mrs. Brown', in *The Captain's Bed and other Essays*, (NY: Harcourt, Brace, 1950), p.96-97.

148 Barry, *The Steward of Christendom* (NY: Dramatists Play Service, 1998), p.5. Further references are noted in the text.

149 Euripides, *Medea*, trans. Rex Warner, in *Euripides I* (Chicago: U of Chicago Press, 1955), p.67.

150 Samuel Beckett, *Waiting for Godot* (NY: Grove, 1954), p.105.

Index